Terminating Therapy

A Professional Guide to Ending on a Positive Note

Denise D. Davis

WILEY

John Wiley & Sons, Inc.

Library of Congress Cataloging-in-Publication Data:

Davis, Denise D.

    Terminating therapy : a professional guide for ending on a positive note / by Denise D. Davis.

      p.; cm.

    Includes bibliographical references and index.

    ISBN 978-0-470-10556-6 (pbk. : alk. paper)

      1. Psychotherapy—Termination. 2. Psychotherapist and patient. 3. Cognitive therapy. I. Title.

    [DNLM: 1. Cognitive Therapy—methods. 2. Professional-Patient Relations.

    3. Psychotherapy—methods. 4. Treatment Outcome. WM 425.5.C6 D261t 2008]

    RC489.T45D38 2008

    616.89'14—dc22

                           2007043557

10 9 8 7 6 5 4 3 2 1

Contents

Foreword

In my first term of graduate studies at New York University in the early 1960s I took my first course in technique of counseling and psychotherapy. The instructor was a tall, thin fellow who wore tweed sport jackets and had a salt-and-pepper crew cut. He looked every inch of what I thought a psychologist should look like. His name was Dr. Claude W. Grant. More than 40 years later I still remember him. The text for the course was Carl Rogers' "Counseling and Psychotherapy," and Grant instructed us on the essential nature of "unconditional positive regard" within the therapeutic relationship. One of the new terms we acquired was "rapport." Grant used the following example of rapport building: "When a client comes into my office I want to make him or her feel at home, and to let him (or her) know that I am paying attention and want to have them feel at ease with me. I might say, 'I notice that you are wearing a Rotary pin in your lapel. Have you been active in Rotary?' This could serve as an icebreaker and get the client talking about their Rotary experience."

I dutifully wrote in my notes, "Ask about rotary." I had no idea what rotary meant, but I was sure that it was important. I could look it up later. I discovered that Rotary International was an organization of business and professional persons who provided humanitarian service. My father and the fathers of my friends were non-professionals and belonged to groups such as the American Legion, Knights of Columbus, Jewish War Veterans, Knights of Pythias, and Veterans of Foreign Wars. Not one Rotarian in the bunch.

Grant spent the term focusing on the establishment of both the therapeutic bond (the relationship between client and therapist) and the therapeutic alliance (the agenda for therapy). The lessons of those classes stay with me still, and I hope that I am half as effective as he was in conveying those skills to my students.

Building on this basic course I took many other courses that emphasized the relationship and alliance. I acquired a many strategies and interventions for rapport building over the years. Few places in my graduate training, my reading, my supervised practice, or discussions with colleagues has the issue of termination of therapy been a major element—until now.

In 1962, Neil Sedaka first recorded, "Breaking Up is Hard to Do." Recorded by many other artists, the song's central message was just that, breaking up is hard to do and most of us would rather avoid it. After spending several (or many sessions) building rapport, helping the client to be open, comfortable, and cooperative, we move inexorably toward ending the therapeutic collaboration. This should, ideally, be a joint decision between client and therapist. It should be appropriately timed, well executed, and be a capstone to the therapeutic encounter; it is far more important, in fact, than the rapport building of the early stages of the therapy. Why is it more important? Given the recency effect, it will likely be what the client takes from the therapy. It provides the client and therapist with a review of what has been gained, changed, improved, reduced, and made better in the therapy. It allows for planning for the future. It allows the therapist and client to develop closure on the therapeutic relationship. It allows the therapist to make "closing remarks," because the therapeutic experience of the client is often to internalize the voice of the therapist and to later have that voice influence the client's actions, feelings, and thoughts. Termination must build on the hard-won experiences of the therapy. With rapport building, there is more time to continue to build the relationship. With termination, the end is in sight. Milton Erickson's volume, "My Voice Will Go With You: The Teaching Tales of Milton Erickson," (1982) capsules, by title and content, this phenomenon.

What Denise Davis has done in the present volume is to advance the field of psychotherapy by structuring and writing a book that focuses on the *process* of termination. The termination of therapy is not a solitary moment in time, but a culmination and synthesis of the entire therapeutic experience.

In Chapter One, Davis describes the importance of the termination process, focusing on the process being impacted by today's managed care practice environment, the role of the therapist's theoretical orientation as a factor in the termination process, and perhaps most important, she defines for the reader what might be considered "good" termination and "bad" termination. With this as her opening, Davis then moves on to describing what she calls a pragmatic termination strategy.

In Chapter Two, Davis addresses the often difficult and confusing issues surrounding the ethics of termination. A graduate student recently questioned me about client abandonment and the ethical position we play as clinicians. The student's understanding of the ethical code was that once a therapist and client start therapy, it cannot be ended even if the client doesn't pay the fee, is physically threatening to the therapist, damages the therapy office, or makes verbal threats to office staff without the client being abandoned. Now I can refer them to Davis's chapter to answer the questions regarding ethical termination. Being a skilled clinician, Davis breaks the termination process down to both types of termination, and identifies the skills of termination.

Davis's approach makes life far simpler for both the experienced and novice therapist. Termination begins with intake and is a central part of informed consent. Chapter Three uses the descriptive phrase "Positive closure from the start: Groundwork for termination." By linking the collaboratively derived treatment goals and a plan for termination, the ending of therapy is set out both as a goal of therapy and as an integral part of therapy. Therapists are often reluctant to discuss termination inasmuch as it will possibly raise the client's anxiety. The client might think, "Here we are at the beginning of therapy, and my therapist is already planning to get rid of me." Davis's plan is to tie the ending of therapy to client needs, goals, and progress.

Chapter Four discusses the specifics of the communication between therapist and client regarding the termination. Davis gives the reader an insightful view of the therapist's internal dialogue. This, too, is something not often discussed by therapists.

Client and therapist resistance to termination is the emphasis for Chapter Five. Davis asks several key questions (e.g., When should I (or should I) insist on termination even if the client resists? What if the client becomes hostile or depressed by the termination? How do I know when I have done enough for the client to consider termination?). She then asks what I believe to be the key question for Chapter Five: What should the therapist do about his or her needs for the therapeutic relationship? How will I (or do I) deal with the ending of relationships? How do I *not* communicate my separation anxiety to the patient? How do I not create a therapy-dependent client?

Chapter Six speaks to the issue of the therapist being culturally aware and culturally competent. The client's socio-cultural schema, personal schema, family schema, gender-related schema, religious schema, age-related schema, health, and stage-of-life schema must all be taken into account in the termination plan. Davis also addresses the client's diagnostic picture and co-morbid psychopathology as factors to be considered in arranging termination.

True to the model that she espouses, the end (termination) of the book starts with Chapter One. With Chapter Seven, the termination of the book is in sight. Davis begins the termination process for the reader. Davis focuses in greater detail on the issues, internal dialogue, and problems of the therapist/provider. Therapeutic errors, crisis termination, therapist fear regarding client safety and well-being, and a therapist perception of a job well or poorly done are addressed. Here again, Davis takes the unspoken and puts voice to these complicated and difficult questions.

Chapter Eight focuses on the complications of therapy that ensue from multiple clients (i.e., working with couples, families, and groups). Some of the issues that are addressed are within the control of the therapist. Others are not within the control of the therapist, such as when a parent or guardian withdraws a child or adolescent from therapy. When one partner suddenly refuses therapy, must the other partner also terminate? Termination with groups presents a thorny problem inasmuch as the problems for termination in individual therapy are exponentially increased in a group. There are multiple needs, multiple goals, multiple demands, and the synergy of the group that works to keep the group intact.

We can easily see how the supervisory relationship and the therapeutic relationship are not only parallel but in many cases it may be seen as an identical process, needing effective termination strategies. Chapter Nine addresses the role definition and the supervisor's responsibility to both the supervisee and to the clients of the supervisee.

In the final chapter, Davis discusses the frequently asked questions of the consumer to the ending or continuation of therapy. This final chapter should be made required reading for all therapists, and if I had my way, I would see it published and distributed to everyone who is beginning therapy.

To say that I am pleased with the work of this talented and skilled clinician, superb teacher, excellent writer, and clever conceptualizer would be an understatement. I am flattered to have been able to be part of this project.

ARTHUR FREEMAN, Ed.D., ABPP

Governors State University
University Park, IL

Preface

Beginnings and endings are important. Termination is one of the most important boundaries in therapy, yet it is one we tend to take for granted. There are many volumes written on planning, beginning, and conducting therapy, but only a handful exist on the subject of termination, and virtually none written from a non-psychodynamic perspective. This book reduces that void with a contemporary cognitive behavioral perspective on termination in psychotherapy.

My perspective in this book is learning-based, and throughout I have developed tools and strategies that will be directly useful in the reader's clinical and supervisory work. I explore current standards of practice and how to meet them, and I look at ways to distinguish good termination from bad. I hope that my consideration of abandonment and professional responsibility will help readers to practice with greater confidence, having gained a clear understanding of this critical concept as it applies in cognitive behavioral therapies. The case examples throughout the book are clinical composites intended to illustrate key points without identifying any specific individual, except where noted for legal cases.

There are many practical concepts developed in the pages that follow: how to conceptualize termination as a task of the therapeutic alliance; how to set termination goals and link them to the treatment plan; how to lay the groundwork for a positive termination even before the client arrives; how to communicate effectively about termination; ways to recognize and deal with your own thoughts, beliefs, and emotions about termination; how to identify appropriate reasons for termination; and six essential steps to ensure that you are doing "enough" for a clinically and ethically appropriate process—to name some of the highlights.

Clinicians of all experience levels may find the extensive consideration of complex termination with chronic, recurrent, and co-morbid conditions, including Axis II problems, to be helpful with challenging clients. Termination issues in the supervisory relationship are explored in depth, including the perspectives of supervisor and supervisee. Concerns that are particular to couples, families, and groups are also addressed. The last chapter is a series of questions about termination that is written and answered from the consumer's point of view. This particular chapter is intended to assist in transporting the ideas and information directly to the consumer through your conversations in therapy or with written materials used in your personal practice. Throughout the book I talk about self-care, clinician reactions, challenges, and ways to protect the safety and effectiveness of one's practice.

The slant of this book is intended to be fresh, hopeful, scientifically grounded, and practical. In essence, I hope that readers will enjoy this book, find it thought provoking and ultimately useful in practice. I invite you to join me in learning how to end with a beginning in mind.

DENISE DAVIS, Ph.D.

Nashville, Tennessee
September 30, 2007

Acknowledgments

I am greatly indebted to Wiley Editors Tisha Rossi and Isabel Pratt who provided the spark for and unfaltering promotion of this project from start to finish. Working with them has truly been a pleasure. Their enthusiasm and dedication is a marvel. I feel fortunate to have come within the scope of their talent and influence. Katie DeChants kept watch over the details and I appreciate her superb editorial assistance at the Wiley home base.

Art Freeman is the wise and inspiring mentor whose support has been an invaluable advantage to me for many years. His gracious contribution of a forward to this volume represents the spirit of giving and encouragement that is typical of Art. I deeply appreciate his comments on this work, his positive impact on the direction of my career, and his many years of friendship and collaboration.

Heartfelt thanks are due to the many friends and colleagues whose generous efforts to read, review, and comment on parts of the manuscript in development energized me and enabled me to move ahead through the long process of figuring out what to say and how to say it. These amiable folks include Laurel Brown, Katy Cantor, Edna Dean, Kirsten Haman, Claudia Labin, Jennifer Mandarino, Jim Rebeta, M. J. Sowinski, Dotty Tucker, Patti van Eys and Jeff Younggren.

I am also grateful to the many colleagues and friends who provided assistance in developing or refining particular ideas and achieving greater clarity in murky or challenging spots. Rebecca Atkins, Jo-Anne Bachorowski, Andy Butler, Stephanie Felgoise, Tobi Fishel, Scott Gale, Michael Gottlieb, Steve Hjelt, Steve Hollon, Karl Jannasch, Dawne Kimbrell, Lawrie Lewis, Marti Mattea, Michele Panucci, Gary Schoener, and Sandy Siedel all had a hand in enhancing the overall scope of this work.

Charlie, Daniel, and Charlie, my husband and sons, each made personal sacrifices to support the work of writing this book. I'm glad they like pizza. Their love and active encouragement was essential to bringing this project to a positive conclusion.

1

Termination Strategy:
A Pragmatic Approach
in Contemporary Practice

Key Questions Addressed in This Chapter

- How does theoretical orientation impact termination philosophy?
- How is termination managed in today's practice environment?
- What makes termination difficult to plan even in brief therapy?
- What circumstances elevate the risks of adverse events at termination?
- What are the main objectives of a pragmatic termination strategy?
- How can we distinguish good termination from bad termination?

THE IMPORTANCE OF TERMINATION

Effectively managed termination is vital to a lasting positive impact, regardless of the type of intervention or when termination occurs. Termination holds the promise of enhancing the benefits and the risk of diminishing these effects of therapy, depending on how well the process is negotiated. In more extreme terms, a good termination can seal the successes of therapy, but a bad termination can sour the best efforts. Even in brief therapy, the process of ending is a crucial part of the experience that helps both client and practitioner to assess their sense of accomplishment and calculate the value of their invested effort. Like any closing effort, termination has special impact on the conclusions, satisfaction, and overall sense of harmony associated with the psychotherapy experience.

Ending therapy is not without challenges. For a mental health professional, termination may be likened to a pilot's task of landing an aircraft. It requires planning, skill, focused attention, nimble responses, vigilance to the risks of adverse conditions or events, and professional composure in action. Just as the pilot needs a flight plan that includes landing parameters, so the clinician also needs a treatment plan with termination goals. The pilot needs to calculate how much distance can be covered given the fuel capacity, and the clinician needs to determine what can be accomplished with the resources available. When it comes to making the final descent, the pilot may have to accommodate storms, winds, and other inclement conditions in order to land safely. Clinicians ending therapy also may encounter high emotions and non-ambient factors, whether those were predicted at the outset or whether they developed unexpectedly at the end of the journey. Professional composure and effective judgment are crucial to both the pilot and the clinician as each carries their respective task to the best possible conclusion. In the pages ahead, we take an in-depth look at the tools and strategies that clinicians need for this important endeavor.

How Does Theoretical Orientation Impact Termination Philosophy?

In psychotherapy, the best point of completion is not easily defined, nor is there a uniform set of procedures for ending. Even with the many types of therapy available today, the comparative literature on termination is relatively sparse (Barnett, MacGlashan, & Clarke, 2000; Goldfried, 2002; Greenberg, 2002; Joyce, Piper, Ogrodniczuk, & Klein, 2007; Wachtel, 2002; Zinkin, 1994). We might reasonably assume that a provider's perspective on when and how therapy should conclude will follow their philosophy of therapy and its perspective on psychopathology. Two broad perspectives on psychopathology aptly summarized by Weiner (1998) provide a way to compare some essential differences in theoretical approaches to termination. According to Weiner, these are the humanistic, developmental perspective, which tends to be more optimistic about change, and the analytic, dynamic character structure perspective, which tends to be more pessimistic about change.

Providers who approach therapy from a humanistic, developmental perspective believe that people are basically capable and resilient. Minimal intervention is often sufficient to facilitate or redirect their natural growth and development. Providers who approach therapy from a dynamic perspective view conflicts and maladaptation as static aspects of a structured character or personality. Problems stemming from character damage often require rigorous intervention for even minimal change and improved adaptation. Concerning termination, the resilience perspective might argue that treatment can be safely concluded at the earliest signs of symptom improvement. Short segments of therapy are considered adequate for the majority of client needs, as it is assumed that even minor changes precipitate a healthier trajectory of ongoing growth. The unyielding character perspective might argue that symptom-focused treatment is inadequate and even risky. Adequate change is assumed to require intensive effort that is commensurate with the extent of the character damage or conflict.

Both perspectives would likely agree that the optimal point of termination is when the goals of therapy have been met. But therapists of either philosophical persuasion will likely diverge in their opinion of what tasks are needed and how the goals will be measured. From the resilience perspective, there is not a specific state or set of tasks that the client has to complete in order to finish therapy. Growth is a continuous process, so the point of completion can be very flexibly defined. For example, if the client learns to apply anxiety management skills to the task of driving to work on crowded freeways and feels more able to cope, therapy could be considered complete. Or perhaps the client stops struggling with anxiety as an emotional state that might occur on the freeway and is ready to move on with other aspects of living. Further treatment is not necessary unless there are other clinically significant problems or concerns that the client wants to pursue. The termination itself may be a task that is accomplished with relative ease, depending on the client's wishes. From the dynamic perspective, however, the anxious client's ability to drive to work is only initial symptom relief. Therapy would not be complete until the client has taken the time to sufficiently understand the roots and patterns of their self-doubt and inhibited achievement.

To date, there is no definitive resolution that either philosophy should prevail. And in real life, all providers do not cleave into this dichotomous separation of optimistic and pessimistic philosophy. We might simultaneously see the growth potential in our clients and recognize the impact of damaging experience. More central to the issue of termination philosophy, however, is the common denominator of scientific perspective. This perspective is alluded to by Wiener (1998) in his assertion that "psychotherapists are most likely to be helpful when they can provide psychotherapy of whatever length appears clinically indicated and when, if their preferences run strongly to either short-term or long-term values, they can keep humbly in mind that not all the correct answers are theirs" (p. 262). This basic experimental approach was outlined some years ago by Goldfried and Davison (1976) as a fundamental strategy for informing clinical work. Rather than adhering solely to the precepts of a particular school or system of therapy, the scientific provider draws from a spectrum of basic research findings to formulate and test a variety of clinical interventions (Goldfried, 2007).

The scientific perspective is not tied to either a hopeful or a cautious position. It simply focuses on what the client has acquired via scientifically understandable forces. Where maladaptation exists, intervention is geared toward what can be acquired as a means of mediating these problems. There are a number of ways this acquisition can take place, including but not limited to various forms of learning and emotional experience in relationship to the provider. The question of treatment completion then becomes, quite naturally, an empirical one. Data from multiple sources help define treatment completion for any given client. There may be evidence from clinical trials that provides a general framework for the types of changes needed and the length of time it might take to achieve those changes. This is blended with vital clinical data to arrive at a reasonable assessment of treatment completion for each individual client.

Simply put, one size of therapy does not fit all clients, even those with the same diagnosis. Some clients will be ready to terminate therapy once the most intense symptoms have remitted, and others will want to extend the effort to deal with other issues. Some clients will appropriately terminate in fewer than five sessions, and their decision is not necessarily "premature." Not all clients need intensive treatment, but some will certainly exceed the provider's predictions for expected length of therapy. Determining an appropriate point of termination is a complex task that involves an integration of clinical, ethical, empirical, and contextual information. Theoretical orientation has a definite impact on the provider's general perspective. But theoretical orientation is secondary to a more fundamental scientific strategy of using multiple sources of relevant data to arrive at an integrated and individually appropriate termination decision.

How Is Termination Viewed in Today's Practice Environment?

Today's standard of care for psychotherapy is based on a health service model. This model includes the following components.

- Documented clinical necessity of services
- Specific goals
- Defined episodes of care
- Evidence-based interventions
- Measurable progress
- Multiple providers
- Focus on consumer satisfaction

These components represent some significant shifts from the standards of care that prevailed even a decade or two in the past. Previous standards of care were based on a system in which providers had more exclusive dominion over clinical decisions. A traditional framework of open-ended therapy with a single provider was most common. Treatment necessity was decided on a subjective basis by the client and the clinician. The goals of therapy were broad and often implicitly held, the timeline indefinite, and the methods were determined by the allegiance of the therapist to a school of therapy.

Changes in systems of service delivery and our clinical and professional standards of care over the past few decades have had a significant impact on therapy termination. These changes have affected how soon, how often, and why we must address the conclusion of service. With these changes, it has become more and more apparent that our assumptions and practices need to be updated. Here is why. Relative costs and quality of services have become primary issues in the health care system. Valid concerns about cost management have given rise to greater emphasis on oversight and accountability in service delivery. Support for open-ended and extended interventions has significantly diminished in the conservation of resources. Measurable gains are now required to justify the use of resources. As a health-related service, therapy must be clearly linked to signs and symptoms of medical necessity and its purpose must be linked to alleviation of those symptoms. Expectations for observable results within defined periods of time have created certain limits and demands for accountability from both client and provider.

In a managed care environment, psychotherapy providers seldom have the leisure of allowing the client time to discover a readiness for termination before they must raise the issue of ongoing medical necessity for authorizing additional services. There is an obligation to establish a compelling need for therapy or in the absence of such to discontinue services. Providing services that are not expected to be beneficial or are no longer needed is unethical, potentially harmful to the client, and fraudulent use of the system. If a provider knowingly facilitates the fraudulent use of resources, he or she assumes the risk of losing professional integrity and possibly the privilege to practice.

At the same time, providers bear a professional responsibility to protect the best interests of the client and must not abandon clients or fail to maintain a reasonable standard of care. Haste or overzealousness in limiting therapy can be just as hazardous as prolonging treatment. Either can be an error that increases the provider's exposure to administrative, ethical, or legal complications. To complicate matters further, clients with the greatest mental health needs often have the most limited access to services. Reasonable termination of clients with long-term needs is one the provider's biggest quandaries. Even brief therapy relationships can be highly emotionally charged and ending therapy can be difficult, particularly when the reasons for termination are not optimal. Attachment is still relevant to successful intervention, even if it is not considered the focal point of change. With tighter time frames, providers have less opportunity to develop the therapy relationship or to provide support throughout a full cycle of change. This increases the risk that something important may be missed or that the client's overall benefit and satisfaction will be diminished.

Protecting the client's best interests has become an increasingly complex task as both treatment options and limits have multiplied in the health care marketplace. Options can include different types of psychotherapy, medication, case management, self-help and support groups, day treatment, sheltered workshops, online support resources, bibliotherapy, family or couples therapy, skills classes, or other medical or allied health services.

Although the options appear to be abundant, these may not all be easily accessible, clearly indicated, or fully effective for all consumers. However, these options represent a range of alternatives that are potentially useful in the client's overall efforts toward self-regulation.

Specific attention to termination strategies in this new context has not kept pace with these expanding and shifting expectations. It has been commonly assumed that if therapy is more focused or time-limited, it should end easily, without as much need to process the affective, cognitive, interpersonal, and defensive reactions that attend termination in open-ended or dynamic therapy (Barnett et al., 2000; Joyce et al., 2007). Both client and provider may expect that the point of completion will be readily apparent when problems are solved. Termination is recognized as important, but construed as a minor closing step. Although these assumptions may hold true in some instances, problem-focused therapy does not always turn out to be brief or affectively uncomplicated.

When the therapist is under direct supervision in his or her work, as in the case of trainees (practicum students, interns, externs, residents) or those in emerging or limited professional roles (e.g., post-doctoral clinicians or master's level clinicians with a limited scope of practice), another layer is added to the termination considerations. Supervisors play a significant part in determining when and how therapy should end, although their vantage point is that of an inside observer who is legally responsible for what happens. In addition, the supervisory relationship itself includes termination issues that run parallel to many of the concerns that can arise within psychotherapy.

Given the demands of today's practice environment, it is clear that new challenges and expectations have made termination more complex. These changes call for a coherent strategy of managing termination decisions across sequential episodes of care, different modes of intervention, varying clinical needs, and conservatively managed resources.

What Makes Termination Difficult to Plan Even in Brief Therapy?

Brief or problem-focused therapy offers a shift away from global objectives such as self-actualization or insight in favor of more behavioral and symptomatic targets that can be operationally defined and measured. Specific changes are expected within relatively short segments of time through the application of focused techniques. It sounds like a simple process, but may not be so straightforward or predictably attainable in practice.

Therapy intended to be focused and brief does not always turn out to be so precise for a variety of reasons. The degree of optimal structure and pace of change will vary from client to client. Clients may not have the skills or motivation to participate in the most efficient ways. The client's beliefs and assumptions may function as barriers to improvement, especially when the client remains passive, avoidant, or fearful of self-disclosure. The scope of the client's problems and the degree of desired change might require multiple interventions or an extended course of treatment, as is often the case with recurrent or co-morbid disorders, especially Axis II disorders.

The provider's skill and deftness in engaging the client is another factor that can alter the course of therapy. Perhaps the provider has limited training in applying specific strategies and lacks confidence in using these methods. Or maybe the provider has a tendency to underestimate the importance of the relationship and other common factors or does not maximize these vital ingredients. In addition, both client and provider may view global objectives as higher order or "real" change and use this as their framework for setting goals. Specific endpoints are then much more difficult to discern as there are no systematic, objective criteria for determining the achievement of global goals (Weiner, 1998).

Even with well-defined goals, behavioral and emotional change does not necessarily occur on a predictable schedule. Empirically grounded interventions are designed for time efficiency, but variability among clients in terms of severity, chronicity, overall needs, beliefs, personal resources and ability to work productively with the therapist all affect the length of intervention for any given client. In addition, the techniques of intervention must be blended into an ongoing interpersonal interaction, another source of variability that is not directly predictable. Other health care services of a technical nature have defined procedures with a clear sequence of action. The provider-client relationship is important but not as highly entwined with the specific service as is the case with psychotherapy. For example, our relationship with our dentist does not affect how our teeth get cleaned and repaired, or how long the procedures take to complete. And few among us would linger just to relax in the dentist's chair once the drilling is done, no matter how much we like the dentist.

In contrast, the process of psychotherapy is less mechanistic and more fundamentally tied to interactive factors. Even with specific, objective goals and tasks, the emotional aspects of the therapeutic bond (Bordin, 1979) act as interpersonal adhesive. When this adhesive is positive, therapy may progress easily, but its conclusion can bring unexpected reluctance and distress. With the relationship as a medium for the service, ending therapy can feel as poignant as saying goodbye to a dear friend or family member. This tension is further complicated by the client's particular style of attachment and by the productivity of the therapy itself, either of which can prolong or shorten the work. Regarding the relationship per se, some clients dread the loss of this emotional connection while others keep a detached stance throughout therapy.

Brief or problem-focused models of therapy typically take a pragmatic approach toward termination. Termination might be considered a developmental turning point or place where a relationship is transformed (Levinson, 1996). In problem-focused therapy, termination is not a final conclusion or loss as much as it is a point of re-evaluation and redirection. From the provider's perspective, the main objective is to create a positive transition that marks the completion of a particular time of collaboration. Future contact is often an option or even part of the plan, as the client can return for "booster" sessions or additional courses of therapy.

To be successful in this endeavor, however, the problem-focused practitioner can not just import the termination strategies of insight-oriented or dynamic therapy. Today's practitioners using cognitive, behavioral, dialectical behavioral, mindfulness-based cognitive, acceptance and commitment, narrative, feminist, solution-focused, prescriptive, integrative, eclectic, or other problem-focused models need a pragmatic approach to termination that is theoretically compatible and consistent with the current clinical, ethical, and practical standards of care. A pragmatic model of termination that addresses these needs is developed throughout this text.

What Circumstances Elevate the Risk of Adverse Events?

Termination may be relatively easy and straightforward when progress is satisfactory and the circumstances of therapy are relatively uncomplicated. The thoughts and feelings of client and practitioner are more or less positive and in harmony. But not all terminations look alike or follow a standard process. Variations, snags, and even stalemates and debacles can result from many different interacting forces, regardless of type of therapy or its intended length. Steady progression toward a natural conclusion may be unlikely or impossible. Such circumstances signal an elevated risk for emotional, practical, ethical, or legal problems, and all providers must be prepared to handle these potential difficulties.

The following is an overview of some of the possible challenges that will be explored throughout this text. These include forced termination, practitioner skill limits, stalled progress, and client resistance to termination.

Forced Terminations Sometimes termination is forced by circumstances that restrict the duration of therapy or compel it to end. Force implies negative pressure and is really a matter of degree, depending on the perspective taken. Alternatively, the term "precipitated" offers a more neutral description of termination that is prompted or hastened by circumstances. A more neutral stance emphasizes the client's autonomy and ability to choose among options, even if those options have realistic limits. There is almost always some degree of choice possible in dealing with the events that are impacting the viability of continuing therapy. One example is a managed care insurance contract that limits the number of compensated mental health visits during a calendar year. If there are changes in the client's or practitioner's contract with third-party payers, the client may be prompted to choose another provider due to prevailing financial considerations. Describing the termination as "forced" automatically makes it a coercive event, as opposed to describing activating circumstances that include options and alternatives.

Various personal circumstances can precipitate termination, such as when the client or provider moves, changes jobs, completes training, becomes unavailable for health or personal reasons, or a conflict of interest develops. Most therapy that is delivered by trainees ends when the training placement is completed. Sometimes clients abruptly leave therapy or they attempt to prolong therapy when it is no longer feasible to continue. Confusion about how to handle these different circumstances increases the risk of impractical arrangements, boundary violations, emotional distress, and possible unprofessional conduct. Here are three very different examples of precipitated termination and some of the possible pitfalls associated with each.

Case Example: Termination Precipitated by Training Status.   Tina was completing a graduate practicum at the university student-counseling center. Although she was excited about moving along in her professional training, she felt sad and vaguely guilty about having to end therapy when her placement was over. Tina had learned that therapy should support the client's growth and self-determination, and that treatment was considered complete *when the client felt ready to end therapy*. Yet her trainee status created a practical time limit on her client relationships. Many of her clients were students and also had practical time limits on their involvement. Therapy had to end or be interrupted at the close of the term, regardless of how ready Tina or her clients felt. Most people accepted this but not without some difficult emotional reactions. Tina and her clients liked one another. They didn't feel ready to let go. This conflict between emotional attachment and practical boundaries confused Tina's clarity of professional action. Tina found herself considering options that could ultimately compromise her professional integrity.

Tina began to ruminate about giving her "favorite" clients her home telephone number and offering to correspond via e-mail or meet for coffee once in a while. That way the therapy relationship could continue. Her anxiety level increased each week as she thought about the approaching end of the term. Several clients finally mentioned their impending departure from campus and need to discontinue therapy sessions. Several others called to cancel, citing a busy examination schedule, or simply failed to show without notice.

Tina ended therapy with all of her clients, but she felt uncomfortable with the forced circumstances. One client asked about the option of continuing to work with Tina, and she explained the practical boundaries that prevented that option. Tina decided against offering the option of casual contact because this could be construed as unprofessional or improper conduct and might actually confuse rather than help the client. In the case of a trainee such as Tina, offering to continue clinical service outside of a formally supervised setting would constitute unlicensed clinical practice. Tina might discover that she is liable for a reprimand from the licensing board that governs her profession, and she could even encounter difficulty in obtaining her license to practice because of a professional misjudgment such as this.

Sometimes termination is prompted by actions of the client that preclude any closing discussion. Perhaps the client simply breaks contact and offers no direct explanation. Or in a more complicated situation, the client may make threats or take adverse actions that compromise the therapy relationship beyond repair. In either situation, the client may still have unresolved problems. However, this does not mean that the therapist is obligated to fix those problems. In fact, when adverse actions have taken place, it is very risky to attempt to continue therapy. The termination strategy in either situation does not have to be complicated or drawn out. The ending may be conflicted, but the practitioner can still map out an appropriate professional course of action. To illustrate, here are two case examples of termination by very different client actions, and the challenges faced by the practitioner.

Case Example: Termination Precipitated by Client No-Show.   Brian is an enthusiastic and caring practitioner. He sincerely wants to help his clients, and he has very high expectations of his performance as a provider. He always tries to do his best and he is prone to feeling personally responsible for snags in the therapy process. If a client declines treatment or does not follow through, he views it as his personal failure. He tends to think, "If I were a better or more likeable therapist, this client would continue working with me." Unfortunately, this self-demanding attitude tends to limit his objectivity and create unnecessary emotional distress over routine aspects of his practice. His reactions to his client Cindy provide a good example.

Cindy entered therapy rather reluctantly at the behest of her family. At age 26, she was having problems with a mildly depressed mood and dependence on her family. Cindy was most upset about family pressure on her to get a job and help out around the house. She viewed coming to therapy as a way to get them off her back. She did not see herself as a person in need of "psych treatment." Her behavior in sessions with Brian was flirtatious and social, and she did not follow through on any homework suggestions, even though he attempted to keep it simple and involve her in the planning. After her third visit, she simply failed to show for her next scheduled appointment.

Brian felt surprised and ashamed that he had been unable to successfully keep Cindy in treatment. He ruminated about what he might have done wrong, and he left several telephone messages with possible appointment times, hoping that Cindy would reschedule. He wondered if he should send her a letter of encouragement. What Brian did not realize was that Cindy was annoyed by his phone messages and deleted them without listening. Her family had eased up on the pressure and she was feeling better, so she had no further interest in therapy. She quite simply was not engaged in a process of self-examination. In addition, she felt physically attracted to Brian, but she had no idea how to discuss or manage those feelings. When he failed to react to her flirtations, she felt rejected and concluded that the whole enterprise was a waste of time.

Understanding the reasons for termination is an important part of adequate closure. When the client ends treatment by failing to return for follow-up, the practitioner may have conflicting emotions and lack clarity about what to do next. Having a plan of action for client communications is only part of the termination strategy. The practitioner also needs a plan for dealing with his or her emotional reactions to termination that is precipitated by the client. Abrupt or unexplained client termination can bring disappointment and trigger painful thoughts about possible professional shortcomings, rejection, or limitations to the process of therapy.

Sometimes termination is necessary because of highly adverse client actions such as demands or threats intended to manipulate or intimidate the provider. Even though these client behaviors may be understandable from a clinical perspective, there is a certain threshold where the adverse actions become pragmatically intolerable. It is especially difficult to reason effectively when one is under attack. Having a clear termination strategy for conditions of duress is absolutely essential.

Case Example: Termination Precipitated by Adverse Client Action.   Kate had been working for more than a year with Jennie, an emotionally unstable, depressed young woman with aggressive and self-destructive tendencies when child protective service investigated a complaint of neglect concerning her young son. Kate did not file the complaint, but rather a family member did so because of concern that Jennie was leaving her son in the care of incompetent babysitters. Jennie demanded that Kate provide a letter to the investigators as a testimony to her emotional stability and capacity to effectively care for her son. When Kate declined to write the letter because of her concerns about Jennie's history and current functioning, Jennie threatened to stalk her, "pop" her, and cause her physical harm. Jennie also made reference to enlisting the help of her gang-involved boyfriend to physically force Kate to write the letter. Kate was frightened and wondered whether she should just write a generically supportive letter or continue to refuse and maybe carry a gun for self-defense. Instead, she decided to schedule more frequent sessions with Jennie to discuss the letter, but also to keep pepper spray and a cell phone nearby at all times.

Kate is unaware that therapist-initiated termination is a viable and correct response when dealing with specific, direct threats to her physical safety. Like many well-meaning providers, Kate is hopeful that increased focus on the triggering issue will be therapeutic for the client. She worries that she could not end treatment at this point because Jennie has so clearly *not* completed treatment in terms of clinical improvements. So her strategy is to intensify clinical contact. However, termination is really the only viable option. Kate is reluctant to pursue this option because she thinks she must not abandon her patient, she does not want to give up trying to help, and she is afraid to confront this threatening patient. She is greatly relieved when Jennie fails to return, but she carries a sense of apprehension about any further contact with her. She worries about possible professional sanctions for abandoning Jennie or that Jennie might actually try to harm her when she least expects it. She is also deeply worried about others who might be harmed by Jennie, and feels disappointed that she did not have a larger impact on this volatile young woman.

This is a confusing situation, as many practitioners believe they must continue to directly manage the interaction and treat the underlying problems or risk charges of client abandonment. They may feel a powerful moral imperative to persist in attempts to contain a client who presents a significant threat to society at large.

From an ethically based risk management standpoint, the therapy relationship is terminated at the point when a threat is made. There is little or nothing to gain by attempting to resolve such a situation through clinical interactions. No further productive therapy is possible because the relationship of trust has been compromised beyond repair. It is not fair to expect the practitioner to continue attempting to manage threats of aggressive action when he or she is an intended target. The actions of the client clearly preclude any further discussion or counseling on the reasons for termination. However, a termination strategy is still needed. Instead of attempting to meet with the client to tie up loose ends, the practitioner needs to establish for the record the fact that termination has occurred and why. If there are other persons in danger, the provider may also need to take steps to warn or take precautions as stipulated by relevant laws and community standards.

There are many different circumstances that can precipitate termination. For any of these, the practitioner needs an appreciation of his or her professional limits and responsibilities, knowledge about possible options for the client, and willingness to bring these issues into the therapy discussion. In instances of a conflict of interest, the practitioner's ability to talk openly about exact reasons for termination may be constrained. However, the discussion can still productively focus on client needs and choices. There may be strong emotional reactions on both sides, but these feelings should not dictate an unprofessional course of action. The practitioner may experience emotions of frustration, disappointment or anxiety and fear. Ending on a positive note does not necessarily mean that the practitioner and the client both feel happy about the termination, but rather that the process is handled in a systematic and professional manner. Even if the client is unable for whatever reason to participate in effective ways, the provider can maintain this tone with his or her strategic professional stance.

Practitioner Skill Limits Well-intentioned practitioners who do not have the specific skills needed to address the problem at hand may confuse persistence with clinically inappropriate continuation of treatment. Doing so risks loss of professional integrity and potential harm to the client. Community standards of care have established the expectation that mental health practitioners should be familiar enough with basic psychopathology and various treatment options to recognize problems that are beyond their personal scope of practice and to provide appropriate referral.

Case Example: Provider–Client Mismatch. Jeremy was troubled by intrusive thoughts that he feared were blasphemous toward God, so he sought counseling at a faith-based clinic. Jeremy had a history of benign rituals of counting and repeating numbers and phrases in his head. When he was under some particular stress, he tended to check repeatedly, including checking doorknobs, door locks, and written work that might contain a mistake. His friends would sometimes find his requests for reassurance exasperating, but otherwise there were no significant impairments to his overall functioning as the result of his checking. His problems were mild and transient, and he never had a need to seek mental health intervention. That is, until his thoughts became blasphemous.

The practitioner at the clinic explained Jeremy's problem as a spiritual war in his head. He recommended intense prayer sessions and offered to meet with Jeremy twice per week to assist him in finding reassurance through contact with his faith. He instructed Jeremy to be very careful at his workplace, a prison facility, because he might inadvertently pick up more spiritual conflict just by interacting with the inmates. To reduce this risk, he recommended that Jeremy should surround himself with pictures or other icons representing angels to provide reassurance of his contact with good spirits.

Jeremy attempted this plan for two weeks. At the end of the second week, he traveled a short distance to visit his family. During the course of the weekend at home, he was hospitalized for an acute suicidal crisis. He started to have more intrusive thoughts about blaspheming God as well as new fears of harming his sister's children in some way. This led to thinking that he should kill himself rather than harm a child. When he admitted to his family that he was preoccupied with the idea he should kill himself, his family initiated hospitalization. In the course of his intake, Jeremy learned for the first time that the name for his problem was obsessive compulsive disorder, and that medication and specific psychotherapy could help.

Jeremy did not bear ill feelings toward the practitioner at the faith-based clinic as he had provided the spiritually focused intervention that Jeremy wanted. However, the practitioner lacked the skills to recognize that the problem was obsessive compulsive disorder, something that was not effectively treated by spiritual counseling. This approach actually exacerbated Jeremy's condition, leading to a crisis hospitalization. Fortunately, with the help of this family, Jeremy was redirected toward treatment appropriate for his particular disorder.

Stalled Progress   Perhaps the most typical termination dilemma is when there is a good rapport but little evident progress. Will additional therapy produce further benefit? It is not unusual for a client to make some initial progress and then stall at a plateau. Both client and practitioner have an emotional investment in treatment and may be encouraged by some initial gains. The therapy relationship is congenial but moving uncertainly toward an elusive sense of completion, maybe lacking a clear or attainable goal. There is risk in proceeding with such a vague sense of direction because the client is less likely to benefit from unfocused therapy. The contact may fade into unstructured meetings that are more social than therapeutic, raising the risk of an inappropriate dual relationship. Other practical risks include an overwhelming caseload with little turnover and practitioner vulnerability to burnout.

Case Example: Is More Therapy Needed?   When it came time to update her will, Melanie wondered, half seriously, if she should make provisions for several long-term clients who seemed destined to continue therapy with her forever. "Maybe," she mused, "they will follow me into the afterlife, showing up for their regular Wednesday appointment in some ethereal office like nothing has happened." These clients were all adamant about the need to continue therapy. Although there were notable differences in educational and economic backgrounds of these clients, each had a marginally stable but fragile existence. Their therapy sessions often had a social tone, but there was no gross distortion of professional or personal boundaries. In their own personal way, each relied on regular contact with "Dr. Melanie" to help regulate chronic emotional problems and manage stress, particularly the stress of social isolation.

Melanie is dealing with patient dependency and unclear treatment goals. She does need a plan for her personal will to stipulate someone who can provide confidential, professional management of client files and assist with referrals in the event of her unexpected death or unavailability. This is responsible and ethical practice management. The treatment relationships are very good, but the "automatic pilot" nature of the therapy indicates a lack of focus that could potentially be redirected in more productive ways. Periodic review and re-evaluation is critical but often overlooked in extended treatment relationships.

Eliciting the client's and the practitioner's thoughts about termination can yield important information about barriers to further progress. Pinpointing specific beliefs or skill issues can provide direction and new energy to the therapy work. For example, the client may be thinking, "I'll never be able to give up therapy. I would be too lonely." Or, "It's too risky to end therapy. I might have a relapse." The practitioner may think, as Melanie did, "If I bring up termination too soon, it might harm this client." Or, "If I bring up the subject of termination, the client will feel rejected." These ideas can be addressed within therapy, as part of an active process of working toward a positive termination, rather than just hanging on to therapy until it feels right to let go.

Melanie and her long-term clients might decide to continue treatment if there is identifiable benefit and relevant criteria for medical necessity are met. Some clients need continuous care, even if their progress is slow or minimal. By talking about the idea of termination, they are in a much better position to strike a negotiated agreement on the proximity or distance of closure and actively work toward this goal. Having a termination strategy for longer-term clients will help focus therapy and mediate any drift toward unproductive or inappropriate interactions.

Providers must make an active decision whether or not to include longer-term treatment within their range of services. If longer-term treatment is offered, treatment objectives that are consistent with a collaborative model can be formulated (e.g., Beck, Freeman, Davis, & Associates, 2004). If extended treatment is not an option, it is even more important to create a positive transition that marks the completion of a particular segment of collaboration. This encourages the client to feel good about the time invested, to be agreeable to returning for further therapy in the future, or to be open to seeking out alternative services or other providers.

Termination Resistance   Some clients are persistently unready and even resistant to termination. When the practitioner attempts to discuss progress, the client has strong emotional reactions and may avoid or subvert the discussion. There are a host of possible reasons for this behavior, the most likely being the presence of Axis II psychopathology (Beck et al., 2004). Some clients react to the mere subject of progress evaluation in an automatically defensive way. Secondary gain may also foster the client's reluctance to let go. Or the client may perceive the therapy relationship in emotionally distorted ways, a situation that some practitioners may not expect or be fully prepared to manage. Perhaps the client construes the end of therapy as an absolute separation, one that threatens their future existence. Being in therapy is "safe," but ending therapy is "dangerous." Some clients attempt to exercise an inordinate degree of power or entitlement in therapy, acting as if the practitioner "belongs" to them and is obligated to meet their demands, reasonable or not. Various idiosyncratic reactions may reflect the client's effort to escape perceived rejection, compensate for a sense of helplessness, or maintain proximity to a source of nurturance and support. Sometimes clients will go to extreme lengths to maintain control and access to the therapy relationship.

Trying to conclude therapy with a termination-resistant client can be likened to our initial aircraft pilot metaphor. Termination without an individualized strategy is like flying on autopilot and then trying to land blindfolded while heading into a storm. The safety and quality of the therapy interaction may diminish rapidly and could become dangerous to one or both parties. The provider can eventually land, but needs help to prevent untoward events. Staying in a holding pattern might buy some time, but it might also complicate the situation as the client's most maladaptive behaviors have prevailed and now control the interaction. Consider the following example of an actual case where control struggles resulted in a nightmarish legal and personal situation for the provider.

Case Example: Harassment as Refusal.   In the case of *Ensworth v. Mullvain*, the client's resistance to termination eventually forced the provider to obtain not one but two restraining orders from the court. At first, the practitioner was persuaded by the client to resume therapy to address the termination issues. When this proved fruitless, a second termination was forced by the client's actions. As a cumulative result of this termination struggle, which took place over the course of several years, the psychologist suffered significant emotional and professional distress.

According to case documentation (Ensworth v. Mullvain, 1990), Ensworth was a psychologist practicing in Pasadena, CA. She worked with Ms. Mullvain for nearly two years and then terminated the treatment. Mullvain resisted the termination, so Ensworth resumed sessions to help her resolve the termination issues and disengage from the provider. Unfortunately, a series of harassing incidents forced the second termination with Mullvain. Ensworth then obtained a restraining order against her former client, which diminished the number of harassing incidents for a period of approximately 15 months, but nevertheless incidents continued to occur. The former client followed Ensworth in her car, tried to stop her car in the middle of the street, circled the psychologist's office building, drove repeatedly around her house, made numerous phone calls to the psychologist, sent threatening letters, and made phone calls to other professionals in the community in an effort to harm Ensworth's reputation.

Shortly after the first restraining order expired, Mullvain sent a letter to Ensworth stating that she would repeatedly violate any restraining order, that she was willing to go to jail, and she was willing to do whatever was necessary to continue contact and ensure that Ensworth did not forget her. She alluded in her letter to committing suicide in Ensworth's presence. Ensworth filed for a second order of protection, which Mullvain appealed in court. Mullvain attempted to argue that she had legitimate business near Ensworth's home. She stated that she had lost money and business as the result of the restraining order as it prevented her from pursuing her work, which included three different door-to-door sales jobs and "all the realms of photographic art and advertising." Her counsel argued against the restraining order, stating that Ensworth had failed to establish emotional damage as the result of Mullvain's actions and therefore the injunction was not supported by sufficient evidence. Further, the injunction would infringe on Mullvain's fundamental right to pursue a lawful calling, business, or profession.

The judgment of the court in issuing the second restraining order was affirmed in the appeal process. In essence, the judicial review found no merit in the client's claim that this injunction would impair her fundamental right to pursue her occupation because she did not demonstrate an *inability* to do her work in places other than near the psychologist's home. The court found that the client knowingly and willingly engaged in a course of conduct that seriously alarmed, annoyed, or harassed the psychologist. The psychologist actually suffered substantial emotional distress by being followed, spied upon, repeatedly contacted by phone and letter, and threatened with being a forced witness to the client's suicide.

The court verified the unacceptable nature of conduct by the former client and provided a means for pursuing further criminal charges if the actions persisted. However, this legal recourse was tantamount to the helping hand pulling the struggling practitioner out of the quicksand just before she sank completely into the pit. She had already endured more than two years of harassment and the effort needed to seek protection via the courts. There are no easy solutions for ending such a power struggle once such intensity has developed. It is yet another reminder of the potentially urgent need to give early and serious consideration to termination strategy.

As these case examples illustrate, progress toward an end of therapy is not necessarily tidy or direct. Many times therapy *does* end because the expectations for a positive accomplishment have been met. However, there may also be disagreement or uncertainty as to when therapy should end, strong emotions or attachments that make the ending difficult and even alarming in some cases, or circumstances that force termination before the client or provider are ready. Failure to directly address termination can leave the provider and client struggling with confusing feelings and uncertain actions. Failure to terminate therapy when it is appropriate to do so can have unproductive or even harmful results. Effective strategy is needed to create the best possible closure, maximize the usefulness of therapy over-all, and minimizing any possible stress or harm.

PRAGMATIC STRATEGY FOR TERMINATION

Paradoxical as it may seem, effective termination begins in the first few meetings. This is when the initial direction of treatment is planned, the informed consent to service is obtained, and the client is oriented to therapy participation (Barnett, 1998; Beck, 1995; Bernstein & Hartsell, 2000; Kramer, 1986). If there are any known circumstances that could affect the course of therapy, perhaps a predictable change in provider availability or insurance coverage limits, it is best to discuss these considerations at the outset. The client's expectations are assessed at this point, including expectations for how quickly change should occur and how long therapy should last. The first few sessions are also a time of socializing the client to the model of therapy and the tasks associated with it.

What happens after this initial orientation varies according to the provider's basic theoretical orientation or philosophy of termination. In the psychodynamic model, termination is conceptualized as an ending phase of psychological and emotional change. This phase of completion happens after certain structural alterations have been established and stabilized in the working phase of therapy (Weiner, 1998). In contrast, the viewpoint proposed here is a pragmatic one where termination is conceptualized as a task of the therapeutic alliance. This perspective allows issues of termination to be dealt with throughout the duration of any episode of care. Termination as a task can easily be incorporated into the initial socialization process, as the client is oriented toward the ways to effectively participate in and conclude therapy. Termination does not necessarily hinge on completion of large-scale changes but rather is a point of re-evaluation and redirection. The client is specifically prepared for participation in determining an appropriate point of termination and primed to expect that this concern will be periodically assessed.

Although there may be common ground between this pragmatic model of termination and a psychodynamic model, especially the common scientific denominator, this model is intended for learning-based approaches. No assumptions are made concerning its usefulness or compatibility with dynamic therapy. Details of a psychodynamic model of termination can be located in other resources (e.g., Barnett, 1998; Barnett et al., 2000; Curtis, 2002; Joyce et al., 2007; Kramer, 1986; Novick & Novick, 2006; Weiner, 1998).

What Are the Main Objectives of a Pragmatic Termination Strategy?

As therapy begins, one primary aim is to ensure its satisfactory conclusion. A pragmatic termination strategy is organized around two main objectives: developing the collaboration and forming a reasoned course of action that will lead to the most satisfactory conclusion that is possible under the given circumstances.

To engage the client's collaboration, the provider presents termination as a component of the entire process of planning and evaluating treatment. Thus, various considerations of ending therapy are an acceptable and expected part of their regular discussions. Some of the commonly encountered reasons for termination may be outlined in the informed consent and discussed early on, such as the achievement of goals or limited time frames. It may be useful to touch upon less common reasons for termination as well, particularly reasons of possible adverse reactions or noncompliance. The amount of attention given to the discussion of termination will likely vary across the course of therapy, but it is clear that this is a shared process of decision-making.

The second objective of a pragmatic termination strategy is to formulate a reasoned course of action for continuing versus ending therapy. As therapy proceeds, it is important that a plan for termination is under consideration. The ending of therapy is not something that just happens, but is incorporated into the overall treatment plan. This plan is determined by a mutually negotiated agreement between client and therapist. Either client or therapist can initiate a decision to terminate treatment, and this can occur for various reasons. If the provider is to effectively initiate termination, he or she must have a clear understanding of the relevant parameters that guide this decision.

Providers typically develop and refine their plan for termination as therapy unfolds over time. Given a vast number of intervening variables that are not fully apparent at the beginning, the terms of the treatment plan usually need to be somewhat flexible. Providers can be alert to potential triggers for termination, and take into account relevant clinical, empirical, ethical, emotional, and practical information as it becomes available. This allows various contingencies to be addressed as "if-then" formulations about ongoing work. If the client participates in treatment and responds well, then therapy will end when the goals are achieved. If the client becomes worse, then discontinuation and referral options should be considered. If the client must work within certain financial constraints, then the goals must be limited to what is feasible in 15 sessions. Routine procedures can be developed for frequently encountered situations, tailored to the practitioner and setting. For example, the routine procedure may be that if a client fails a scheduled visit, then he or she will be encouraged to reschedule. But if a client fails three scheduled visits, then treatment may be terminated without further contact. Templates based on typical situations and policies can then be modified as indicated by special circumstances or clinical judgment.

Thus, a pragmatic termination strategy is distinguished by two key elements: active collaboration on the task of termination and the use of a reasoned course of action to achieve the best possible conclusion.

How Can We Distinguish Good Termination from Bad Termination?

There is no specific definition of a good or bad termination that consistently holds across different theoretical orientations. However, there are some commonly accepted ideas about termination that shape a basic distinction between desirable and undesirable conditions. One commonly accepted idea is that good termination occurs either when therapy has achieved its goals, reached its maximum potential, or is no longer needed. Bad termination occurs when there is harm to the client, the provider, or both. Termination that occurs too early or too soon might fall within the scope of undesirable termination. This is often referred to as "premature" termination, when therapy ends before the client can benefit from the service.

Premature termination has many negative connotations and difficulties as a concept. It is viewed as a problematic waste of resources, a source of discouragement and evidence of ineffectiveness of services (Reis & Brown, 2006). Yet our understanding of premature termination has been hampered by the lack of a uniformly reliable description of the phenomena. For research purposes, termination that occurs after one to four sessions (Garfield, 1994) or before completion of a predetermined number of sessions (Pekarik, 1992) has defined "premature" termination. A more qualitative approach describes premature termination as therapy that ends without the sense of psychological closure associated with having resolved problems or at least understanding the reasons for ending therapy (Kleinke, 1994).

Although the term "premature" may be useful to describe some instances of termination, it implies a number of things that are not necessarily accurate for all of the instances to which it is applied. The word "premature" refers to something that takes place before a proper (Merriam-Webster, 1984), customary, correct, or assigned time (American Heritage, 2001). Clients who stop therapy after a few sessions or before they achieve the changes sought by the provider represent a heterogeneous group. The judgment of a termination as "premature" may be due to a mismatch of the expectations of provider and client, where the provider is biased toward longer-term treatment and skeptical of quick fixes, but the client expects and prefers brief intervention (Reis & Brown, 2006). The negative implications for the client are largely inferred by the provider's assumptions, whereas the negative effects on the provider are aggravated by perceptions of ineffectiveness or uselessness of their efforts.

If we conceptualize change as a cyclical rather than a linear process (Prochaska & DiClemente, 1992; Prochaska, DiClemente & Norcross, 1992; Prochaska & Norcross, 2003), we can better understand the progression of client change across time and through interaction with multiple influences, one of which may be formal psychotherapy. Even a single session of therapy can activate skills and motivation that continue to foster change without further contact with a therapist. Termination of therapy before the complete resolution of a problem may be reasonable and appropriate, and indeed is typically the case (Prochaska & Norcross, 2003). Termination after a limited period of time, after circumscribed tasks are accomplished or in response to compelling circumstances, is not necessarily improper, uncustomary, or incorrect.

What we lack is a descriptive perspective on termination that will allow more relative judgments about various conditions of termination. Such a perspective would illustrate reasonable termination actions in operational and qualitative terms, and avoid priori assumptions about correct or customary length of time and extent of change needed to complete treatment.

The beginnings of a descriptive perspective can be found in the definition of termination offered by Younggren and Gottlieb (in press). They define termination as "an ethically and clinically appropriate process by which a professional relationship is ended." If we direct our attention to the collaboration between provider and client as the medium of this ethically and clinically appropriate process, we can develop a dimensional perspective on the range of possible conditions.

The following five types of termination collaboration are proposed here to describe the process of communication between client and provider. The five types of termination collaboration are:

- Prospective termination
- Flexible termination
- Complex termination
- Oblique termination
- Unprofessional termination

Prospective termination is planned in advance and agreed to by both parties. It occurs most often when the client has reached the planned goals and has no further need for service. Prospective termination might also occur in well-defined situations where there is a known endpoint determined by circumstances. An example of this is the clinician in training who must terminate services at the end of their assignment. Another example is the managed care situation where the number of sessions is significantly limited and there are few if any degrees of freedom for negotiating different financial arrangements with the client. As noted by Younggren and Gottlieb (in press), there is usually little conflict associated with this type of termination and it presents little risk to the clinician or the client.

Flexible termination describes those situations where there is relatively little advance planning, but the decision to conclude is mutually agreeable and generally without conflict. The provider and client communicate about the issues of continuing or ending and decide that a proximal conclusion is appropriate. This may be negotiated with the intent to pick up again at a later point, but without an explicit commitment to do so. Flexible terminations may be implemented in response to unanticipated circumstances, and are often accompanied by recognizable improvements in the client's presenting problem. Flexible terminations intentionally maximize the client's autonomy in determining the duration, intensity, and focus of therapy.

Complex termination refers to sensitive, protracted, or volatile communications about progress and the conclusion of therapy. This type refers to the difficult termination where there is likely to be some conflict or intense client emotional reactions that have a negative or complicating impact on the termination process. Client issues are the main precipitants of complex termination, but there are other factors, including the therapist's reactions and the situation, that interact with the client's difficulties. Complex terminations are very important and will receive closer consideration in chapters two and six.

Oblique termination, on the other hand, is cloudy, evasive, and unilaterally enacted by the client. There is little or no discussion or response to the provider's attempts to address the client's absence. The client exercises autonomy, but does so without involving the provider or gaining closure within the collaboration. Providers might attempt to follow up or gain closure, but they can not force the client's cooperation. Complex terminations may be difficult or frustrating, while oblique terminations can be haunting and worrisome if one lacks a reasonable degree of discernment about respective responsibilities of the client and provider.

There is only one type of termination that is categorically "bad" and that is an unprofessional one. Unprofessional terminations are not purely a matter of insufficient termination skills. It is incredibly rare to have a bad termination of good therapy. "Bad" terminations tend to flow directly from a provider's failure to manage the course of therapy and maintain appropriate professional standards of conduct and practice (Hjelt, 2007). Unprofessional terminations do not happen because of small misjudgments or differences in clinical opinion that arise at the end. Bad terminations are more typically situations where the provider veered significantly off-track earlier in therapy, even from the beginning. Unprofessional actions or complaints of such concerning termination are in effect a marker for a trail of errors. Perhaps the overall treatment plan was inadequate or an unstable client was allowed an inappropriate degree of control over the relationship and the provider failed to take corrective action. As an example of grossly unprofessional termination, consider the provider who fails to show up for sessions and does not respond to any of the client's attempts to communicate about the disposition. The therapist is simply gone, checked out mid-therapy without a word of good-bye or explanation. Such cases of true abandonment are rare, however. Situations where steps were taken to terminate properly but conflict or complexity was mismanaged are more common. Other potential errors include inadequate notice, improper self-disclosure, failure to refer, or failure to consult. Attempting to provide service beyond the scope of the provider's competence is frequently a core mistake that produces a pattern of therapy mismanagement (Hjelt, 2007). Burn-out, impairment, poor coping and stress management, inadequate skills or professional socialization and therapist character problems, such as narcissism, are all possible antecedents to provider misjudgments and professional error (Freeman, Felgoise & Davis, 2008).

Because of potential confusion with various connotations, the label "premature" is not used in this descriptive spectrum. Premature termination may be a relevant clinical phenomenon, but it is highly intertwined with potential biases toward long-term interventions, and it does not describe the processes of provider-client collaboration.

SUMMARY POINTS FOR APPLIED PRACTICE

1. Effective, positive termination is not a matter to leave to chance. It takes planning and discussion, beginning with the informed consent process and continuing throughout therapy until its conclusion.

2. As in most relationships, either party has the right to bring the interaction to an end. The client has the right to terminate therapy at any time, without cause. The provider is professionally responsible for advancing the best possible termination, given the particular circumstances.

3. Views on the optimal length and aims of therapy can vary a great deal among providers of different philosophical perspectives and between providers and clients.

4. The limits and parameters of today's health care environment require careful attention to the necessity and effectiveness of therapy, thus raising the bar on termination responsibilities.

5. Completion of treatment is not a clear-cut matter, but rather a contextual decision that is negotiated between provider and client.

6. Emotional attachments, practical concerns, treatment goals, clinical progress, and ethical limits are all part of the context that affects termination decisions.

7. Both haste and procrastination can increase the risks of error in termination.

8. Some terminations hold a greater risk for adverse events. These include terminations stemming from precipitating circumstances, stalled progress, limited provider skills, or clinical complexity.

9. Pragmatic termination strategy is a proactive tool for orienting both client and provider to the task and process of ending the professional contract in problem-focused models of therapy. Two main objectives of the pragmatic termination strategy are to foster the client-therapist collaboration and to use that collaboration to form a reasoned course of action for concluding their work.

10. Good termination is negotiated by the provider and client. Truly bad termination occurs when the provider's actions fall below acceptable professional standards. Bad termination is usually not just something that accidentally happens at the end of good therapy. Most often it has antecedents in other errors, such as failure to properly manage the course of therapy.

2

Professional Skills and Termination

Key Questions Addressed in This Chapter

- What is a collaborative stance toward termination?
- Is it useful to distinguish types of termination?
- What are the standards for ethically responsible termination?
- What is client abandonment, and how can it be avoided?
- Can termination be broken down into specific applied skills?

BUILDING A BASE OF COLLABORATION

There are a number of professional skills that form the foundation for competence with a pragmatic model of termination. These include being well grounded in the use of collaboration in termination planning, understanding some of the variations that are likely to be encountered in termination communications, and being informed of relevant ethical standards concerning termination. It is also necessary to understand client abandonment and how to avoid it. Finally, the provider needs to have a good grasp of specific applied skills needed to implement termination actions.

What Is a Collaborative Stance toward Termination?

A collaborative stance means that the provider actively encourages discussion of termination and frames the decision as a mutually shared responsibility. Closure is regarded as an ongoing process more than a distant event or phase. It is woven into the goals and tasks of therapy right from the start, and the termination decision is forged bit by bit through interaction and progress. Various options are weighed for how well they serve the client's clinical needs in the context of other relevant considerations. When contact ends, it might complete an extended episode of therapy or it might be a transition between smaller segments of focused work. It might be open-ended with the option to return to therapy, or it might be specifically closed to any further contact. Competent management of this collaborative process requires clinical sensitivity, sound communication skills, a thorough grasp of professional standards, and clarity in the provider's practice policy.

Provider and client are the primary collaborators, but there may be other parties with a vested interest in the termination decision. With rare exception, it is safe to assume that all concerned parties want therapy to be successful and to come to a desirable end. Despite this common objective, there are apt to be vast differences of opinion on how to define success and how long therapy should take. Each different vantage point includes a certain tension between opposing forces. Clients want to relieve distress and achieve a variety of personal changes, but they come to therapy in varying stages of readiness for change. Practitioners are committed to helping those in need, but they must also attend to professional responsibilities. Insurers or other third-party payers seek top quality service but at lowest possible cost. Agencies strive to fully meet the needs of specific individuals yet balance this with fair access for their designated population. Employers want their benefit programs to enhance worker stability and productivity, but they must contain discretionary spending. Significant others care about the client's well-being, but also have their own agenda and limits. Thus, the primary collaboration does not operate in a vacuum that is free of external concerns or pressures. A collaborative stance also means being cognizant of the multiple and perhaps conflicting interests that impinge on the termination decisions and finding ways to address the client's best interests in this context.

A collaborative stance is already part of the basic clinical approach in many problem-focused modalities, such as cognitive therapy (e.g., Beck, 1995; Beck and Weishaar, 2008). In general, the learning-based clinician aims to make each and every session a useful contribution to the client's overall self-management and skill development. There is no specific assumption that therapy is only useful when it involves intensive contact over a long period of time or resolves all of the client's maladies. The model for therapy is that of *coping* with life's challenges in a positive way, and treatment is flexibly structured around the client's specific needs and resources. The practitioner's challenge is to engage the client in productive efforts during the time available and to work together toward drawing a positive conclusion within each session and across the episode of therapy. To accomplish this, the provider is consistently open and positive about discussion of termination, bringing it up and following it up at appropriate times.

Is It Useful to Distinguish Types of Termination?

The quality of a termination is important. However, a single description can not sufficiently capture the qualitative variations that are possible. Terminations do not all look alike. There are many ways to view or describe this multidimensional process, as we discussed in Chapter One. Because there are differences in the way that termination is presented, discussed, decided upon, and enacted, it is useful to have a systematic way of describing common patterns. Variations in the features of termination can be linked to three general factors: (a) the nature of the therapy itself and the circumstances surrounding it, (b) the client's conduct in relationship to the therapy and the provider, and (c) the multitude of therapist variables impacting the provider's availability and competence (Younggren & Gottlieb, in press).

Many current descriptions are based on a single dichotomy. Termination decisions are considered either voluntary or involuntary/forced (Sperry, 2007; Weiner 1998). Two categories of contract dissolution—treatment completion and premature termination—are outlined by Younggren and Gottlieb (in press). Other authors describe a combination of reasons including finances, lack of benefit, potential harm, subtle terminations, or unavoidable terminations (Bennett et al., 2006). Empirical data on termination suggests that clients terminate unilaterally or without notice about 37 percent of the time in clinics, whereas termination is mutual about 63 percent of the time (Tryon & Kane, 1995). Many, if not most, mutual terminations are triggered by satisfaction with gains or external constraints unrelated to therapy. Of those who terminate with notice, dissatisfaction is apt to be the reason among less than 10 percent. Interestingly, these investigators report that less than 1 percent of the terminations were therapist initiated (.8 percent) (Renk & Dinger, 2002), but this low figure and the level of dissatisfaction (8.5 percent) may be a function of the clinician's novice skill level in this study.

As we have discussed, a basic distinction between good and bad termination is useful for separating acceptable from unacceptable conditions. It would also be useful to have a means of describing the variability across good or reasonably good terminations as well. Capturing possible qualitative variations can help us refine our termination strategy to meet different client needs and prospectively manage various challenges and risks. The five descriptions proposed here focus on the process of communication as an essential component of termination. These are termination collaborations that are (a) prospective, (b) flexible, (c) complex, (d) oblique, and (e) unprofessional. The most desirable types of termination are prospective and flexible, and these are most common. Complex and oblique terminations are less common but unavoidable at times. The objective with the latter two types of termination is to improve the quality of collaboration to the extent that is possible. Provider stress is elevated with complex or oblique termination and needs to be included as a factor in the termination strategy. The fifth type, unprofessional, is least common but always a matter of serious concern. Understanding the parameters of each type can orient the provider toward ways to ensure quality and reduce the risk of bad termination.

Prospective Termination   *Prospective termination* refers to advance plans for ending that typically culminate with one or more closing sessions. The decision to terminate therapy is an intentional one, based on deliberations between client and provider. In these deliberations, client and provider review relevant clinical, practical, and ethical issues and attempt to make the best possible choice given all things considered. Prospective termination is usually linked to some logical point of conclusion, such as symptom improvement, goal attainment, or agreed circumstantial limits. Prospective termination is a key consideration in any treatment provided under a managed care contract, as time limits are established at the outset. Providers can facilitate prospective closure by periodically discussing termination from the point of informed consent forward. Such discussion can be brief and is perhaps most easily accomplished in the context of progress reviews. As progress reaches a plateau or agreed contract limits or goals are encountered, a collaborative discussion about the next steps should include the option of termination. Providers will, of course, use care in their clinical demeanor to minimize any potential misinterpretation of their actions as rejection or unfounded dismissal of the client.

The amount of time needed to process the closing will depend on the overall duration and scope of treatment and the client's perspective on termination. Those clients who are ready and willing often need relatively little time to navigate this transition. Others may want several sessions to address their various concerns. For many clients, a gradual tapering of session frequency allows time to anticipate and prepare for termination and helps both client and provider evaluate any need for further treatment. Ideally, a final face-to-face meeting is planned in advance, where the main item on the agenda is imminent closure. Prior to this point, termination has been discussed as an anticipated action that would follow a future session.

Hopefully the decision to terminate is mutually acceptable, but total agreement is not necessarily required before discontinuation of contact occurs. It is helpful to keep in mind that both client and provider have some veto power over the therapy relationship. Clients have the right to end therapy at any time, and thus have absolute veto power. Clinicians, on the other hand, must operate within the bounds of professional duty and have a reason to end therapy. However, there are many reasons why the provider must end therapy for practical and ethical reasons (Bennett et al., 2006; Younggren & Gottlieb, in press). This can be accomplished prospectively if the clinician engages the client in a direct dialogue about discontinuation, discusses the reasons to the extent possible, encourages questions and expression of feelings, and provides a clear disposition. Providers, who obtain informed consent to various conditions of termination at the beginning of therapy, including time limits, have a potentially legally binding contract that stipulates the client's agreement to these conditions for termination. Discussion of these parameters from the first session is a key strategy for increasing the client's understanding and reducing the potential for negative reactance.

It is possible in some instances that neither provider nor client is actually happy about the planned termination, but they have identified, discussed, and forged some understanding of reasons for the action. The client feels adequately informed and not "blindsided" by an unexpected ending or unknown policy. There is no specific expectation that all problems have been permanently resolved as a prerequisite for prospective termination, but there is a rationale for the action taken. The client has been able to check his or her perceptions and ask pertinent questions, as well as express feelings of satisfaction or dissatisfaction. Even if there is a range of conflicted emotions, the provider fosters a tone of positive interaction and psychological integration. By using a caring, dignified, and respectful approach, the provider can create a transition that closes the therapy contract in a way that is supportive to both participants.

Sometimes clients do not think that a final face-to-face meeting is a priority. It is not uncommon for this client to either cancel or fail to schedule the proposed last session. Providers can recommend attendance at this termination session, but they can not force the client's participation. Such non-response is an example of client action that precludes an exit interview. However, the client's informal departure is still consistent with a prospective termination in that the decision was discussed in advance and a plan for ending contact was established.

In prospective termination, provider and client have the most clarity about the closing disposition. Clients will certainly vary in their need for further services depending on the nature and extent of their problems and the supportive resources that will be available once therapy ends. The option of following up on an "as needed" basis is often included in the closing disposition because any client has some potential for needing or wanting follow-up contact or further service. As the saying goes in medicine, we are all potentially "pre-op," meaning that even those who are in good health could have some unpredictable need for surgery.

Clients with a higher likelihood of needing further service because of chronic or recurring disorders can be encouraged to seek booster sessions, or to activate a new episode of treatment, without carrying a stigma of failure. However, following up with the same provider may not always be feasible because of personal changes, as people move and redirect their lives. It is useful to review some of the possible ways that the client can access other resources without the direct help of the specific provider, if needed. It is also helpful to ensure that the client knows how to gain access to information in his or her official health record once therapy has ended.

Clinical Example of Prospective Termination.   As a graduate student, Luis was a low-income client whose health insurance would fully cover

18 sessions of outpatient therapy per calendar year. The limits of coverage were clarified at the beginning of treatment, and Luis and the provider determined that they would do as much as they could to treat his depression within the bounds of that time frame. They noted the option of adjusting the frequency of sessions over the course of treatment to maximize the availability of support. They could attempt to time sessions so that additional visits beyond the initial 18 would roll into the next calendar year. Luis also had additional insurance benefits that covered medication management without subtracting from the 18 visits for psychotherapy and a provision for inpatient hospitalization should that be necessary.

Luis's response to therapy was positive and steady improvement was noted in progress reviews at 4 and 12 sessions. At each of these reviews, the provider explicitly mentioned the number of remaining sessions so that he and Luis could assess whether or not termination was still on track for the 18th session. After 12 visits, they decided to taper the frequency of contact to every 2–3 weeks, and then to once per month. At the 17th session, they discussed Luis's overall progress, his strategies for maintaining this progress, his reactions to ending sessions, and his options for follow-up contact or access to his record. They agreed to preserve the one remaining session for an "as or if needed" consult.

Flexible Termination   *Flexible termination* is an ending that occurs in response to immediate, salient plans and contingencies. This decision may deviate from earlier targets, but new considerations prompt a flexible reassessment of those earlier plans. Perhaps a change in client circumstances triggers termination at a point sooner than anticipated or before reaching a state of resolution that the provider would prefer. Or there may be other clinical or ethical factors that bring termination to the forefront of discussion. Perhaps the client is making little progress and appears to have reached maximum benefit for the time being. When the termination is structured as an experimental, "try it and see" option, there may be less direct discussion about the process of ending because the possibility of returning is explicitly left open.

Flexible termination allows for maximum client autonomy and participation in the treatment plan. When dealing with circumstances such as insurance contract limits, the provider outlines available options as clearly as possible and encourages the client to take responsibility for choosing among the options. If termination is precipitated by unanticipated limits or circumstances affecting the provider, it can be most helpful to offer the client a choice among reasonable options where feasible. For example, if a provider must abruptly take a brief medical leave, the client can be offered a choice between waiting until the provider returns to practice (if clinically feasible) to complete termination or resume therapy (and a back-up provider is available for interim contact if desired) or transferring immediately to an alternate provider.

When it is the client who raises the idea of stopping therapy, the provider is sensitive to the client's needs and resources. Flexible termination may be an appropriate and useful choice if the client does not have the energy to focus on active change or is entering a maintenance phase and can rely on other resources for support. The client says, either directly or indirectly, "This is enough for now. I'll be back later for more," or "This might be all I need, I'm not really sure and I need to find out." As with prospective termination, the provider can encourage the client to follow-up as needed without fear of a failure stigma.

There are cases where the provider might propose the idea of taking a break from therapy to foster the client's independence and self-management skills, with the option of resuming sessions as needed. This strategy emphasizes the client's role in choosing to make use of therapy as a resource for active change, and it can minimize the tensions that can develop when progress is at a plateau. It is important that this option be presented as opportunity for exploration and discovery and not as a rejection of the client.

Sometimes clients will initiate termination by informal communication such as telephone or e-mail. Providers typically encourage the client to schedule a session formally dedicated to termination issues, but clients do not always agree or comply with this plan. It may be that authorization for payment has expired and the client is unwilling to assume the expense of even one more session. In this case, many providers will consider the option of offering an additional visit at reduced or no cost, if possible, to ensure that the client's needs are adequately addressed. Or it may be that the client is ambivalent or unclear about the termination decision and purposely wants to leave things open-ended. Providers can use contextual information to determine an appropriate course of action in such instances. For example, a client may have made some reasonable short-term progress when she encounters a change in circumstances, such as children out of school for the summer. So she does not formally terminate therapy, but instead leaves a message indicating that she will call for follow-up as needed after the school year resumes.

Clinical Example of Flexible Termination.   When Helen changed jobs mid-year, she also changed health care plans, and her therapist was not in the provider network of the new plan. It was going to take at least six months for her therapist to join the new plan, if he was even accepted at all. Helen was not enthusiastic about transferring to a new therapist, so the provider appealed to the insurance plan for an extension of her benefits. The insurance carrier allowed payment for one session for closure and transition. There was no provision for further sessions because the insurance carrier determined that there were plenty of other in-network providers within the client's geographic area. So with no specific advance notice, Helen and her therapist met for what was to be their last session.

Several issues were discussed during this session. These included Helen's current status and situation, her overall progress, skills she had acquired, and her thoughts and feelings about continuing or ending therapy at that point. She assessed her strengths and accomplishments, and reviewed some ideas for maintaining and continuing her progress. The clinician reassured Helen that he would provide records and information to a new provider should she request that in the future. Together they reviewed a list of alternative providers and identified three good candidates should Helen decide to continue. Helen expressed overall satisfaction with therapy and with the provider's effort to ensure a termination process. Based on her current status, she decided to wait and see about continuing therapy.

Complex Termination   *Complex termination* occurs when client factors significantly confound or distort the communication about termination and the negotiations and discussions do not proceed as expected or needed. Clients with personality impairments and poor coping skills tend to have the most difficulty in negotiating this transition. They may be very reactive to the idea of termination and confuse things that the provider says or fails to say. Clients with severely limited resources, multiple or co-morbid disorders, chronic stresses, or exploitive motives may have corresponding difficulties with the termination process. Complicated reactions to termination often stem from the client's primary beliefs and the coping strategies associated with these cognitive patterns. A range of clinical factors that complicate termination is explored in greater detail in Chapter Six.

Providers can further confound the termination process with an ineffective approach, poor handling of their own needs and limits, and unproductive reactions to the demands or idiosyncrasies of particular clients. Being too lax or casual about termination can allow easily preventable problems to escalate into larger and more difficult problems. Being defensive and controlling about termination can disempower the client and induce a mind-set of dissatisfaction with service, a stance that actually increases the provider's risk of client complaints. Eschewing termination in favor of prolonged therapy is not a foolproof professional default choice either. Providers are professionally compelled to continually determine if it is safe, reasonable, and effective to continue therapy or end it if those conditions can not be met.

The clinician's tasks in complex termination are fourfold: (a) to create and maintain reasonable professional boundaries; (b) to communicate as effectively as possible given the client's particular clinical issues and sensitivities; (c) to pay particular attention to the level of emotional arousal generated by the termination—the client's, their own, and that of any other involved party (a supervisor, the agency, a family member, etc.); and (d) to develop an individualized termination strategy based on this client's clinical needs, ongoing behavior and situational limits and stick with it even if the client objects.

For example, if a client is easily overwhelmed by a profusion of affect and reacts strongly to change, the clinician can approach termination through more gradual exposure. With this client, discussing termination well in advance of the imminent event and enlisting the client in setting the plan for a termination date may increase the client's sense of control. If the client is apt to depart abruptly because of rejection sensitivity, the provider can tie termination to accomplishment of multiple functional goals that are defined operationally and tracked on a regular basis. This may help to counteract the client's tendency to misinterpret various interactions as indications that the provider wants to dismiss them.

Clinical Example of Complex Termination. A number of examples of different complex terminations are presented throughout this volume. In Chapter One, the case of *Ensworth v. Mullvain* illustrated some of the very real power struggles that can occur when a client feels anguished and entitled, and the provider must deal with exceptional challenges to the termination boundaries. Other examples are presented in Chapter Six. The following example illustrates the challenge of a client with very low self-esteem who idealizes the provider and tends to cope with interpersonal anxiety via avoidance and other impulsive strategies.

Gail often worried that she was "a pain" to her therapist, and she expected to be dumped or fired as a client at any time. This was a significant pattern in Gail's life, as she was hyper-vigilant to signs of impermanence in relationships and believed herself to be unworthy of interest. One of her primary coping strategies was to dwell on her own shortcomings in dealings with others and to impulsively withdraw at the slightest hint of uncertainty to protect herself from the stress and humiliation of rejection. Gail's mood was consistently depressed, and her functional impairment varied from moderate to severe. She was hardly ready for termination on the basis of clinical improvement. Nevertheless, Gail was making progress and had recently achieved a significant goal of visiting her children during the holidays. While she was recounting details of the visit, she interpreted the therapist's attentive listening as an indication that therapy was over. As the session was wrapping up, Gail abruptly said, "Well, I guess this means we're done." With that, she bolted out of the office without confirming her next appointment. When the therapist phoned her about rescheduling, Gail acted surprised. "I thought when you were quiet for so long, that meant you were tired of listening to me. I'm probably a boring client. Now that I was able to see my kids, therapy must be over." The provider reminded Gail that termination would not occur in such an abrupt way without discussion or clear reasons. For their next session, they agreed to discuss the specific set of goals that could determine the reasons for a prospective termination.

Oblique Termination   *Oblique termination* refers to discontinuation that is unilaterally enacted by the client without discussion, explanation or response to follow-up. The client may abruptly "no-show" and not respond to follow-up phone or e-mail messages. Perhaps this departure was preceded by lateness and cancellations that portended the ending, but there is little direct information about the client's rationale. The client might cancel with no reason or with a circumstantial reason that averts termination discussion and then fail to request or follow through on rescheduling the cancelled meeting. There is an unsettled aspect to this ending, at least for the provider, as the lack of communication implies a negative tone, but this is unconfirmed. This type of termination can occur at any point in therapy, but most often after relatively few sessions. It may be the prototypical termination labeled "premature" where the client ends things without the provider's concurrence. The range of emotions triggered by this outcome can be difficult for providers, from relief for an end to an unproductive alliance to discouragement by the poor collaboration and disappointment at the client's dismissal of the treatment opportunity.

There are many possible reasons for oblique termination. One is that the client did not understand or like the process of therapy and did not know how to raise questions with the provider. Perhaps the client felt intimidated by the situation and the mysteriousness associated with psychological treatment. Or there may have been a provider-client mismatch or problems with the rapport. The client may have taken offense or dislike toward some action, statement, or characteristic of the provider. Poor communication skills, conflict avoidance, or confusing emotional reactions are also possible reasons why the client unceremoniously terminates contact. It is difficult to explain or defend reasoning that is based on personal embarrassment or discomfort, so the client avoids the possibility of having to offer an explanation. Some clients are cynical about such abstract services or inclined to treat the contractual relationship in a very impersonal way. It is also possible that disruptive events in the client's life interfered with returning, and this is simply unknown to the provider.

Obviously, providers want to reduce the likelihood of an oblique termination, and hopefully can do so by encouraging the client to collaborate from the beginning on this important decision. Otherwise, providers do not have a legal or ethical duty to hotly pursue clients who fall away from therapy. Clients have a responsibility to determine their participation in therapy and providers do not need to make undue efforts to adapt to client conduct. However, the severity of the client pathology does increase the provider's responsibility for attempting to follow up with the client, as we discuss in Chapter Five. Self-management strategies are important for the provider in resolving emotional residue and gaining closure with an oblique termination.

Clinical Example of Oblique Termination   Hunter was walking to his car after his fourth therapy session when he received a text message about a family crisis with his mother having a stroke. In the flurry of heading out of town to be with his family and covering his work responsibilities, he forgot all about his next therapy visit. Knowing nothing about the family situation, the therapist left a voice message for Hunter following his "no show." Two weeks later, the provider left a second voice message that encouraged Hunter to call back at his convenience. Unbeknownst to the provider, Hunter had decided that he was just too preoccupied to be in therapy, and he was ambivalent about his possible future need. He did not want to close the door, but he did not want to feel pressured into continuing. As Hunter was somewhat guarded in therapy, he viewed the follow-up messages from the provider as attempts to "keep him coming back." So he did not respond and simply deleted the messages, thinking "I'll call him when and if I decide I want to."

Unprofessional Termination   *Unprofessional termination* occurs when the provider fails to uphold reasonable standards of conduct for the mental health profession. This involves actions that are exploitative, capricious, inadequate, and damaging or potentially damaging to the client. Reasonable standards of conduct are a matter of judgment and are sometimes difficult to ascertain. Because of this, it is very important to consider a range of reasonable versus unreasonable behavior and to explore the nuances of various clinical dilemmas with experienced colleagues. Peer consultation is especially useful for developing perspective on practical challenges and establishing consensus for reasonable action.

The examples of unprofessional termination offered here are only possible illustrations of such action. Whether or not an action was or is unprofessional can only be determined by someone qualified to make such observations and with a full understanding of all information and context pertinent to a particular case. Because it is a potentially career-altering or career-ending charge, the label of unprofessional action should not be rashly applied. Nor should it be breezily ignored as a remote or trivial concern. It is not a weapon for intimidating or manipulating others, although some will attempt to use it as such. It is, however, important to have some concept of what an unprofessional termination might look like.

Clinical Example of Unprofessional Termination   Dr. Kathryn's client, Martina, was starting a new custom jewelry business and wanted a managing partner. Dr. Kathryn had an interest in jewelry, office space in her building that would be suitable for a retail store, and a desire to develop some management skills. Both Martina and Dr. Kathryn thought that their business partnership was a terrific idea, since they "already worked so well together." Wanting to avoid an inappropriate dual relationship and foster maximum client autonomy, Dr. Kathryn presented Martina with a choice—therapy or business relationship, but not both. Martina elected to go for the business opportunity.

Despite their high hopes, the business failed and both lost money. Martina became depressed and wanted to resume therapy with Dr. Kathryn. However, she was also angry about the lost money and expected Dr. Kathryn to "pay her back" with free therapy. Dr. Kathryn refused to accept her back in therapy, citing a professional conflict of interest. Dr. Kathryn was also angry with Martina and blamed the business failure on her lack of drive. When Martina requested a copy of her record to take to another therapist, Dr. Kathryn said she would send it but never complied with the request. Angry and confused, Martina filed a complaint of unprofessional conduct with the state licensing board.

Dr. Kathryn appears to have good intentions but bad professional judgment. Consultation with a trusted colleague might have helped her to recognize the essentially exploitive nature of discontinuing therapy to pursue a joint business venture. Although she wanted to avoid a dual relationship, she was willing to sacrifice the primary commitment to therapy in the interest of pursuing a secondary relationship that promised personal gain. This opportunity was only available because she knew Martina as her client. Martina did not understand the reasons why she could not resume her prior therapy relationship, and she felt abandoned by Dr. Kathryn. Dr. Kathryn failed to anticipate the complications that could develop should the business fail, which it did. This affected her handling of professional responsibility for ensuring a clear case disposition and management of Martina's clinical record, resulting in further professional error.

APPLYING REASONABLE PROFESSIONAL STANDARDS

As licensed professionals, mental health providers are expected to adhere to professional standards of conduct as stipulated by state laws that grant the license to practice. It is common for a specific professional ethics code to be incorporated into the rules and regulations of that discipline to articulate its expectations for professional conduct. Across the different mental health disciplines of psychology, psychiatry, social work, advanced practice nursing, pastoral counseling, counseling, and marriage and family therapy, there is much similarity in the ethical codes for general professional conduct and the provision of therapeutic services. Although there are variations in detail and emphases, the general standard of care is similar.

Termination tends to fall into an area of legal and ethical regulation where there is considerable room for professional judgment. Although many of the ethical standards for professional practice have implications for termination, there are only a few direct references to specific circumstances or actions. These references tend to use qualifying language such as "reasonably clear" or "as appropriate" to allow for clinical discretion. Thus, providers must draw upon broad ethical principles to form and authorize necessary judgments.

Along with the freedom of discretion comes greater risk for error or misjudgment. There are definite risks associated with poorly handled termination or a failure to terminate when indicated. The client may be harmed or perceive that harm occurred. The effectiveness of the prior work may be diminished. The client may be confused or upset and discouraged from seeking further therapy. The client may believe that a personal relationship is forthcoming or has already begun. The client may come to resent the investment of time and money and feel cheated of expected results. The client may become angry and pursue adverse action against the professional via any or all of several avenues. These circumstances all represent professional risk.

When a client is unhappy about when, why, or how therapy ends, there are several options he or she might pursue. These include filing a consumer complaint with the state professional licensing board, filing a malpractice lawsuit, complaining to the professional's employer, complaining to the insurance company or managed care organization, or filing an ethics complaint with the provider's national professional organization. With the growing popularity of web-based clinical directories and web sites that allow consumers to post ratings and comments on providers, the Internet is a readily available outlet for disgruntled clients. Familiarity with ethical guidelines is crucial in avoiding unprofessional termination, real or perceived, and its adverse effects.

What Are the Standards for Ethically Responsible Termination?

In any termination, the provider's professional actions are guided by an ethically based standard of care. The primary underlying ethical principles are beneficence, non-malfeasance, autonomy or respect of the client's right to self-determination, and concern for fair or just access to service by all persons. These four principles function as a common framework for all health care ethics (Beauchamp & Childress, 2001). Although each mental health discipline (e. g., psychology, counseling, nursing, etc.) has its own formal code of ethics, all incorporate these four basic principles and specifically refer to promoting client welfare, respecting dignity and self-determination, preventing harm, and providing non-discriminatory access to service (AAMFT, 2001; AAPC, 2005; ACA, 2005; ApA, 2006; APA, 2002; ICN, 2005; NASW, 1999).

Providers of each discipline are typically held accountable to the ethics code of their own particular discipline. Because the respective codes are based on the same underlying principles, their directives are highly consistent.

Together they illustrate a common standard of care within mental health practice. In our discussion of standards for ethically responsible termination, the longest and most detailed (APA, 2002) will serve as a primary resource for explaining the principles that are common among mental health disciplines. Where other codes offer further interpretation of these principles, this will be noted.

Termination-Specific Ethical Responsibilities   The first responsibility concerns interruptions to ongoing service. Providers are responsible for making reasonable efforts to facilitate services in the event of interruptions to therapy (APA, 2002, 3.12; ACA, 2005, A.11.a; AAMFT, 2001, 1.11; AAPC, 2005, III.A.). Such interruptions might be anticipated or unanticipated in nature. The provider is expected to facilitate orderly and appropriate resolution of responsibility for client care in the event that their employment or contract ends, with paramount consideration given to client welfare (APA, 10.09).

When a conflict of interest or potential conflict of interest interrupts therapy, termination and proper referral is expected (NASW, 1999). A conflict of interest is any situation that might "interfere with the exercise of professional discretion or impartial judgment," (NASW, 1999, 1.06 (a)). Providers are expected to refrain from any role where other relationships or interests might reasonably be expected to "(1) impair their objectivity, competence, or effectiveness in performing their functions," or (2) "expose the person or organization with whom the professional relationship exists to harm or exploitation," (APA, 2002, 3.06).

Multiple relationships can create a conflict of interest when the provider is simultaneously in a professional role and in another specific role with the client or someone closely associated with or related to the client (APA, 3.05 (a)). Random, incidental contacts are not likely to constitute a specific role and thus do not trigger a conflict of interest termination (see Ebert, 2006; Younggren & Gottlieb, 2004; Zur, 2007).

Providers are generally expected to "terminate therapy when it becomes reasonably clear that the client/patient no longer needs the service, is not likely to benefit, or is being harmed by continued service," (APA, 2002, 10.10 (a)). If the provider determines that he or she is unable to provide professional help and offers clinically appropriate referrals that are subsequently refused, the provider is directed to discontinue the relationship (ACA, A.11.b).

Providers are prohibited from terminating therapy for the pursuit of sexual intimacies with clients, relatives, or significant others of current therapy clients (APA, 2002, 10.05; 10.06). Termination for the purpose of pursuing other social or financial relationships with the client may be expressly restricted (NASW, 1999, 1.16 (d)), or restricted by the calculated risk of impairing the provider's objectivity, competence, or effectiveness, or exploiting or harming the client (APA, 2002, 3.05).

In the interest of preventing exploitation or harm, providers also have a right to self-protection. Non-payment of agreed upon fees for services can be an acceptable reason for termination (ACA, 2005, A.11.c). However, it is wise to ensure that the financial arrangements have been made clear to the client, the clinical and other consequences of nonpayment has been discussed, and that the client does not pose an imminent danger to self or others (NASW, 1999, 1.16 (c)). If the client threatens or otherwise endangers the provider or creates jeopardy of harm, or another person with whom the client has a relationship threatens the provider, termination is permitted (ACA, 2005, A.11.c; APA, 2002, 10.10 (b)).

To complete termination in an ethical and professional manner, providers offer termination counseling prior to ending contact, and they suggest alternative service providers as appropriate (APA, 2002, 10.10 (c)) and discuss the benefits and risks of options for the continuation of service (NASW, 1999, 1.16 (f)). The exception to this provision is when it is precluded by actions of the client or third-party payers (APA, 2002). There is no inherent expectation of prolonged discussion, extended treatment, or elaborate matchmaking efforts. Rather, the intent is to provide communication that fosters the client's informed self-determination, if that is not deterred by the client's own threatening or non-cooperative behavior.

When termination or interruption of services can be anticipated, it is appropriate to notify clients promptly and seek resolution in accordance with the clients' needs and preferences (NASW, 1999, 1.16 (e)). Pre-termination counseling should include (a) advance notice of termination when possible, (b) discussion of the reasons for termination, (c) an opportunity for clients to ask questions about termination, and (d) referral information as appropriate (Fisher, 2003).

As a whole, the ethics codes of the mental health professions are highly consistent in stipulating consumer protection by limiting risky, unreliable, incompetent, or unnecessary service and prohibiting termination for the sole purpose of exploiting the client. Providers are expected to anticipate circumstantial interruptions to service whenever possible and to notify clients as to those conditions as soon as feasible. Arrangements for back-up coverage during an interruption or referral in case of discontinuation need to be offered. Therapy should be interrupted if a conflict of interest develops, including a potentially exploitive, harmful, or conflicting multiple relationship. Clients should be offered pre-termination counseling, unless they are unwilling or unable to participate.

Providers have the authority to initiate termination if the client is not benefiting from service, is not likely to benefit, or no longer needs the service. In a similar vein, the provider must determine if he or she is a competent and compatible match for the needs of the client and, if not, discontinue and recommend alternative resources. If a provider is not capable of handling the client's difficulties or is a mismatch, then the likelihood of the client's benefit from treatment is low and the risk of some form of harm is elevated. Providers also have the authority to initiate termination if the client does not cooperate with the terms of their agreement either by making productive efforts—which makes it unlikely he or she will benefit—or meeting financial obligations. Providers can and should terminate treatment with a client who threatens their personal or professional safety and integrity. The primary prohibition against termination concerns ending therapy for the sake of pursuing an exploitive relationship with the client or the client's significant other.

What Is Client Abandonment, and How Can It Be Avoided?

Client abandonment is universally recognized as an adverse event, yet its exact definition is elusive. Abandonment is a term that refers to bad or wrongful termination and is associated with harm to the client and cause for professional sanction. However, the conditions that qualify the provider's action as abandonment are not clearly established. Blurriness in the parameters of abandonment may unfortunately push many conscientious and compassionate providers to unnecessarily postpone appropriate termination. Wary of this egregious professional error, the providers become overly cautious in their stance. Presumably less frequent but still possible is the error of being insufficiently sensitive to the client's need for assistance in concluding or redirecting the therapy relationship. Termination is defined by Younggren and Gottlieb (in press) "as the ethically and clinically appropriate process by which a professional relationship is ended" and "abandonment represents the absence of that process."

Traditionally, mental health clinicians have assumed that completion of treatment occurs when the client reached a state of resolution and readiness to end. At the heart of this position is the theoretically driven assumption that powerful dynamic processes develop during therapy, of which the client may be unaware. By virtue of having established a professional relationship, the provider assumed a fiduciary duty to manage these dynamic processes and to prevent damage to the client in the process of closure. However, the professional standards for discharging this duty have, for several decades, contained an unresolved ambiguity between the potential need for providers to terminate therapy and the client's right to self-determination (Younggren & Gottlieb, in press).

From this perspective flows the admonition that once a client is accepted, therapy becomes a non-cancellable contract because dynamic forces have been set in motion. Because of these forces, providers must hold client concurrence or readiness as the imperative condition for reasonable termination. Anything short of this could be abandonment, at least as it is practiced within a dynamic orientation. This creates a serious bottleneck for the provider when dealing with situations where it may be ethically appropriate to recommend, initiate, or even insist on termination.

Abandonment worry is a provider's dilemma that stems from the unresolved ambiguity surrounding one's professional rights and responsibilities for termination. Termination might be appropriate for a variety of reasons, yet the provider hesitates out of worry over the possibility of abandonment as defined from a single, absolute perspective. Without an operational definition, the provider may worry about when and where abandonment occurs and whether or not damaging effects could result. Is going on a vacation potential abandonment? If the client complains of feeling abandoned, does that mean the client has been harmed? Does non-reinforcement of maladaptive behavior constitute abandonment if it makes the client uncomfortable? Perhaps most difficult of all is the worry that stopping a non-productive treatment effort will be construed as client abandonment. Is the provider entitled to determine when treatment is no longer needed with or without the client's full agreement? The necessity of continued treatment is very difficult to determine and apt to significantly differ across theoretical perspectives. When viewed as a process of learning, psychotherapy could last an hour or a lifetime. There is no uniformly defined endpoint. Nevertheless, providers routinely face concrete situations where they must weigh the benefits and risks and decide whether or not to proceed.

Our understanding of abandonment as a legal concept in psychotherapy has been drawn mainly from a medical malpractice model. In this context, a mental health provider may be found liable for wrongful termination or abandonment when the professional relationship is ended in a fashion that is below the standard of care and there is damage as a proximate result (Hjelt, 2007). Hjelt acknowledges that the standard of care can be fluid and elusive and has considerable grey at its margin. However, the issues of professional duty, breach of duty, and damage will determine the standard of care to which the provider is held. Various appellate rulings have established that more than mere termination is needed to prove abandonment; there must also be evidence that the action was taken without reason or sufficient notice to enable the client to obtain other care, and that the client was injured as a result. Court opinions have also established that providers have a right to withdraw from a case provided due notice is offered, and that there can be no abandonment when the client voluntarily chooses not to return to the provider (Hjelt, 2007).

If we use the process definition of termination proposed by Younggren and Gottlieb (in press), abandonment occurs when the provider fails to "take clinically indicated and ethically appropriate steps to terminate a professional relationship." This definition of termination focuses on appropriate process rather than clinical judgments about treatment completion, thus increasing the degrees of freedom for individual determinations. Inappropriate process is defined by Sperry (2007) as ending needed therapy without giving the client adequate notice or time to prepare for the end of the relationship.

In its literal meaning, abandonment refers to deserting or forsaking a duty. Once a client-therapist relationship is established, the provider assumes a generic "duty of due care" that is defined by law. Although this is really a bundle of duties that vary according to the nature, scope, and duration of the professional relationship (Hjelt, 2007), we can speak of three primary obligations as stipulated by practice statutes and regulations. These are (a) to protect against known, imminent physical harm; (b) to create and maintain a professional record of services; and (c) to provide due care for which the provider was consulted to the extent of his or her skill and expertise. Duties pertaining to termination are subsumed within each of these three primary areas.

Duty to Protect   Practitioners are expected to assess for the presence of imminent risk of physical harm and take appropriate steps to fulfill the duty to protect any identifiable potential victim, including the client (Fulero, 1988; Sales, Miller & Hall, 2005). Terminating therapy with a client without assessing for *imminent* risk of harm to self or others could be construed as an abandonment of this duty. If a client has a history of self-harm, previous suicide attempts, or violence toward others, the average provider would be expected to inquire about such risks before discharging the client. Because emotional crisis can increase a client's potential for impulsive and potentially violent actions, it is generally unwise to terminate anyone who is at the peak of a crisis. The exception to this would be if the client is directly threatening to harm the practitioner. Termination may appropriately occur at some point before a crisis is completely resolved, but imminent risk of harm has subsided or further steps such as hospitalization have taken place to reduce the imminent risk of dangerous action.

A practitioner who believes that a client is not benefiting from treatment still should not terminate the service during an acute phase of a crisis due to the risk of abandonment of protection. For example, a provider may become frustrated with a client who is in the midst of an acute manic episode, believing the client to be unresponsive to any intervention. The provider would be very unwise to abruptly terminate the client without allowing the client to arrange for transfer of care. Instead, the provider has a duty to address the client's immediate safety and to provide information that will facilitate the transfer of care. Depending on the client's level of risk and other potential mediating factors, it may be necessary to take steps such as involving significant others or initiating involuntary hospitalization. In such a high-risk situation, consultation is a necessary part of any reasonable termination action.

Duty to Create and Maintain a Record   Providers have a duty to construct, maintain, and dispose of client records as per state and federal laws (HIPAA) designed to protect privacy and preserve the client's timely access to this personal information. Practitioners can avoid most if not all risks of abandonment of records by adhering to these regulations. This duty does not have a direct relationship to decisions of termination, but it does affect professional actions during and after termination. Client records must be maintained in a secure and accessible location for an extended period after therapy is over. Termination of the professional relationship does not terminate one's responsibility for protecting the client's record.

Problems are most likely to occur when the practitioner relocates or leaves a practice. Typical professional standards would have either the practitioner or persons responsible for an agency or group practice provide notice to recent (i.e., active within the prior 18 months) clients regarding the provider's departure, along with information on how to obtain or transfer records. There are no uniform standards on how this notice should be provided as it may take the form of a personal letter, phone call, or published general notice in a community resource such as a newspaper. The essence of the duty is to make reasonable efforts to provide client access to records and not to simply abandon the record in an unsecured, inaccessible, or unknown location. Failure to adequately provide for maintenance and disposal of this information could result in charges of abandonment of records.

Duty to Provide Due Care   The third duty pertains to upholding public trust and providing the services that are offered. Professionals are generally expected to behave in an orderly, predictable, ethical, and fair manner and only offer services for which they are qualified and that they can reasonably provide. When the provider behaves in ways that are inconsistent with this expectation, there is apt to be dissonance and a greater risk of client dissatisfaction or harm, regardless of the rationale for the provider's actions. This is why an orientation to therapy and adequate informed consent procedures are so important. Informed consent procedures form the basis of the therapy contract that specifies the provider's limits, expectations for the client's participation, and the client's overall understanding and acceptance of the contract. If either party can not fulfill the terms of this agreement, the professional is responsible for re-evaluating, renegotiating, or potentially terminating the contract. Having established expectations from the beginning can be very helpful if and when these discussions occur. Details on termination and informed consent are discussed further in Chapter Three.

The provider's right to set and enforce limits is implied in the presentation of their policies. This discourages the client from thinking that the provider is available "on demand" or that therapy must continue regardless of the client's potentially unresponsive, uncooperative, or hostile actions. Such policies form an agreement between both parties and serve as notice for the conduct that is expected of the client. If a client behaves in a way that constitutes "inconsistent conduct," the provider has a right to make decisions about the relationship without client concurrence (Younggren & Gottlieb, in press). Many providers do not realize that they have a right to expect certain things from their clients, cooperation and integrity among them. The client's counterproductive actions are grounds for a clinically and ethically appropriate termination.

Managing this sort of termination, however, takes both skill and preparation and may be among the most difficult and risky transactions. For example, in a review of disciplinary actions concerning termination and abandonment, one instance of inappropriate termination was related to the use of e-mail notification. The psychologist was reprimanded and placed on one year of probation with supervision and continuing education (Younggren & Gottlieb, in press). The psychologist's defense had countered that the client was verbally abusive in a telephone call. It appears that the regulatory board did not find this instance of client behavior threatening enough to justify immediate termination without further discussion or notice, nor did it accept the informal electronic message as a sufficiently professional means of communication for termination notice.

If the provider must conclude therapy for personal reasons or because the client's concerns fall beyond their scope of competence, reasonable steps can be taken to draw the work to a conclusion and assist the client in locating other resources if needed. Termination is in fact an appropriate fulfillment of one's professional duties when the initial goals have been reached and there are no new goals, the client no longer needs therapy, is unlikely to benefit, a conflict of interest has developed, or the quality of service is insufficient to produce any benefit. The client does not have to agree with termination, although it is certainly preferable to seek reconciliation of opinion. The practitioner is not compelled to continue services until the client feels ready to accept the termination or until an unresponsive client improves. In fact, continuation of therapy is clearly contraindicated when there is no benefit or there is potential harm to either client or provider.

If termination occurs because the practitioner's employment contract has been terminated, the practitioner is not obliged to continue working without pay to avoid accusations of client abandonment. What the provider must do, however, is approach termination in a professional manner, provide as much notice as possible, and help each client understand the options for continued services.

Pragmatic Guide to Abandonment Risk Management

- For abandonment worry, seek consultation from a qualified colleague.
- Approach all termination communications in a professional manner.
- Be alert for predictable interruptions that will trigger termination.
- Include termination policies in informed consent.
- Fulfill duties to protect against harm, create and protect records, and provide due care.
- Understand the conditions where providers should consider or initiate termination.
- Be sure to provide due notice when initiating termination.
- Review termination policy with client as part of ending process.
- Offer appropriate referral information as needed.
- Do not terminate therapy in order to pursue an intimate or business relationship with the client.

Can Termination Be Broken Down into Specific Applied Skills?

Good termination judgments require sound professional and clinical strategy and knowledge of relevant ethical, legal, and clinical factors. But knowledge alone will not determine the provider's competence in carrying out effective terminations. The clinician needs to be able to consistently and skillfully use this knowledge to work effectively with the client in drawing therapy to a close, sometimes under highly challenging conditions.

Becoming both proficient and comfortable with the clinical and ethical process of termination is possible if the provider develops the following applied skills.

- Articulate a practice profile that reflects a specific scope of competence and philosophy of practice.
- Screen prospective clients for appropriate fit.
- Use informed consent to orient clients toward reasonable expectations for the professional relationship, including provider availability, communications, their expected cooperation and effort, and conditions of termination.
- Establish a termination policy and follow it.
- Link the treatment plan and goals to operational criteria for termination.
- Track progress, benefit, and potential harm of therapy and routinely assess the estimated proximity of termination.
- Talk about termination with the client on a periodic basis.
- Respect and plan for your own personal limits; maintain routine consultation—don't go it alone.
- Defuse, contain, or terminate volatile situations.
- Initiate termination when appropriate and provide sufficient notice.

- Adapt the termination process to the client's cultural, clinical, developmental, and practical needs.
- Document pertinent information about termination and supporting information in the client's record.

Illustration of each of these applied skills will be taken up in the chapters to follow.

SUMMARY POINTS FOR APPLIED PRACTICE

1. Termination occurs with every client, but terminations do not all look the same.

2. A collaborative stance toward termination helps to reduce the risk of conflict, dissatisfaction, or poor outcome.

3. Therapist and client are the primary collaborators when it comes to termination, but they usually must operate within a context of multiple vested interests such as agencies, insurance companies, family members, or significant others.

4. Closure is a developing process that is woven into the goals and tasks of therapy from the start. As a process, it is multidimensional and interactive.

5. Different types of termination communications can be described as prospective, flexible, complex, oblique, or unprofessional in terms of the collaboration between client and provider.

6. The risks of bad termination can include distress, confusion, increased mistrust, resentment, and loss to the client. The provider may also be emotionally distressed and vulnerable to professional penalties in the form of complaints to the licensing board, malpractice action, complaints to the employer or insurance carrier, reports of ethics violation to professional associations, and bad comments on public blogs.

7. To complete termination in an ethically appropriate manner, providers offer advance notice and pre-termination counseling whenever possible, and suggest alternative providers as appropriate.

8. Providers have both authority and responsibility to determine if treatment is no longer needed, not beneficial, not appropriate to the client's needs, or if the client's conduct is inconsistent with the safety and integrity of clinical intervention.

9. Abandonment is a much feared and misunderstood concept. Current thinking defines abandonment as the absence of a clinically and ethically appropriate termination process. Terminating therapy under clinically and ethically appropriate conditions, even without client concurrence, is not abandonment of one's professional duties, but rather the fulfillment of them. Abandonment does not occur if the client voluntarily discontinues therapy or if there is reason for the termination and due notice.

10. Specific applied skills can help the provider ensure the implementation of an appropriate termination process.

3

Positive Closure from the Start: Groundwork for Termination

Key Questions Addressed in This Chapter

- How does a practice profile help to manage terminations?
- Can a provider ethically screen referrals?
- Should termination be included in informed consent?
- How can I estimate the length of therapy at the outset?
- What is a termination plan, and how is it linked to the treatment goals?
- How can I assess client motivation and use it in the termination plan?
- How do I know if the client is benefiting or likely to benefit from therapy?

OPTIMIZE THE MATCH

As therapy begins, our first objective is to develop an effective working relationship: one that prompts the client to make psychological changes. Rather than simply deciding what must be done *to* the client, we work *with* the client to forge an agreement and engage in processes that will realize his or her goals (Bordin, 1979). Sufficient technical skill and cognitive effort is only part of what is needed to successfully do this job. Good professional communication skills are also needed to shape the consultation into a productive experience that begins *and* ends on a positive note.

The effort to create a positive experience really starts even before the client arrives for intake. In this preparatory stage, the provider's task is to develop a profile of competencies, philosophy, and specific practice policies, including termination policy. This is the provider's opportunity to articulate the basic beliefs and assumptions that guide decisions in the applied practice context. Having clarity in this practice profile aids in concrete tasks such as creating the marketing and informed consent materials that communicate the provider's qualifications to prospective clients. These written communications are tools that summarize key information and thus help to structure an effective working alliance. Marketing tools help consumers

47

select a potential provider but they do not establish a contract for services. Informed consent tools stipulate the formal agreement between client and therapist.

Communications about termination at the beginning and throughout therapy are essential to effective management of this important task. Brief but explicit discussion of termination and sharing of your practice policies at the beginning can greatly enhance smooth consideration of this issue throughout therapy. Orienting the client toward collaboration in determining goals and points of completion is a vital first step. In the middle section of therapy, ongoing review of benefits and progress is important to keep the interaction focused and avoid unhelpful digressions. As therapy progresses in time, discussion of potential endpoints becomes a more proximal issue. Determining termination may be easy or difficult, depending to a large degree on the progress and collaboration already established. The following sections examine specific steps that will maximize the chances of a positive collaboration on termination as therapy unfolds.

How Does a Practice Profile Help to Manage Terminations?

A practice profile spells out what services the provider offers, what particular method or philosophy of practice is used, and other pragmatic aspects of clinical service such as office hours or insurance acceptance. Making such information available to prospective clients helps pre-select those who will be most appropriate for the provider's skills and mode of practice. The seeds of a positive alliance are sown when the client begins therapy with the belief that the provider will meet their needs and expectations and they find this to be true. By publicly sharing practice information, the provider has already engaged the client in making decisions that reduce the risk of early termination due to incompatibility. A well-defined scope of practice increases the likelihood that the provider will relate to the client confidently and effectively within the earliest sessions, thus beginning therapy on a positive note.

One useful way to articulate the essence of one's practice profile is to develop written marketing materials. Public statements such as those offered in brochures, directory listings or web sites usually emphasize the provider's areas of expertise and particular relationship skills that will attract and maintain a psychotherapy clientele. Although the provider's philosophy of *termination* is not usually stated directly in these marketing forums, it is implied by the types of services offered and objectives pursued. For example, a provider who offers global services with broad goals implies a philosophy of open-ended therapy with non-specific endpoints. A provider who offers specific treatments, such as social skills training for socially anxious teens, implies that termination may be appropriate when these skills are improved.

Creating a written profile that includes philosophy of practice and specific policies is useful as a personal exercise even if you do not distribute it in a brochure or on a website. Writing down key parameters creates an internal framework of consistency for ongoing decisions and communications with colleagues, prospective clients, and the community at large. Boundaries that are clear and specific, rather than vague or ambiguous, will enable you to best manage both professional risk and personal stress.

The written practice profile forms a nucleus of information that can be woven into a separate informed consent document used in routine practice. It is important to note that providing general practice and scope of competence information on a website or in a clinical directory is very helpful to consumers, but this does not establish an informed consent contract. This necessary contract is established in a specific document containing a description of services where the client's signature attests to his or her understanding and agreement. Describing your practice profile in the informed consent document helps to reduce the risks of clients misunderstanding the scope or parameters of your services. All providers should review written materials that represent their practice on an annual basis to evaluate the need for updating or correction as one's range of services is likely to shift as skills are developed and refined over time.

Scope of Competence   The first step in crafting a practice profile is to specify the types of clients and problems that fall within the scope of the provider's current competence. This usually includes certain populations and certain diagnostic groups. Populations served can be divided into age groups, such as children, teens, adults, or elders. Problems or diagnostic subgroups may be broad, such as "mood disorders," or may be more specific, such as "civilian post-traumatic stress" or "health anxiety." Those with very specialized expertise may want to make that clear as well, as in treating "child perpetrators of sexual abuse."

Equally important is clearly establishing what problems and clients are currently outside the provider's scope of competence. In a public statement, the provider might only specify excluded populations or services when doing so will reduce or avoid consumer confusion. Problems or clients *potentially* within the range of services can be evaluated on a case-by-case basis.

Philosophy of Practice   The next step is to specify a philosophy of practice. This part of the profile is often more challenging to construct. Ideally the provider offers a description of his or her primary theoretical approach in terms that are understandable to a non-professional. This statement should also convey a sense of personal style. The philosophy not only reaches out to potential clients to encourage their involvement if appropriate, it offers a basic idea of how you think and what it might be like to work with you. When the client's actual experience is consistent with those expectations, satisfaction and trust are enhanced.

It is useful for the provider to offer a philosophy of practice so that prospective clients can match their own preferences to the working style of the provider. This reduces the risk of abrupt termination or other problems due to mismatch of service, incompatibility of style, or large divergence between expectations and reality.

Consider the following examples of public statements of practice philosophy, based on actual examples from Internet-based directories, to compare the differences in how these providers might approach treatment and termination.

Therapist A

My primary goal is to create a relaxed, comfortable atmosphere that fosters a solid working relationship. My role is to be a partner and consultant in your personal discovery. I view therapy as a safe haven for exploring connection, understanding and positive change. My approach is eclectic, holistic and geared to the needs of the individual and the nature of the problem. I honor the spiritual growth and development of each individual as I help with learning new, more effective coping strategies. Clients with issues in various areas including anxiety, depression, frustration, sexual abuse, substance abuse, grief, relationship problems, women's issues and existential issues are welcomed.

Therapist B

I am an experienced professional who will help you with life's struggles. I am committed to helping you work your way out of feeling miserable. Clients served include adolescents, adults and elderly persons with problems of depression, health, chronic pain, eating disorders or cutting. Together we will develop a customized treatment plan based on your needs, one that is designed to diminish symptoms in a reasonable amount of time. Treatment methods include behavioral, cognitive and relationship and other methods as needed.

Therapist C

I offer evidence-based treatment designed to achieve concrete, measurable results. Using a supportive, humanistic framework, my approach is active and goal-oriented. We will collaborate on a treatment plan tailored to your needs and issues and designed to obtain relief from symptoms as rapidly as possible. My clientele is limited to adults with anxiety disorders and anger problems. I do not accept referrals for domestic violence offenders.

The practice philosophy of the following provider suggests a basic theoretical orientation of an open-ended, personal growth approach to therapy, in contrast to the more directive, focused approaches of the preceding examples.

Therapist D

As a therapist, I enjoy watching people grow and change in how they deal with other people and issues. My belief is that people are fundamentally cut from similar cloth. We all long for authentic connection to others and ourselves. Somehow life gets in the way and we lose connection to our natural ability to operate out of our true self. When this happens, we have anxiety, depression, eating issues, a lack of passion or a host of other emotional health problems. In individual or group therapy, I will tap into a range of approaches to help you feel and live better. At the deepest level, therapy offers a new understanding and reconnection to aspects of yourself long ago obscured, allowing you to make peace and finally feel whole.

The philosophies of practice offered by these providers create different impressions of how each might approach the tasks of beginning and ending therapy. This is helpful to potential consumers and other referring providers who want to have a better understanding of what to expect from a given provider's unique style. Some clients primarily want a warm and supportive relationship as a starting point, while others are specifically seeking a goal-oriented approach to contemporary problems. Some want to have the option of an open-ended therapy relationship while others desire a more concretely structured experience with a targeted end-point. It is important to ensure that each client understands and agrees to your particular approach by including a relevant description in your informed consent statement. Providers who practice in a setting with generic consent forms might consider using an additional contract that describes their profile for a more individualized informed consent.

Can a Provider Ethically Screen Referrals?

It is certainly ethical to pre-screen, or evaluate clients during the first few sessions, to determine if there is an appropriate match for your skills and scope of competence. The psychology ethics code (APA, 2002) clearly outlines the necessity of practicing within the scope of one's competence (2.0), based on skills, training and experience (2.01) as well as personal functioning (2.06). This prescreening is not, however, always a straightforward task. Stating what one can or can not do and with whom sounds easy, but these decisions can become complicated by various pressures of the workplace, the ambiguity surrounding many clinical referrals, and the professional duty that comes with a clinical relationship.

If the client's needs are unclear, it may be reasonable for the provider to begin an initial consultation to sort out the issues and determine what services would be appropriate. However, limitations on the availability of other suitable providers can create substantial pressure to retain the client, even if the provider is beyond their skill set. Clinicians sometimes mistakenly believe that once a client has been accepted for consultation, they are ethically bound to continue therapy if needed, unless the client *chooses* to go elsewhere. On the contrary, providers are ethically bound to withdraw from those responsibilities that they can not competently handle. It is certainly reasonable to evaluate clients whose needs may fall near the boundaries of one's expertise, and to get more information before making a decision on skill match and compatibility.

Knowing what one can do for whom and making every reasonable attempt to limit practice to those areas will greatly reduce the risk of termination challenges that occur if the client fails to improve or becomes worse. Articulating and practicing within such general limits can substantially reduce clinical or practical errors, and relieve the stress associated with trying to work productively in an unproductive treatment match.

This means saying "no" to intriguing opportunities, demanding bosses, pleading clients, or encouraging colleagues when the problem is most likely beyond one's scope of competence. Internal pressures, such as the desire to be all things to all people or anxiety about slow times in practice, can compromise one's ability to maintain reasonable limits. Every psychotherapy client has to be evaluated as a suitable match for the provider's skill set and re-evaluated as the work progresses. Those who fall outside the range of provider competence must be redirected to more appropriate resources when needed. Those who are at the margins can be evaluated more carefully on a case-by-case basis. In essence, the provider asks, "Is it appropriate for me to accept this client?" As more information becomes available, the provider then asks, "Is it *still* appropriate for me to work with this client?" There will certainly be times when the provider can reasonably extend his or her limits if it is feasible to do so with the support of additional learning and consultation. Otherwise, therapy should stop if it becomes clear that the problem is beyond the provider's abilities, and the client should be directed to other, more specifically qualified resources.

SET POLICY AND SHAPE EXPECTATIONS FOR TERMINATION

The nature and scope of the provider's practice usually shapes the key parameters of termination policy. In an independent or loosely affiliated group practice, providers usually have the direct authority to decide whether or not breaks or interruptions are incorporated into ongoing therapy or are considered termination of service. Generally, the independent practitioner decides the client's disposition on a case-by-case basis. Agencies or managed group practices with high demand for service and waiting lists must establish a consistent termination policy to ensure that they can best serve the greatest number of clients. All providers, regardless of setting, must have some way of managing the flow of client demand and the availability of provider time.

Termination policy begins with the basic expectation that termination will most likely occur by mutual agreement when goals have been met or service is no longer needed. Further policy on other conditions of termination is likely to vary according to the nature and setting of the provider's practice. An independent practitioner might consider therapy terminated if the client does not reschedule an appointment within three months unless a follow-up agreement stipulates otherwise. An agency might establish termination after a failure to reschedule within 30 days or after two failed appointments (e.g., Reis & Brown, 2006). Individual providers have considerable latitude in how they want to handle multiple cancellations or no-shows, although all providers need to limit schedule disruptions in some way. Agencies are more apt to have a standard policy on attendance to minimize wasted time and assist providers in setting expectations for client participation. The independent practitioner might choose to allow any client to return for more therapy if clinically indicated and attempt to accommodate the client immediately, while an agency might require the returning terminated client to start at the bottom of a waiting list for another initial intake session. In uncomplicated situations, the independent practitioner might establish a record of termination with a brief note in the client's record. An agency might require a more formal documentation of case closure, perhaps including a letter of termination that is sent to the client.

Should Termination Be Included in Informed Consent?

In any practice setting, it is wise to develop a written termination policy that is included in the informed consent agreement to be signed by the client. Those in independent settings have more latitude in setting and adjusting policies, but this freedom brings with it the risk of errors and omissions resulting from the lack of systematic policy. Although inclusion of a specific termination policy is not clearly stipulated by law or ethics, it is an implied aspect of informed consent. Ensuring informed consent to the process of treatment is expected of every mental health provider. If termination policy is not currently written into informed consent materials, consider adding this item at your next update.

There are several advantages to including a professional termination policy in your informed consent contract. It can help to bring up the subject right from the start and diminish the risk of misunderstanding or disagreement on future actions. Spelling out policies in writing can also assist in tactfully and supportively managing the ambiguity of therapy closure. In addition, the client's signed agreement with this policy can provide support in the event that an adversarial situation develops.

The actual text of the policy should cover basic parameters of what to expect in terms of who initiates termination as well as when and how this might occur. Specific mention of billing, scheduling, or limited number of visits as triggers for termination can be included here, even if these points are repeated in other parts of the informed consent document. These decisions, as noted, are particular to the provider or the agency or practice and the nature of the practice. Termination decisions are typically made in advance by a mutual agreement, although either client or therapist can establish a reason for initiating termination, in some cases without mutual agreement. The following is a possible set of termination parameters that could be written into the termination policy.

Possible Reasons for Termination

- By mutual agreement when:
  - Treatment goals have been met
  - Contract limits such as the number of allowed visits are reached
  - Transfer to another provider or service is appropriate
  - Other environmental circumstances make it necessary
- By client discretion via any of the following actions:
  - Failure to initiate rescheduling within 90 days of a session, a no-show, or a cancellation
  - No-show (no notice) of more than two scheduled appointments
  - Cancellation of three consecutive appointments
- By therapist discretion when:
  - Circumstances compromise the feasibility or quality of service
  - Services are not benefiting or may be harming the client
  - Client conduct is inconsistent with the safety and integrity of the work (noncompliant with expectations for fee payment or clinical participation; any form of threatening or fraudulent behavior)

Variation of specific terms of termination can be adapted to the parameters of the setting and the clientele served. The following examples illustrate two potential adaptations of termination policy as per informed consent policy for different providers and settings.

Example Termination Policy A

Termination of services typically occurs by mutual agreement when treatment goals have been met, or when maximum benefit has been reached. We will periodically discuss termination as we track your progress. However, you have the right to terminate at any point. If possible, it is best to discuss therapy termination prior to ending contact. Please feel free to discuss with me any concerns or questions you might have about the benefit of your therapy or if, when, or how it should end. If I think that you no longer need my services or might be better served by other resources, including a more intensive level of care, I may initiate termination. I will consider therapy terminated by your actions if you do not reschedule as recommended or planned, have missed two appointments without notice, fail to make timely payment as per our agreement, or otherwise compromise the safety and integrity of our relationship and work together.

Example Termination Policy B

For psychotherapy to be effective, consistent attendance at sessions and active participation in treatment is a must. However, we also give consideration to the needs of our clients who travel considerable distance to therapy and may be combining multiple consultations with health care providers in a single trip. Please notify our offices at least one hour prior to your scheduled appointment if your arrival has been delayed and we will attempt to accommodate you on the same day or reschedule your appointment at the next available time. Termination of psychotherapy will typically occur when you feel that your needs have been met or when your provider advises that the maximum benefit from treatment has been reached. In the interest of best service, we recommend that any termination decision be given a 30-day consideration period to allow for at least one closing consultation where the end of therapy is specifically discussed. It is our policy that the provider may initiate treatment termination for any of the following reasons:

• Client is not actively participating in therapy by bringing up important issues, being open in discussion, or following through on recommended homework
• Client does not make an effort to attend sessions on a regular basis and has a pattern of missing or canceling appointments
• Client is persistently uncooperative or has become hostile to the provider
• Client's behavior threatens the safety or integrity of the practice in any way
• Client defaults on the established responsibility for payment or co-payment

Clients who wish to return to therapy after termination may be accepted onto our waiting list as a new intake. We reserve the right to refuse to accept returning clients after termination for non-compliance, default, or threatening behavior.

In keeping with sound ethical practice, written informed consent to therapy is administered at the initial consultation. As the plan to proceed with therapy is discussed with the client, key aspects of the consent process are verbally reviewed. This is an ideal time to include the topic of termination. Lengthy explanation of all possible reasons for termination is probably not necessary or appropriate at this point. Rather it is the provider's opportunity to initiate an open dialogue on this important task of the collaboration. Key limits that are known at the outset, such as a finite number of visits or a provider's anticipated departure, should be discussed to establish the client's adequate understanding.

This discussion marks the beginning of a specific termination strategy with any given client. As provider and client explore possible therapy objectives and the provider gains more information about the client's readiness to change, an image of potential points of termination will begin to emerge. Having an early dialogue fosters an effective working relationship between provider and client with respect to the task of termination. Various parameters can be explored, including the client's expectations for the length and direction of therapy, priorities for outcome, and practical barriers that affect treatment continuation.

With a personal profile that outlines areas of competence, an articulated philosophy of practice and specific nuts-and-bolts policy on termination, the provider has set a strong foundation for effective collaboration on this important task of therapy.

Provider Checklist for Practice Profile

- Specify/update client populations served.
- Specify/update types of clinical problems treated.
- Know the populations and problems that will *not* be served.
- Plan for potential clients to consider on a case-by-case basis.
- Describe the type of therapy and the philosophy of practice used.
- Outline practice policy on termination.
- Add the practice profile and termination policy to informed consent documents that client signs.

How Can I Estimate the Length of Therapy at the Outset?

New or prospective clients often zero right in on the matter of termination by asking, "How long is therapy going to take?" At the outset, it is appropriate to estimate some length to the contract for service, again for the purposes of informed consent and a strong working relationship. Clients typically want the provider's opinion on how soon relief from distress might be expected and a general estimate of the time it will take to reach their overall objectives. Clients with undefined objectives may simply want to know how long they will need to be "in therapy."

Making an estimate of therapy duration is a very challenging task, especially with limited information. This requires the practitioner to apply a standard, linear judgment to a highly variable process. Typically, progress toward goals is circuitous, following a path of starts and interruptions, new problems, redirections, and unanticipated challenges (Prochaska & Norcross, 2003). Rather than being a discrete occurrence, change is a process that happens through a collection of internal and external events accruing over time. The amount of time needed will depend upon the client, the nature of the problems, the resources available to support and encourage change, the scope and nature of the desired changes, and the quality of the treatment relationship. Although these estimations may be difficult, the provider has an obligation to assist the client in understanding the potential length and benefit of therapy.

Problem-focused therapy is designed for discrete episodes of treatment that directly pursue observable results. Because therapy begins with specific issues, there is an expectation that it will be limited to a relatively brief time frame. There is substantial evidence that relatively brief, focused interventions produce effective symptom remission and sustained effects over time for a number of disorders (Chambless & Ollendick, 2001; Chambless et al., 1998). However, the overall process of change remains a long-term phenomenon that may require more than one episode of intervention, particularly with co-morbid or recurrent disorders. Assuming that short-term treatment is entirely sufficient for long-term change in all cases is just as faulty as assuming that short-term treatment is inevitably inadequate.

Some clients are able to change quickly but some are not. A single episode of therapy may be adequate for some while others seek multiple episodes of intervention. Extended episodes of therapy may have either brief or prolonged breaks in active contact. A single practitioner may provide all the therapy, or multiple providers may be consulted. Along the way, both practitioner and client will grapple with questions about the appropriateness of termination. How much and what type of change must be completed before discontinuing contact? Limiting therapy to focused episodes of treatment may have several distinct advantages, such as encouraging client action and independence, conserving resources, and focusing on results. However, both practitioner and client may feel perplexed and uncertain when it comes to making a logical and non-arbitrary decision about the timeliness of ending an episode of care versus the need for extending their work. This uncertainty is no surprise, given that perspectives on adequate treatment duration vary according to the stakeholders and that criteria for treatment completion tend to be vague and implicit rather than systematic and explicit (Jakobsons et al., 2007).

Skillful management of each episode is what gives shape, substance, and a sense of productivity to the therapy endeavor and sets the stage for positive termination. Ideally, practitioner and client work together to plan or negotiate an acceptable duration for pursuing reasonable goals. This plan is actually a decision that is continually re-evaluated. As therapy proceeds, every session holds some question of whether or not another session should be scheduled. If additional sessions are scheduled, the certainty of the client's attendance is not established until he or she appears at the appointed hour. If the plan is sound and the work productive, it is likely that there will be only minimal attention to any questions of continuation.

Along the way, both participants have to decide whether or not the work is usefully contributing to the intended purpose. Their ability to productively work together accounts for a significant portion of the success of therapy, about 30 percent (Lambert & Barley, 2002). The client's effort, consistency, progress, predictability, and preferences all likely influence the practitioner's estimation of the usefulness of more sessions. The practitioners' warmth, compatibility, and expertise in turn influence the client's estimation of the usefulness of more sessions. There is growing evidence that the practitioner's flexibility in responding to the client's specific difficulties and concerns within the context of a coherent treatment plan is a distinct skill with implications for the client's motivation and improvement (e.g., Huppert et al, 2006).

Collaborating on the Estimate of Therapy Duration   Good decisions about therapy duration depend on having sufficient information and giving appropriate weight to relevant factors. Collaborative discussion is the primary means for optimizing these deliberations. When the practitioner and client exchange ideas, more information is considered and the relative weight given to any one factor can be negotiated or adjusted. Without such discussion, there is greater risk of lopsided or unilateral decisions that omit important factors.

There are several component skills that the practitioner taps in fulfilling his or her role in this discussion. First, the practitioner draws out the client's thoughts, feelings, and agenda. Next, the practitioner offers professional perspective on problem conceptualization and empirically supported options for accomplishing therapy objectives. The practitioner also understands how specific client factors can enhance or complicate progress and helps the client to recognize this important context for setting reasonable expectations. Finally, the provider takes the lead in initiating discussion at appropriate times, sharing information, summarizing points of agreement on goals, and checking for the client's endorsement or reservations. The provider will also take the lead in seeking informed consultation for resolving any specific challenges that may arise in the course of this ongoing discussion.

When the provider transports the technology of empirically supported treatments into a general clinical practice, he or she uses an overall template that is based on a manual or set of manuals to formulate an individualized intervention. Most manuals (e.g., Beck et al., 1979; Beck, 1995; Barlow, 2001) outline treatment of a specific clinical problem, such as depression or panic disorder, within a single episode of approximately 12 to 25 outpatient sessions. This time frame is not rigidly bound but rather an estimate of potential treatment duration for single problems or uncomplicated cases. Treatment that includes extended relapse prevention (Young, Weinberger & Beck, 2001) or more complex personality disorders can be expected to last a year or more (Beck et al., 2004; Goldfried, 2002; Linehan et al., 2001).

The clinical trials that support the efficacy of an approach are by necessity time-limited and controlled. Treatment has a shorter duration and a more selected population than may be characteristic of the provider's practice. Further, some clinical reports focus only on a segment of treatment that was designed for a significant component of a complex clinical problem. For example, a 10-session segment of cognitive therapy specifically targeted to suicidal thoughts and behaviors was reported to successfully reduce suicide attempts by 50 percent and significantly reduce hopelessness for depressed individuals who had recently attempted suicide (Brown et al., 2005). These 10 sessions were not considered a treatment for depression per se, but rather a specific module designed to reduce the most lethal aspects of depression among clients at high risk. Clients were all encouraged to seek additional mental health care for depression and for any other associated problems such as substance abuse. Thus, a treatment manual is an important starting point for empirically grounded interventions, but it does not stipulate over-all treatment duration for individual clients. It is a systematic way to select promising types of treatment and estimate a minimum duration.

One empirically grounded practical strategy is to recommend an ini-tial trial period of at least 3 sessions beyond intake to gauge the client's personal pace and compatibility with the provider and the approach. Duration can be more accurately estimated once the initial impressions are consolidated. This introductory trial is short enough not to over-whelm the client who is uncertain about participation, yet it is long enough to allow basic socialization to the purpose, structure, and expec-tations for therapy. A few sessions may be long enough to introduce a skill component to the client's coping repertoire or formulate a strategy for handling a specific problem. Clients who attend at least four sessions total have significantly better outcomes than those who only attend one or two sessions (Pekarik, 1992). If these early sessions include efforts to explain the therapy process and offer guidance on how to prepare for and effectively participate in sessions, the practitioner will likely enhance client attendance, persistence, motivation, improvement, and completion of therapy (Orlinsky, Grawe, & Parks, 1994; Reis & Brown, 2006; Zwick & Attkisson, 1985).

Starting with an initial trial of several sessions allows room for both client and practitioner to evaluate the client's needs and to engage the client in the activities that make therapy productive. From there, labeling the size of the treatment episode provides a logical way to think about the bound-aries of therapy across time. This helps to shape the client's expectations for a commitment of time and energy and may deter unrealistic wishes for instant transformation or allay fears of interminable therapy. The following is a typical framework for describing therapy duration.

Problem-Focused Therapy Duration

- Minimal Episode: 1–4 sessions
- Brief Episode: 5–25 sessions

- Extended Episode: 26–50 sessions
- Continuous Support or Linked Episodes: 51 sessions or more

Once the provider has initiated a collaborative decision-making exchange and provided a reference point for possible therapy duration, a framework is established for setting the treatment plan and re-evaluating the proximity to the finish line as therapy proceeds.

FORMULATE A TERMINATION PLAN

What Is a Termination Plan, and How Is It Linked to the Treatment Goals?

A client may have no idea when therapy should reasonably come to an end, but a therapist can not afford this same naiveté. If the therapist has only a vague idea when the therapy should be concluded, it is quite likely that the treatment plan is non-specific about possible points of closure. Instead, termination should be a component of the treatment plan in some defined way. The termination component of the plan needs to be anchored in operational criteria of time, task, symptoms, functional state, or some blend of these.

For example, if the client has a limited number of sessions or there is a point on the calendar where therapy will have to end, the termination plan will be anchored to this criterion. A timeline might also be a useful termination criterion when the treatment objective is to assist in coping with an ongoing stressor or development issue. For instance, if the treatment plan is to improve coping with a stressful work environment, the termination plan might be to re-evaluate in six months, after the client's yearly work evaluation. The termination criteria do not necessarily dictate the ending, but they serve as an operational trigger for re-evaluation and redirection.

In the absence of specific situational constraints on the length of therapy, it is useful to use an objective procedure for assessing termination readiness. Although this is a critical issue in treatment planning, there is to date relatively little specific guidance in the cognitive behavioral literature. Usually termination readiness is identified by reduction of symptoms or achievement of goals. A structured framework of seven criteria for termination is offered by Jakobsons et al. (2007). These include clinically significant symptom decrease, stability of symptom decrease for eight weeks, clinically significant decrease in functional impairment, symptom reduction linked to new skills, ability to use new skills in high-risk situations, an attitude of excitement about new responses and options, and finally, new responses as a habitual way of coping with different stressors.

Meeting all seven of these criteria would, according to Jakobsons and colleagues, be analogous to hitting the bull's eye on a target, an ideal readiness for termination. Preferably termination can be deferred until the client meets minimal criteria of stable symptom decrease, significant functional improvement, and evidence of ability to use adequate skills under provocative or stressful circumstances. Benchmarks for measuring any of these components are subject to negotiation between provider and client.

Either at intake or in the early planning sessions, the provider can connect the therapy goals with termination by asking the client, *"What do you want to accomplish before we end our work together?"* Or the provider might ask, *"When we have reached the close of therapy and consider the effort a success, what changes have been made?"* This begins to define the client's priorities for change. To bring the consideration of time limits into the discussion, the provider might offer the following question: *"What is your top priority for the first 10 sessions?"* Or perhaps, *"If we have only 10 sessions, what are the most pressing concerns you want to address?"* The client's global objectives can be assessed by asking, *"Time limits aside, what do you hope to gain before stopping therapy?"*

Other primary considerations that have an impact on termination can also be discussed at this point. Simply asking, *"Are there any barriers to your being able to work toward those goals?"* can open up a dialogue about factors that might precipitate early discontinuation. An orientation to productive use of therapy can flow directly from this line of questioning as well. The provider might ask, *"Would you like to know how to make the most out of each session and get good results?"* Presuming that the client will answer yes to this question, the provider has a logical opening for brief socialization to the therapy process.

It is quite simple to add mention of termination as part of the client's orientation to ongoing progress reviews. The objective is to include the tasks of concluding as an important and expected part of therapy. However, care must be taken to do this in a way that does not make the client feel less secure, rejected, or threatened. Sensitive providers know that there can be a vast difference between having a dialogue about general plans and issuing a set of disclaimers and limits. The provider might ask whether or not the client has any questions about the written policies, encourage the client to raise termination concerns at any point, and reinforce the idea of talking about termination as part of progress assessment.

It is also helpful to summarize key aspects of the discussion of therapy goals and offer a statement of positive expectation for the work ahead and its eventual conclusion. This might sound something like the following: *"I think I can help you with (reducing your worry and coping better at home). Let's work together as we've discussed and see what kind of progress we can make in the 10 sessions we have planned. If our initial approach works as expected, that's great; we'll keep going toward your goals. If it doesn't, we'll figure out what changes to make to keep you moving in the direction you want to go until you get there. Along the way, we will decide how much is enough and where you want to stop. How does this sound to you?"*

In commentary such as this, the provider establishes confidence in helping the client toward specific ends and an expectation that they will decide together how to draw therapy to a close. The disclaimer that initial plans are not a guarantee of results and should be evaluated for effectiveness along the way is included. An agreement to therapy is not a commitment to striving for the sake of striving and it is not presented as such. Instead, it is an agreement to pursue certain results as long as there is a reasonable expectation these can be attained. The essence of verbal orientation is to clarify this purpose and to establish some systematic and mutually understood plan for determining if and when the purpose is accomplished.

Possible Anchors For Termination Criteria

- Time
  - Number of sessions
  - Calendar date
  - Season
- Task
  - Client action completed (e.g., find a job, speak in public, complete a project or procedure)
- Symptoms
  - Clinically significant decrease or return to normal baseline
  - Stable decrease for defined time (e.g., eight weeks)
  - Decrease in frequency and belief in maladaptive thoughts
- Functional State
  - New skills transferred to novel situations
  - Life satisfaction improved
  - Resilience to stress increased and emotion regulation improved
  - Role adjustment or acquisition as per objective and subjective benchmarks
  - Adaptive behavior maintained for defined time (e.g., six months)
  - Adaptive cognitive regulation and shift in core beliefs
  - Developmental progression (e.g., milestones encountered)
- Blend
  - Combination of above

How Can I Assess Client Motivation and Use It in the Termination Plan?

The client most likely to make direct progress toward a mutually agreeable termination is one who is "motivated" to benefit from therapy. This client actively participates and has positive expectations as well as adequate social and practical support. As much as 55 percent of the client's improvement in psychotherapy may be attributable to personal factors such as his or her expectations and readiness for change, prior skills, and ongoing life circumstances (Lambert & Barley, 2002). On the other hand, progress may be limited and termination delayed when problems are severe or chronic, there is notable social stress or a lack of social support, or secondary gain associated with symptoms. Hopelessness, passivity, avoidance, or guardedness and mistrust are also impediments to progress.

Although the client's motivation has long been recognized as a key factor in productive therapy, understanding of this motivation has been greatly advanced by delineation of predictable stages of change. Most well known in the area of stages of change is the work of Prochaska and DiClemente (Prochaska & DiClemente, 1982, 1992; Prochaska, DiClemente & Norcross, 1992a, 1992b, 1994). Therapy is likely to be more efficient and effectively directed toward a specified conclusion if the interventions are chosen with sensitivity to the client's stage of change and context of social and personal support.

Stages of Change   There are six stages in the Prochaska et al. (1992a, 1994) transtheoretical model of change. These are (a) pre-contemplation, (b) contemplation, (c) preparation, (d) action, (e) maintenance, and (f) termination. The presenting client may be at any point at intake and may have cycled through the stages in prior attempts to change. Recycling through stages is common and should not necessarily be viewed as treatment failure. The amount of progress that a client makes during and after therapy tends to be a function of his or her pretreatment stage of change and ability to move out of one stage and into the next. For example, if the client can progress just one stage in the first month of therapy, the chances of further action within six months is doubled (Prochaska & DiClemente, 1992a).

In pre-contemplation, the individual is unaware or under-aware of personal ownership of a problem and has no intention to change any time in the foreseeable future. Pre-contemplators might wish for different conditions but focus on external factors as the source of what needs to change. Or the person in pre-contemplation may be demoralized and lacking self-efficacy and thus avoids thoughts about change. The hallmark of pre-contemplation is resistance to recognizing that one has anything to change (Prochaska & Norcross, 2003). The primary reason that someone in this stage might present for therapy is overt pressure from outside circumstances or other people. As we might predict, the client's psychological state of readiness for change is likely to be a significant factor in therapy continuation versus premature termination. On average, 40 percent of clients who present for therapy will prematurely terminate, and most if not all of those will be persons in the pre-contemplation stage (Brogan et al., 1999). Although the definition of premature termination can vary considerably, it usually means attending only one to four sessions when longer treatment was recommended by the practitioner (Garfield, 1994).

Contemplation is the next stage in which the person more deeply considers the possibility that an internal problem exists and gives serious thought to personal behavior change. Clients presenting at this stage typically have some discomfort and are seeking relief, but lack clarity in the focus, direction, or effort needed. The client's motivation is beginning to build momentum, but could just as easily diminish. A significant commitment to action has not yet been made, nor has a clear plan for behavior change. The client is ambivalent and may feel an anxious uncertainty about choices. Attempts to implement an action-oriented intervention at this stage may be ineffective or even detrimental. Contemplation is thus a critical, meaningful stage that requires sufficient energy and attention to successfully resolve ambivalence about action.

Preparation is the point at which intentions and actions begin to overlap. The intention to take action is more immediate or close at hand, with significant action expected within days or weeks. Slight but definite movement marks this stage, helping to solidify the intention for efforts to follow. Motivation may increase as change is more fully conceptualized as a series of possible behaviors and ambivalence is diminished. Motivation could also decrease, as the bulk of the effort remains ahead, and the client may cycle back to a previous stage of contemplation or pre-contemplation. Support and encouragement of change, and focusing on specific small, manageable steps, can facilitate the client's successful negotiation of the preparation stage.

The action stage is the key point at which observable changes in behavior, experiences, or interactions gain momentum. The client is making changes within him or her self to overcome a problem. Some clients will enter therapy at this point, having worked through the contemplation and preparation stages on their own with the assistance of friends and other supports, or through previous and related treatment efforts. These are the clients who will respond rapidly to action-oriented techniques, and who will progress quickly in therapy, perhaps completing treatment in 10 sessions or less. However, it is a mistake to assume that any client entering therapy is at the action stage. Many have not yet reached this stage of readiness and need therapeutic assistance in developing adequate reasons and motivation to change as well as effective action plans.

In the maintenance stage, behavior change is stabilized into an enduring new pattern or lifestyle. Although it might be tempting to view this stage as a static one with an absence of change, it is more precise to consider it an ongoing effort with unique challenges. One of the most significant challenges is avoiding relapse or re-activation of previous problematic behaviors. Clients will vary with regard to presentation in this stage of change. Some will actively recognize the importance of support while others may be prone to taking the permanence of their changes for granted. An important therapeutic topic in this stage is consideration of what is needed to maintain change, and recognize vulnerability to reversal of change or relapse. This is also a point where issues other than the presenting complaint may become a therapeutic focus. If this is the case, a review of the treatment plan and goals is important.

The termination stage refers to when the problem has ended and the client considers him or her self as "recovered." When the problem is one with a high rate of relapse, there is difference of opinion on whether or not it is ever appropriate to consider it terminated. For example, many in the field of addictions consider the maintenance of recovery as something that would continue in perpetuity. However, there is research evidence that supports a concept of problem termination for some clients with addictive behaviors (Miller, 1995). Termination of the problem is a stage reached by some when they are no longer troubled and not making any explicit effort to maintain this state.

Understanding how people move through the stages of change has significant implications for effective termination. How do people move through the stages of change? The first step appears to be consciousness or awareness of a problem, whether the problem is biological (physical symptoms or impairments), psychological (emotional distress, cognitive impairments, behavioral dysfunctions), or social (interpersonal, role, family, or community impairment), or some combination of these dimensions. At the pre-contemplation stage, little time or energy is invested in self-evaluation. If there are negative aspects to a problem, the individual does not react much to them. At this stage, the person is rather closed to new information and will resist owning the problem or planning behavior changes, perhaps dropping out of therapy or presenting a hostile or dismissive attitude.

The most helpful therapeutic stance for pre-contemplation is likely to be a nurturing and supportive approach that gently draws the client into a consideration of his or her circumstances by piquing their curiosity or interest. Offering an opportunity to examine thoughts, feelings, and ideas in a very accepting and non-demanding atmosphere may help the client move toward greater recognition that a possible problem exists. Providing the client with information about the attitudes and behaviors of others may also be useful in this stage as a reference point for self-evaluation.

Intellectual recognition alone is not likely to compel progress toward contemplation of change. Some emotional connection to the problem is needed. The problem has to matter in some affectively relevant way. A variety of affective techniques such as guided discussion, validation, or expressive dialogue might draw the client's attention to emotional implications of the problem. For some, information on normative parameters is most emotionally provocative, especially when it pertains to a preferred social reference group.

A significant number of clients can be expected to terminate treatment at pre-contemplation. Sufficient rapport, pacing, and encouragement may mediate this for some. For others it may be an appropriate point of termination if the client does not have the interest, motivation, or resources to proceed further in the change process. To insist that the client remain in therapy would be unethical, as the client is not likely to immediately benefit from service. Using four sessions as a recommended minimal contact creates an acceptable context for early termination. The practitioner should communicate a positive and accepting attitude toward the termination so that the client feels welcome to return at any point in the future. Having a favorable impression of the interaction with the practitioner will help to make it easier to return to therapy if the client decides to do so. If the practitioner takes any actions beyond the mildest attempts to "keep the door open," there is a risk that the client will feel coerced and become alienated from therapy as a resource.

The contemplation stage is marked by increased seeking of information and self-evaluation. Clients entering this stage will respond well to activities of thinking, reflecting, and self-exploration. Bibliotherapy and information gathering are useful strategies that are consistent with client expectations. However, some clients become stuck in the contemplation stage, substituting repetitive thinking for action and in effect become "chronic contemplators" (Prochaska & Norcross, 2003, p. 516). Practitioners can also get stuck in the chronic contemplation stage, endlessly nurturing the discussion of conflicts and feelings without moving on to the implications of action versus non-action. Both client and practitioner may believe, mistakenly, that this repetitive review will eventually reduce distress and produce clarity of direction. Clients who have more complex problems and less preparation for change are likely to need more time for contemplation and a more extended course of therapy. Chronic contemplation, however, can be identified as a liability that produces ongoing discomfort and may forestall active preparation.

If a client terminates therapy in the contemplation stage, it may be because he or she is unready or unwilling to move toward action. This may be an appropriate termination as it the client's right to choose whether or not to change. Change may need to be postponed until circumstances are more supportive. If therapy must be drawn to a close because of contract limitations on the number of sessions, a positive closure will summarize the issues that have been considered and prompt the client to continue with independent efforts. Other resources such as self-help books, support groups, or specific skills training might offer useful assistance in the client's self-directed progress.

At this stage, a plan to return for another "course" of therapy when resources allow might also work well. For example, a client may have used up the sessions allowed within a calendar year under his or her insurance plan, so the current therapy is terminated but another course in the next calendar year may be feasible, if the client wishes to return. Finally, the practitioner may suggest termination if the client seems stuck in chronic contemplation and unlikely to make productive use of the therapy in the foreseeable future. Here also the therapist can summarize the issues and offer guidance on self-directed efforts that will facilitate entry into the preparation stage, possibly with an option to return for a new episode of treatment after completing some small steps toward action readiness.

In the preparation stage, the client formulates a plan for what to change and how to change it, with specific directions beginning to take shape. The path of change may not be detailed down to the tiny minutiae, but there are goals and priorities and some idea of how to achieve these objectives. The practitioner continues to offer support and encouragement, and to coach the client on specific methods or procedures to facilitate success. Small efforts are recognized and highly encouraged. The practitioner can help focus the effort and provide crucial reassurance and guidance. Clients may be hesitant and overwhelmed at this point and often need liberal doses of support.

Preparation is a stage where it is very useful to directly solicit the client to stay in therapy long enough to gain confidence in his or her skills. If the client has made previous efforts that were ineffective and is prone to link those with the current therapy when frustrated (e.g., "I've been trying so hard for so long"), the practitioner can gently point out the brief history with newer tactics and emphasize the need for skill development. If termination must occur, the practitioner can assist the client in focusing on particular skills for continued practice.

In the action stage, practitioners help to maintain the affective and cognitive foundations of the earlier stages, and provide technical support for the behavioral change efforts. They can help the client effectively apply techniques of counter-conditioning, stimulus control, contingency management, and cognitive restructuring or defusion. Encouragement, accountability, and partnership are all important in the action stage. Clients are surrounded by advice on the action of change, and may be drawn off track by distraction or misdirection. Significant others may be quite helpful and right on target with suggestions, or they may be poorly informed or sabotaging of the client's intentions, despite intentions to the contrary.

Thus, an effective therapeutic stance is that of an informed (and patient) consultant who knows the particulars of the client's situation and is keeping track of both progress and direction of change. The practitioner can reinforce persistence when the effort becomes difficult, tedious, or questionable. When one method doesn't seem to be working, the practitioner can be helpful in trouble-shooting and offering alternative strategies if needed.

Many practitioners and clients alike will begin to consider termination during the action stage and will appropriately diminish the frequency of therapy contact. Practitioners of problem-focused therapy will often encourage a tapering of sessions at this point, meeting biweekly or monthly to monitor progress and implementation of change.

Maintenance begins when change has been substantially established for a noted period of time, anywhere from one to six months or longer. The issues of lapse and relapse and ways to cope with these stressors through redirection are important. Developing a new or adjusted sense of identity is also important for success in the maintenance stage. In other words, the client begins to see him or her self as a changed person. As a changed person, he or she is motivated to prevent a change back to old ways, and may even have significant apprehension about the possibility of relapse. Relapse prevention strategies are organized around skills of self management (Marlatt & Gordon, 1985; Roberts & Marlatt, 1998).

Risks at the maintenance stage include overestimating the stability of the behavior change and underestimating the need for any ongoing action. To reduce the risk of relapse, the client learns that persistence and intention are needed to achieve a balanced, moderated lifestyle. High-risk situations and early indications of behavior shift are observed. The deployment of effective coping skills is encouraged with an emphasis on minimizing harm and learning from the experience. In maintenance, termination is ideally achieved by tapering sessions over some period of time that is determined by mutual agreement between practitioner and client. Some clients with non-terminating problems or fragile support systems may need open-ended or indefinite maintenance contact. For these clients, primary considerations are keeping therapy focused over time, demonstrating ongoing benefit, and making optimal use of available resources.

If the client has reached a point where the problem can be considered terminated, it seems obvious that therapy should be terminated as well. There may be other issues or problems that suggest continuing therapy, which is perfectly reasonable. However, this should be explicitly discussed or the therapy may become fuzzy and lose direction. For example, a client with panic disorder may have reached the goal of termination of panic attacks but continues in therapy for a related problem of general health anxiety or interpersonal difficulties. Conversely, many clients wish to terminate therapy when the original problem terminates without continuing work on other problems. The therapist should remain cautious about infringing on the client's right to choose to accept or reject an option for treatment continuation. Using an established therapeutic influence to sway the client's decision toward remaining in therapy might be viewed as an exploitive action that serves the provider's economic or personal interests while diminishing the client's autonomy.

Positive conclusion to therapy can be drawn at any point during the process of change with sufficient recognition of the client's progress through stages. Because most therapy will terminate before the actual problem completely terminates, it is natural that the client or practitioner may feel some anxiety about the stability of change (Prochaska and Norcross, 2003). Viewing change as a continual process, however, allows for segments of work such as negotiating a shift from one stage to the next or changing some parts of a larger problem. The practitioner can define therapy as a consulting resource that serves clients all along the continuum of change, at different or multiple points in time.

Perhaps the client has alleviated the most troubling symptoms and will return to address self-esteem or quality-of-life issues in another episode of therapy. Or it may be that the client lacks the resources or support to move into the next stage of change. Contact with the therapist is just part of an ongoing process that has the potential to encourage the client toward contemplating change at a later point when resources are more available. Those clients who seem to be prematurely terminating may simply be signaling that the attempt to engage in further change is premature. For these reasons, it is critical that the practitioner approach every closure from a positive perspective even if change is far from complete.

How Do I Know if the Client Is Benefiting or Likely to Benefit from Therapy?

As therapy proceeds from the initial to the middle sessions where the bulk of the work takes place, it is important to track whether or not the client is making any progress or otherwise benefiting from the service. If there is no progress within a reasonable amount of time, or no likelihood of progress forthcoming, then treatment can not ethically continue. Unfortunately, there is no specific definition of a reasonable amount of time to allow for the possibility of progress. Pragmatic concerns such as managed care authorization or insurance coverage limits also have a bearing on this assessment as progress must be demonstrated in order for treatment to continue. Client and therapist are not only asking, "What kind of progress are we making?"; they are also considering, "What kind of progress are we making given the time we have available?" and "Is progress likely in the foreseeable future?"

There are several possible benchmarks for tracking progress in therapy. Even though the client's goals might be broad in scope, the practitioner has several vantage points for assessing gains produced by ongoing work. Standardized measures such as symptom rating scales or structured interviews are wonderful for capturing major improvements, but alone may not always be sensitive enough for tracking smaller changes on a session-by-session basis. In addition to routine administration of standardized measures, clinicians might note any of the following evidence of clinical progress.

Benchmarks of Clinical Progress

- Subjective sense of purpose and value linked to therapy sessions; verbal statements that therapy is beneficial
- Positive alliance and productive collaboration
- Stabilization or re-stabilization following contact
- General symptom reduction
- Focused symptom improvement and improved emotional self-regulation

- Functional or behavioral changes, including improvements in role adjustment or performance
- Improved family or other system functioning

Noting benefits in one or more of these areas is vital to an ethical practice. If there is no benefit in any or most of these areas over a sustained period of time, then ethically the provider is obligated to consider termination as the client is either failing to benefit or no longer needs the service.

Subjective Sense of Accomplishment Linked to Therapy Interaction   In a collaborating relationship, the provider regularly asks the client for feedback on whether or not therapy is producing useful results. Progress with presenting problems is checked, along with the status of new issues. This brief review keeps both participants oriented to an overall purpose and direction for therapy as the activity moves forward in time. Many times the sense of purpose is something that develops out of the interaction between the provider and client as they transform the client's complaints and global strivings into a more specific and concrete problem list with an action plan.

Although this is a subjective benchmark, it reflects a critical, "gut feeling" on the part of both client and provider that they are, in effect, getting somewhere worth going. The provider may be most attuned to the level of emotional arousal within the session and whether or not the content of sessions is dealing with emotionally salient issues and moving toward clinical change. Clients provide validation of this salience with spontaneous comments or solicited feedback that verifies their perceptions of value in the work. For example, the client might say, "I'm glad we finally talked about that. I think that is one of the main things that have been bothering me for a long time." Or perhaps, "I didn't realize how significant this is until it came up today. But now that we've taken the time to discuss this, I can see how much this has affected me."

When the client experiences a cognitive shift during a session, he or she might acknowledge this with a comment such as "I've never thought about it that way until just now. That's a really different way of looking at this that makes a lot of sense." The comment might be accompanied by some non-verbal indications of emotional arousal such as a welling of tears, a shift in vocal inflection, a "catch" in the voice tone, or a thoughtful pause and a shift in the client's gaze. The client might make other reflective statements such as, "I feel like I'm getting some good ideas on things I can try, and I don't feel so lost. This is helping." Any statement similar to these is an indication of the subjective sense of purpose, an important benchmark for progress. These can be monitored by listening carefully to the client's spontaneous comments and responses to direct inquiry and to one's own automatic thoughts in and after the sessions.

Positive Therapeutic Alliance   Closely related to the subjective sense of purpose is the positive therapeutic alliance that is so strongly linked to satisfactory outcome. This complex phenomenon can be essentially summarized by its affective, cognitive, and behavioral components. First, there is a warm and positive rapport between the participants. Interaction generates positive feelings. If there is tension or discomfort, this is usually related to the content of the problems, not the process of therapist-client interaction. When there are disruptions in the positive tone of the interaction, these are resolved in a way that preserves the good alliance. In a good alliance, the client views the therapist as caring, helpful, and competent as a resource. The behaviors of a positive alliance include making and keeping regular appointments, preparing for the session, behaving in a respectful manner during the session, reflecting on the session after it is over, and planning ways to respond or follow-up on matters of the session.

For the relationship to be a positive *therapeutic* alliance the client needs to actually confide something and the interactions between client and provider focus on clinical matters. Social rapport is one of the provider's fundamental tools, but its purpose is to promote a directed therapeutic experience. If the therapy drifts into a primarily social exchange and the therapeutic content can not be readily discerned, it is likely that little or no progress is being made. This might indicate that further progress is unlikely; it might indicate that important issues are being actively avoided, or it might indicate that the original problems are sufficiently resolved. This is often a very perplexing situation for the provider, as one must balance the client's need to set the pace and direction of change with the need to keep therapy moving toward a purposeful end.

A positive alliance fosters progress in many ways, not the least of which is encouraging the client to attend to and disclose the sources of distress. Turning to the therapeutic relationship as a resource is a sign of progress away from avoidance, isolation and withdrawal. This is a relationship in which the client is building or restoring interpersonal functioning in terms of trust and emotional disclosure as well as productive communication skills. As the provider encourages the client toward the next step in his or her process of change, the client is willing to accept and act on suggestions or recommendations, carrying out homework or making an effort to make productive use of the therapist's input.

Stabilization and General Symptom Reduction   The most evident type of progress is usually when immediate symptoms begin to remit and the client becomes more stable. Hope and positive expectations are activated, even though problems are not completely resolved and there may be a significant ways to go. A crisis is resolved, or a plan for addressing more chronic and pervasive problems begins to take shape and the client begins to feel noticeably better. Some objective measure of this benchmark is typically useful, such as a symptom checklist matched to the client's presenting problems.

The course of such improvement is not always smooth and direct, as there will likely be exacerbating experiences and new struggles along the way. Such is the nature of human change. However, persistent worsening of symptoms or a lack of stabilization or re-stabilization following sessions is a cause for concern. The reasonable caution that "things may get worse before they get better" is meant to acknowledge the likelihood of some distress related to the process of self-examination. This caution is not meant to dismiss evidence that a client is not benefiting or possibly even being harmed by the ongoing work.

Focused Symptom Improvement and Improved Emotional Self-Regulation   Sometimes progress needs to be measured by focused bits of change rather than broad improvements. Clients with multiple problems, long-standing impairments, or a limited range of resources may be most likely to show these sorts of smaller, incremental gains over time. The overall level of depression or anxiety, for example, may remain at elevated levels, yet improvement is made in specific areas such as reduced suicidal ideation, less pervasive guilt, increased tolerance for uncertainty without jumping to conclusions or an increase in day-to-day decision-making. When combined with a productive alliance and a good subjective sense of purpose, these gains should tip the balance in favor of therapy continuation over termination whenever it is pragmatically possible.

Intermittent symptom assessment as well as client subjective reports are good sources of information regarding these changes. For instance, the client might report that certain predictable triggers feel less provocative and more manageable. Perhaps the client has more enjoyment and fewer "meltdowns" during the typically tumultuous afternoon hours between school pick-up and dinner. Or a single but highly disruptive symptom diminishes or disappears, such as migraine headaches or panic attacks. The provider may also see evidence of changes in the client's focus of attention or in-session interactions that indicate progress in certain specific areas. For example, the client might stop dwelling on the nuances of medication and its side effects and start talking more about the content of her fears and frustrations.

Functional Changes   Notable signs of progress may be observed in functional improvements made by the client over the course of therapy. Interestingly, these can sometimes escape the client's awareness or may be dismissed as simply doing what is expected. Functional changes usually have an observable behavioral component, and should relate to the values and long-term best interests of the client. For example, becoming more active is usually a positive functional change for a depressed client. However, engaging in more activities with a high risk for self-damage such as drinking or gambling is not a positive functional change. On the other hand, small increments of positive changes, such as playing with the children, getting the laundry done, eating in response to hunger, making it to work on time, attending a football game, or less aimless Internet use, may be important signs of progress.

Functional change may be evident in the recovery of more normalized everyday activities and relationship interactions as well as in the client's reactions to unexpected stressors. For instance, the depressed client is able to enjoy time with unexpected houseguests. The critical parent is able to acknowledge the teenager's "C" in history without exploding and still have a pleasant family dinner. Functional changes may not be continuous or permanent, but these behaviors are typically strong signs of progress and can be identified as such to the client.

System Changes   Important system changes should not be overlooked as identifiable signs of progress, even in individual therapy. Such changes can denote shifts in the client's interaction patterns and response to stress, even if the client is not able to describe or report his or her specific impact on the system. Perhaps the family is able to eat together at the kitchen table and interact instead of avoiding one another and eating in front of the television. Or the client reports that the work environment is improving and there is greater productivity and less conflict among his or her group of co-workers or between levels of the work hierarchy. System changes might occur before or after the client realizes notable improvement in symptoms or other functioning, as sometimes the system is responsive to even slight alterations in the client's behavior. For example, a client reported a noticeable improvement in marital communication and affection as soon as she began a behavioral activation exercise of grocery shopping.

Conditions of No Improvement   If the client is experiencing little or no benefit from therapy, it is highly likely that one or both participants will recognize this via a sense of frustration and lack of purpose or direction. Sessions may be pleasant enough, but aimless or stuck. This needs to be distinguished from the expected frustrations that often accompany an uncertain and sometimes tedious process of psychological change. Clients often need encouragement to persist in the endeavor when it is likely that they can and will benefit.

Progress in therapy is always relative to its overall goals and purpose. If the client can not identify a use, purpose, or intended direction of therapy, it will be difficult to see progress. The goal then becomes helping the client learn how to make productive use of therapy or choose termination.

If the provider does not clearly see the purpose of therapy, a reassessment of client needs is in order. This is also a prime time to seek case consultation to facilitate a better understanding of potentially useful directions. Relevant goals can sometimes be located in the client's current stage of change, where the purpose is to help the client advance to the next level.

Keep in mind that one is ethically bound to make a reasoned appraisal of the client's actual and potential benefit and offer a suitable recommendation. There are possible biases that can complicate this judgment. One potential bias is overestimating the benefit of treatment, based on conviction and a personal investment in the enterprise. Some providers may believe that therapeutic benefit is solely a reflection of their personal competence, and they feel compelled to "make" therapy work with every client. Others might base their estimation of potential benefit on allegiance to a particular model of therapy. Although enthusiasm and commitment are very important to the helping stance of the mental health professional, an over-investment in client success can be linked to stress and professional burnout (Freeman, Felgoise & Davis, 2008). Alternatively, the provider might approach this task with an attitude of *commitment* to the client's best interests and high professional standards while remaining *objective* about the assessment of benefit.

If the client fails to improve, worsens, or reaches a sustained plateau yet remains clinically impaired, the provider will want to assess the barriers that might be interfering with a positive response. The following series of questions can aid in assessing these potential obstacles.

Questions to Pinpoint Barriers to Progress

- Do I fully or accurately understand the current problem?
- Has the client developed another clinical disorder that I have not detected?
- Is my approach likely to be effective with this type of problem? Would another type of therapy be more effective?
- Does the client have sufficient trust, confidence, and positive rapport with me? Would the client have a more productive match with a different provider?
- Are the treatment strategies consistent with the client's current stage of change?
- Is the client stuck in chronic contemplation and avoidance of action?
- Have new and unexpected stresses overwhelmed the client?
- Has the client received sufficient instruction or socialization into the tasks of therapy?
- Does the client have expectations for a different type of therapy or a different pace of interaction?
- Does the client have beliefs that interfere with the tasks of therapy (Beck, 2005)?
- Do outside circumstances or other problems interfere with the client's effective participation? If so, how can that interference be resolved?

- Is there significant secondary gain associated with not improving?
- Has the client developed an undetected medical problem?
- Would alternative services better meet the clients' needs (e.g., speech therapy, vocational rehabilitation, inpatient drug treatment)?

Candid responses to these questions will help determine whether or not termination is the appropriate next step. If the barriers can be resolved or the goals of treatment readjusted, then therapy might be continued with greater benefit. If the barriers can not be resolved or only with great difficulty, termination may be the most viable option. Continuing therapy might be a barrier to the client seeking other appropriate solutions to the problem.

When termination is recommended due to no improvement, the termination discussion should most likely include recommendations for an alternative course of action. This will depend on the specific situation, but might include referral to a different provider, referral for a different type of professional service, referral for further medical evaluation, or encouragement to address a personal concern and reconsider psychotherapy at a later point.

The following are some clinical examples where termination due to lack of improvement was followed by positive responses to alternative options.

- Jason felt frustrated by attempts to explore his difficult childhood. After lengthy discussion, Jason and his therapist agreed to termination and transfer to a different therapy. Jason found the new approach both pleasant and useful.
- Lisa had an extremely difficult time opening up with her therapist because he reminded her of the uncle who tried to molest her. She had trouble putting her feelings into words, so she was greatly relieved when the provider raised the idea of the option of talking with a female therapist.
- Mabel had symptoms of cognitive disorientation along with agitated depression following a major loss when she was fired from her part-time job. Psychological assessment suggested her disorientation was pseudo-dementia secondary to depression. However, her response to a standard regimen of treatment for depression was minimal. Psychotherapy was discontinued after nine sessions, pending further medical evaluation by geriatric medical specialists. Within months, Mabel was diagnosed with pre-senile dementia. Her family hired an in-home day companion who assisted Mabel with personal grooming and activities such as shopping and outings.
- Tyler was generally well adjusted but complained of mild social anxiety as a result of his hearing impairment. There was a hearing aid of higher quality than his current device that would be much easier to use, but he was conflicted about spending the money. The therapist suggested that Tyler consider investing the money in the better hearing aid and then evaluate whether or not therapy was necessary. Tyler telephoned a few months later to express appreciation for the encouragement to justify the expense. The better instrument

had indeed vastly improved the quality and comfort in his social interactions, and he felt no further need for therapy.

As initial problems are resolved, other concerns may take their place. This is not unusual. There is nothing wrong with extending the treatment contract and in fact this probably happens quite often. However, it is important to review the treatment plan as the original goals of therapy are met, and consider if termination would be appropriate.

SUMMARY POINTS FOR APPLIED PRACTICE

1. A written practice profile can sow the first seeds of a positive therapy alliance. This tool helps you define your scope of competence and communicate that to prospective clients.

2. Say "no" to clinical referrals that are beyond your scope of competence, no matter how intriguing or beguiling the request. If the referral is near the margins of your zone of confidence, make time to do the necessary homework.

3. Add a termination policy to your written consent to care and verbal informed consent process.

4. Estimating the length of therapy is a primary concern of most clients. This can be addressed as a reasonable request and taken as a task of the collaboration.

5. Termination should be a component of the treatment plan in some defined way, anchored by time, task, or symptomatic or functional criteria.

6. The track to termination is significantly influenced by expectations, readiness for change, prior skills, therapeutic alliance and collaboration and ongoing circumstances. Include these factors in your estimation of treatment duration.

7. Orient the client to the task of planning for conclusion as part of formulating the treatment plan. A clinical stance of encouragement and guidance is apt to be more effective than one of admonishment and forewarning.

8. Add a decibel of caution to your treatment duration estimate for every complicating element including chronic problems, recurrent episodes, co-morbid disorders, Axis II problems, social stress, secondary gain, hopelessness, avoidance, and guardedness. Adjust the goals according to the client's needs and resources (see Chapter Six for discussion of termination strategy in complex circumstances).

9. If possible, match the intervention and the termination plan to the client's stage of change at intake. Change is a continual process. Therapy is a consulting resource that serves clients all along the continuum of change.

10. Progress can be marked by routine standard symptom assessments and by observing in-session indications and reports of certain benchmarks, including subjective value, positive therapeutic alliance, stabilization, general and focused symptom reduction, role adjustment, better performance, improved behavior or emotional self-regulation, and healthier system functioning.

4

Talking about Termination:
A Closer Look at Communications

Key Questions Addressed in This Chapter

- What makes termination difficult to discuss?
- What is the "culture of expectations," and how does it impact termination discussions?
- Are there beliefs that affect the provider's approach to termination?
- What are clinical, practical, and ethical reasons for termination?
- Are there any conversational targets to help structure termination?
- What documentation is necessary?

ORIENTATION TO THE TOPIC OF TERMINATION

An uncomplicated termination can be easy, fluid, and pleasant. Both parties accept the decision and have positive feelings about it, even if those feelings are mixed with ambivalence. Having reasonable expectations that are grounded in the practical realities of today's health care system contributes a great deal to a smooth closure. Sequential segments of therapy are the current norm, creating the necessity of addressing termination at multiple points. There is no less emphasis on the client's best interests, but there is greater obligation to attend to termination planning throughout therapy and a greater need for the client to effectively utilize services. Where premature termination was once the primary bane of an optimal therapeutic process, prolonged therapy or neglected termination has become the new peril. Providers must discern the clinical circumstances that indicate highest need for extended care and find the best ways to assist all clients in titrating their use of formal intervention.

Communications between client and provider throughout therapy provide the structure for termination. As previously discussed, an optimum termination strategy includes some explicit attention to talking about termination as part of the overall treatment plan. Although this task does not appear particularly daunting, it may not be easy, comfortable, or automatic. Because it can be easy to avoid or neglect talking about ending despite the various elevated risks associated with poor termination, it is useful to routinely ensure that this essential communication takes place.

The provider's confidence and finesse in discussing termination is likely shaped by many factors, including theoretically based expectations, assessment of client needs and resources, and individual skill in managing anxiety and inducing collaboration within the conversation. Just thinking of termination as an approachable topic does not automatically translate into deftness and skill in knowing when to discuss it or how to productively understand and manage the conflicts that may surface with the topic. The following sections will explore reasons why termination may be difficult to discuss and suggest some specific conversational targets for talking about termination in a systematic and positive way.

What Makes Termination Difficult to Discuss?

Both client and provider have an ongoing stream of thoughts and appraisals on the process of therapy. Often these slip by with only slight notice or comment. Most therapists make some ongoing effort to attend to these thoughts and evaluate them as a source of constructive information. Automatic thoughts that pertain to progress and satisfaction or dissatisfaction with the work or the relationship are especially important to capture. If things are going well, thoughts of ending therapy are apt to be only brief and fleeting if they occur at all. Termination might come up only when prompted by cues from managed care time limits or when goals are achieved; it is not particularly difficult to talk about and initial signals are easily recognized.

Nevertheless, there might be circumstances where the topic of termination feels more sensitive than money, sex, or personal satisfaction with therapy. This discomfort can have many components, including the avoidance of uncomfortable affect, under-assertiveness with the subject, lack of clarity about possible reasons or criteria for termination, discomfort with interpersonal change, or a fear of precipitating some harm by discontinuing treatment too soon. Finding the right time to broach the subject and knowing what to say and how to say it are all skill issues. We might reasonably expect the therapist to be better at doing this than the client.

At the heart of such difficulty may be distorted beliefs pertaining to emotional fragility and a desire to preserve the therapeutic relationship. The client and therapist both may fear that talk of termination will produce "hurt feelings" that cause the other to feel rejected or take offense. There could be a very strong attachment that has become fundamental to the client's overall support system. "Breaking up is hard to do," as the well known popular song by Neil Sedaka and Howard Greenfield (1962) reminds us. Both client and provider may fear the other will be angry or defensive, or overreact to the idea of discontinuing the ongoing relationship.

It may be that expectations of emotional profusion are not a distortion. Talk of termination really will precipitate a firestorm of abreaction from the client, and the therapist feels stuck in the conflict between confronting a therapy stalemate and containing a potentially volatile reaction. Recognizing that the topic is not being addressed in a normal fashion is the first step in developing an effective strategy under these conditions. From there, the therapist's task is to bring the topic into the discussion and work toward clarifying a plan.

Another major reason for difficulty in talking about termination might be that things are not going well clinically and something is significantly off track in the client's progress. Either therapist or client could be ruminating about termination as a means of resolving the tension or frustration associated with the non-productive or counterproductive clinical interaction. Yet they are reluctant to raise the idea of termination because this establishes their current efforts as a failure. If the therapist thinks, "We are going nowhere" or "We are not together on the plan," these are both potentially viable indications of a need for termination (Younggren & Gottlieb, in press). It is not surprising that both therapist and client want to avoid reaching these conclusions, but avoiding the subject does not make the problem go away.

At any given point, the idea of ending therapy is influenced by the rate and degree of progress, how chronic and pervasive the disorder, positive or negative valence of the ongoing interaction, strengths and vulnerabilities of the client, the overall context of client resources and competing needs, the provider's relative availability, and the views of both on reasonable expectations for therapy. Termination is easier to discuss when it has been established as a task of treatment from the beginning and obviously when therapy is progressing as hoped. Termination is more difficult to discuss when there are highly charged emotional attachment issues, greater client dependence, more complex problems overall, and when progress is inconsistent with initial plans and expectations.

What Is the "Culture of Expectations," and How Does It Impact Termination Decisions?

There are many commonly held expectations about what it means to be "in therapy" and what the experience should entail. These shape the prospective client's expectations of their relationship with the provider and how therapy will end. Clients bring assumptions with them based on prior personal experiences in therapy, experiences they have heard about from others, stories they have read or seen depicted in the media, or general observations drawn from the culture at large. Provider assumptions draw from the same general culture but also include the influences of their professional acculturation, personal therapy, consultations with colleagues, and ongoing experience as a provider.

Historically, the general cultural expectation for psychotherapy has been a relatively long-term treatment process in the context of an intensive, protected relationship. For decades, this was the expected general standard of care. This standard emphasized the importance of avoiding "premature" termination, retaining clients in therapy over an extended duration, and providing a consistent relationship with a single provider. Once accepted into therapy, the cultural expectations emphasized the provider's duty to be available to the client until the client was ready to complete treatment. Over the last two decades, there has been a gradual paradigm shift in commonly held assumptions about the nature and duration of psychotherapy as a restorative endeavor. Because of shifts in the way that health services are delivered, current standards call for coherent management of termination decisions across multiple and complex situations. Both client and provider may be unprepared to anticipate or manage these decisions, particularly if their expectations are rooted in the traditional view of termination as the final culmination of working long term with a single provider.

In the provider's professional culture of training and practice, activities that are considered standard techniques may in fact reflect a long-term psychodynamic standard of care. For example, the provider may think it necessary to limit talk of termination or avoid bringing it up "too soon." This agenda is most consistent with fostering transference. In a learning-based collaboration, the provider uses a more directive approach to help the client build functional skills, including decision-making skills. Among the important decisions to be made are those concerning how to use the time in therapy and when to draw it to a close. Yet when it comes to guiding a discussion of termination, even highly collaborative providers sometimes default into a neutral or waiting mode. The culture of training expectations has embedded the notion that termination will be initiated by the client when a state of readiness is achieved. Waiting for the client to control the ending of therapy has the unfortunate risk of shifting too much responsibility to the person in therapy with the least experience or skill in making this judgment. A contemporary culture of expectations holds the provider accountable for establishing the necessity of care and for collaborating with client to determine when it is appropriate to end service.

Are There Beliefs That Affect the Provider's Approach to Termination?

Clinicians who are otherwise directive in their therapy stance may hold certain beliefs that constrain their actions with regard to termination. Without a clear orientation to action, the prudent provider is naturally going to err in the direction of caution. Effective planning of termination may be impeded by beliefs that (a) inhibit reasonable action, (b) prolong therapy, or (c) promote procrastination in broaching a difficult subject. On the other hand, termination may be more easily approached when it is viewed as an important opportunity to foster collaboration and a component of the standard of care.

Beliefs That Inhibit Reasonable Provider Action

"I should not terminate therapy as long as the client wants to continue."

"The client must indicate an interest and willingness to terminate before we can discontinue therapy."

Some providers feel a strong internal sense of resistance to raising the issue of termination. It is as though the provider is simply not allowed to take this action. One possible reason for this reluctance is the belief that the client must initiate termination for therapy to be truly completed. Once a client has been accepted, the provider perceives an obligation to maintain the relationship until the client determines that service is no longer needed. Otherwise, the therapy process may be distorted by the provider's needs. However, offering such unconditional availability is not typically possible or consistent with current practice realities. There are clinically and ethically appropriate reasons that providers might consider or even mandate termination. Today's standard of care expects the provider to periodically review the continuing need for services with the client. The provider is not only allowed but expected to prompt the client's initiative toward termination.

A related belief that fosters the provider's internal resistance is the notion that the client will recognize an internal readiness for termination and initiate discussion about ending therapy. However, many clients look to the provider for signals and recommendations concerning the appropriate reasons for termination. The provider is viewed as the one with the authority to determine when the client should be "discharged." The provider can be alert to these possible issues and without being dictatorial take the lead in guiding termination planning.

"It is extremely risky for the provider to raise the idea of termination."

Termination is a point where professional risk of adverse action is elevated (Younggren, 2007). Although it is important to be cognizant of risks in professional practice, magnification of such risks without effective coping strategies can have the net effect of inhibiting ordinary and reasonable actions. When the provider magnifies the impact of emotional arousal or the likelihood of negative consequences for either the client or himself, termination may be perceived as having more potential harm than benefit. Even though the realistic probability of harm may be quite low, possible outcomes are perceived as severe emotional, psychological, or professional threats. First and foremost, providers may worry that the stress of emotional arousal in discussing termination will be aversive or damaging to the client.

"My client might misunderstand my intent and feel rejected."
"My client might feel inadequate or unprepared."
"I don't want my client to be unhappy."
"The client might become angry and upset."

Providers may also be apprehensive about their own emotional or professional risks.

"I will get punished for trying to terminate therapy."
"The stress of a termination confrontation will be too much for both of us."
"The client might seek other services and speak badly about me."
"The client might complain to the licensing board or try to sue me."
"I don't want to be guilty of client abandonment."

Conflict or a difference of opinion with the client concerning termination may feel emotionally uncomfortable as well as professionally risky. Fears of upsetting the client or making an error are often associated with predictions of devaluation and professional reprimand. There may be anxiety about damaging one's professional reputation, destabilizing one's source of income, or being subject to legal action. These predictions of adverse action actually have a low probability unless the termination is associated with some other form of professional misconduct such as inappropriate multiple relationships (Hjelt, 2007; Younggren & Gottlieb, in press). Nevertheless the anxiety will persist if the provider deals with perceived risks by avoiding discussion of termination.

What the client and provider believe about abandonment plays a pivotal role in how actively they approach termination. As noted in Chapter Two, it may be that the understanding of abandonment is vague. If a client feels abandoned by the ending of therapy, exploration of these feelings often reveals anxiety about symptom return or loss of functioning without ongoing contact with the clinician. The client may be unclear about reasonable points of termination and opportunities for follow-up contact. Only through an active discussion about these concerns can a reasonable plan be developed. Clients who tend to be hostile and dominant may use accusations of abandonment as a tool for controlling the therapist, thus creating a high-risk situation that requires a different approach to the termination communication and plan.

The provider's apprehensions about client abandonment may reflect various professional performance anxieties. One worry may be that therapy is incomplete or imperfect in some way. Without absolute certainty that therapy is complete and successful, the provider may fear that termination is a terrible mistake that will bring psychic harm to the client. Or the provider may fear that initiating termination will trigger unmanageable anger and disagreement from the client, which in turn paves the way for dreadful professional consequences. In the provider's anxious ruminations there may be vivid images of hostile courtrooms, angry cross-examinations and humiliating verdicts that lead to job termination and economic impoverishment. Avoiding this ugly scenario by avoiding termination seems to be the most certain coping strategy. On the other hand, it is possible that there are other effective solutions to this dilemma. Compassionately confronting the client's angry or defensive reactions can open the door for a better understanding of remaining problems. This can establish a productive focus for any potential continuation of therapy, if it is determined to be feasible.

Beliefs That Prolong Therapy

"Therapy should continue until it is absolutely clear it is no longer needed."

"Therapy should be terminated only when it is clear that permanent and lasting changes have occurred."

"We can't be certain that the client has no further need for therapy."

Another reason that either the provider or the client may be reluctant to initiate termination is the belief that prolonged therapy will produce curative results. Prolonged therapy occurs when there is no relevant direction to the sessions or identifiable benefit other than social contact. This should be distinguished from long-term therapy that includes both a directed plan and an expected benefit from the service. Therapists and clients alike may be tempted to prolong therapy in an effort to reach some ideal point where they both can be certain that the client will not encounter further difficulties. Any residual problems or emotional reactions become potential "evidence" that the client is not permanently protected and therefore not ready for termination. The exact nature of what establishes this guarantee is elusive, and therefore the interaction is vulnerable to drifting into aimless or casual directions.

Ethical providers will certainly avoid exploitive or capricious termination. However, enticing clients to remain in therapy by offering an undefined cure is unethical as well. There are no criteria for final completion of therapy. There is no evidence-based procedure that mediates *all* potential future need. On the other hand, it certainly can be appropriate to close therapy even if the finish line is fuzzy and uneven. To begin moving toward this closure, it may be helpful for the client and provider to formulate ideas of specific tasks or objectives that could lead to a reasonable termination. This can prompt a fruitful exploration of the client's basic expectations of control, well-being, personal vulnerability and freedom from uncertainty. The task of implementing termination creates a context for the client to apply skills acquired in the course of therapy.

A related idea is that prolonging therapy will overcome a poor response or a lack of progress.

"Things are not progressing very well, so we should keep trying."

"I must give the client more sessions to help her understand the limits of therapy."

"My client needs and depends on me, so we should continue."

Progress may be lagging overall, or there may be a specific area where progress is stagnant. For some reason, both provider and client are expecting to get different results by doing more of the same therapy. Perhaps additional sessions could be quite useful, if there is a goal and a workable agenda for reaching that goal. Without a reasonable plan for producing different functional results, prolonged therapy is contraindicated. Providers making this judgment are encouraged to be mindful of their ethical responsibility to provide services only when there is a reasonable expectation of benefit. If the client does not accept or actively participate in the alternative plan, then it is fair to assume that the agenda is not workable and the expected benefit is on shaky ground. There is a fine line to discern between encouraging the discouraged client to persist when benefit is possible and respecting the client's autonomy in deciding whether or not to participate in a specific therapeutic approach.

Finally, it may be that the client is prolonging therapy because it is socially reinforcing and the situational costs are not sufficient to trigger the client's interest in termination.

"I like you and I don't have anything else to do."

"If I stop therapy, my family will start expecting more from me."

The client enjoys the positive relationship and, for whatever reason, is unconcerned about or insulated from the financial cost. A client with considerable free time might find therapy easier and more interesting than other possible activities. There may even be secondary gain such as increased services or reduced demands that are associated with being in therapy. Thus, the "cost" of termination might outweigh the "cost" of maintaining the status quo.

Sometimes interpersonal contact is a very central part of a long-term therapy plan. For example, highly isolated clients might use the interpersonal contact for reality testing and stabilization. Some clients may need extended support in managing chronic conditions, using their emotional regulation skills while negotiating developmental tasks, reducing self-defeating behavior, or managing chronically stressful life circumstances. In planned long-term therapy, sessions are directed toward such specific purposes and personal social limits are maintained. However, if the client is simply choosing to come to therapy for a pleasant social interaction and nothing more, termination may be indicated. The desire to continue a positive social connection is quite natural and something to appreciate. In the context of therapy, however, there are no goals or tasks that are linked to a purely social agenda, and therefore no progress. The only remaining task is to redirect the client's social efforts.

Beliefs That Promote Procrastination

"I'll wait until a better time to bring up termination."

"Better to leave well enough alone."

"It's too stressful to discuss right now."

"The devil you know is better than the one you don't."

Procrastination might be more than just another item on the client's list of life problems. Procrastination can invade the process of therapy as either or both of the participants put off talking about important but uncomfortable and potentially conflicted issues such as termination. Their assumption is that termination will be difficult, so it may be better to delay discussion in the hopes that it might somehow get easier over time.

On the other hand, procrastination may stem from an overall complacence about the therapy process.

"Termination doesn't really need to be discussed."

"Sooner or later, it will come up naturally."

"Termination is arbitrary anyway, so why bother planning for it."

Termination is assumed to be something that will automatically fall into place, so little time or attention is really needed. This benign neglect can be the wellspring of much misunderstanding and at the very least an abrupt or minimally processed termination. Circumstances where the number of sessions is limited at the outset demand that termination be considered at regular intervals.

Procrastination in dealing with termination can also be a form of protest and control. Termination is viewed as an unreasonable demand being forced by uncaring or unscrupulous third parties.

"It is not fair that we have to deal with these imposed limits, so we'll just ignore them."

"It's wrong to force termination so I'm going to put it off as long as possible."

"No third party is going to tell us what to do."

There is no doubt that economic factors or other circumstances may cause less than optimal timing of termination. However, these factors are not entirely under the control of the client and the provider. Refusing to give practical consideration to such parameters is a disservice to both client and provider. Not only is the focus on an attitude of disgruntlement, but there are distinct economic, ethical, legal, and administrative risks in noncompliance with established contracts.

Beliefs That Facilitate Direct Discussion

"Bringing up the idea of termination can be encouraging and productive."

"It's part of my role to ensure that the tasks of therapy, including termination, are handled in a professional way."

"Discussing possible endpoints will help us assess the client's progress and pinpoint the most important goals."

"Termination can be a positive experience if we talk about it, share information, and try to make a reasonable decision with all things considered."

If the provider believes that the idea of termination is not particularly harmful, but instead views it as an important and positive task of collaboration, it may be easier to approach the topic. Raising the idea of termination can elicit important information about the client's view of his or her progress and hone in on remaining concerns.

Approaching the idea of termination encourages the client's independence and provides evidence that the provider has the client's best interests in mind. The client may appreciate the attention to this important decision, including concern about various practical considerations. The provider is not simply prolonging therapy or holding onto the client for his or her own benefit, either financial or emotional. Instead, the provider wants the client to have the satisfaction of achievement and closure as soon as is feasible. The provider also realizes that the very task of discussing, planning, and implementing termination can yield a valuable opportunity for integrating the work of therapy.

MAKING THE DECISION TO TERMINATE

What Are Clinical, Practical, and Ethical Reasons for Termination?

Termination occurs either by mutual consent, at the client's discretion, or at the therapist's discretion. For any occurrence, there is a clinical, practical, or ethical reason, or some combination of reasons, for the termination. Termination for clinical reasons occurs when the maximum benefits have been realized and service is no longer needed, or when the clinical benefit of service is insufficient or unlikely. The client might have the wrong service, wrong provider, or incompatible expectations for therapy. Termination for ethical reasons occurs when the provider determines that the conditions for safe and effective service can no longer be met. According to the provider's professional judgment, the risks outweigh the benefits and termination is necessary to protect the safety of any participant or the integrity of the work. Although this might be discussed with the client, it is up to the provider to make a final determination on whether there is an irresolvable compromise to the quality or benefit of services and to take the appropriate action. Termination for practical or circumstantial reasons occurs when concrete situations have or will affect the feasibility of continued treatment. Failure to adequately deal with practical issues raises the risk of clinically or ethically inappropriate arrangements.

Being able to recognize, understand, and discuss these various reasons is important to the task of terminating at the right time for appropriate reasons. Seven reasons identified by Younggren and Gottlieb (in press) are treatment completion, reimbursement limitations, psychotherapist-patient mismatch, lack of progress, non-adherence, boundary violations, and absence of the psychotherapist. A summary set of reasons similar to that outlined by Younggren and Gottlieb are discussed below in the form of questions that can guide the provider's assessment. These are, "Are we there yet?" "Are we stalled or going the wrong way?" "Are we traveling together?" "Am I (still) the right provider for the job?" "Are we out of time or money?" "Have our circumstances changed?" and "Am I being manipulated, threatened, stalked, or harassed?"

Are We There Yet?   Arriving at the end of the road is the ideal termination. It is most gratifying to end therapy when the client's goals have been met, symptoms have diminished, and adaptive personal functioning has been restored or improved. But only perfectionists need to lay *all* concerns to rest before termination can be entertained. The realists among us are glad to make progress toward the primary objectives. We really have no way of knowing maximum benefit for any given client, so we have to discern a tipping point of diminishing returns and reasonable discontinuation. However, the criteria for recognizing this destination tend to be vague or implicit. It is important to select measurable benchmarks to help determine when we might say that the service is no longer needed. For example, the destination benchmark could be something as specific as a 50 percent reduction in baseline symptoms. Or it could be something more subjective such as an increase in job satisfaction.

Sometimes the positive experience of therapy can lead both client and provider to travel right on past the exit signs at initial goal attainment. Without an acknowledgement of these accomplishments and a refocusing of the itinerary, however, we might find ourselves traveling down an unmarked path without direction or purpose. When you have arrived at where you intended to go, it is important to consider either ending the journey or setting a new destination.

The provider may be the first to recognize that the client is approaching readiness for termination by the degree of improvement noted in key areas. The client may happily see the improvements, but have reservations about the sustainability of this change. If so, the provider can check the client's predictions about what could happen if therapy were to terminate in the foreseeable future. Specific reservations or concerns can be addressed within the remaining time in therapy, including plans to maintain and extend the improvements. They can also consider what, if anything, needs to happen to help the client feel ready for termination.

Clients give many conversational cues that signal interest or readiness to discuss termination. Some of these are quite obvious, but many will be subtle. Direct questions or statements, such as "How much longer will I need to be in therapy?" or "I think I'm ready to wrap this up," clearly draw attention to the task of termination. To ignore or deflect such bids from the client misses a crucial opportunity for collaborative work. When a direct bid is offered, the provider can follow the flow of this conversational initiative and begin assessment of termination concerns. Opening a dialogue, even if it is brief, is likely to be more productive than making deflecting statements that close off the discussion. Consider the following examples.

Example A

Client: How much longer do I need to be in therapy?
             Deflecting statements:
Provider: As long as you want to be.
             I don't really know, but I think we have a long way to go.
             It's too soon to talk about that.
             Opening a dialogue:
Provider: That's an important question. Let's take some time to sort out what we've accomplished so far, what else you may need or want, and where we want to draw our work to a close.

Example B

Client: I think I'm ready to wrap this up.
             Deflecting statements:
Provider: OK, then let's go ahead and schedule our next appointment.
             Well, I guess that means we're done.
             That's what I've been waiting for you to say.
             Opening a dialogue:
Provider: Do you mean ending this session, working on the current problem, or therapy overall?
Client: Well, I'm not really sure. I wonder when I will be ready to end therapy.
Provider: I'm glad you brought this up. It's important to talk about your progress and the plan for ending our work. Let's consider what you think would have to happen for you to be ready to end therapy.

The provider may not have the benefit of such direct solicitation of the topic of termination. Softer signals to discuss the treatment plan occur when there is a lull in progress or the client's participation. Perhaps the client has achieved some important gains and has little more than a status quo report for the session agenda. The overall energy or attentiveness to the sessions may seem to lag. Other minor commitments are given priority over scheduling sessions or completing homework. The provider may generally sense that the client is starting to "drift" as there is a feeling of detachment in the client's presentation. Rather than silently assuming that there must be some reason that the client keeps coming, this is a place where the provider might appropriately open a review of the termination plan.

Because soft signals are ambiguous, it is important to keep in mind that this may indicate other important issues beginning to surface rather than necessarily assuming termination readiness. Consider the following comments as an example for bringing focus to these soft signals.

Provider: For the last couple of sessions, I've been noticing that our agenda does not seem as full or as pressing. Have you noticed any changes?

Client: Yes. I'm doing better overall, and I've been wondering what I should talk about. When I get here, I always seem to find something though.

Provider: I think we're both happy about your progress, would you agree or disagree? (Client nods agreement.) This is a good time to regroup and review where we are on the list of issues that we started with. Perhaps you might have a different perspective now, and maybe there are other issues that need attention. Otherwise, it could be time for us to consider a plan for wrapping up. I'm not sure it's time to stop yet, though. What are your thoughts?

Client: I am feeling better, but I don't want to stop therapy now. It seems to be helping.

Provider: I'm glad to hear that. How about if we use the rest of our time today to go over the original list of issues, see where you are, and update our goals?

Client: That sounds good to me.

Are We Stalled or Going the Wrong Way? Oddly enough, a common response to poor progress or deterioration is to continue therapy rather than considering termination. It is as though the last thing either client or provider wants to consider is that their effort really is ineffective or harmful. Persistence is important when dealing with difficult emotional and behavioral problems, but unproductive therapy is both a clinical and ethical reason for termination. Providers are ethically bound to terminate therapy when it becomes reasonably clear that the client no longer needs the service, is not likely to benefit, or is being harmed by continued service (AAPC, 2005, III.C; ACA, 2005, A.11.c; APA, 2002, 10.10 (a); NASW, 1999, 1.16 (a)).

Unfortunately, there is no reliable way to establish with any objective certainty that there is no benefit or likelihood of benefit whatsoever to the service. Potential harm from treatment can be difficult to separate from a general worsening of a condition that could have occurred regardless of the intervention. Nevertheless, it is incumbent upon the provider to determine whether or not therapy is going anywhere or if it is harming the client in any way. Termination needs to be considered if the provider believes "we are not getting anywhere."

Providers are advised to regularly review the benefits of continuing therapy as well as the potential risks of discontinuing service, using relevant evidence-based information wherever possible. For example, clients with double depression, that is major depression superimposed on antecedent dysthymia, are at high risk of relapse and warrant continued intensive treatment of the dysthymia even if major depressive symptoms have resolved

(McCullough, 2000). But practicing clinicians often encounter situations where evidence-based recommendations do not yet exist. Predictive judgments still must be made concerning needs and benefits, and the provider's best option is to link continuation with a relevant clinical benchmark of progress such as those listed in Chapter Three.

It is important to involve the client in a discussion of progress and therapy options, both to support the client's autonomy and to continue the informed consent process (Younggren & Gottlieb, in press). A divergence of opinion between client and therapist can significantly complicate this discussion. Therapy might seem stalled or stuck from the therapist's point of view, yet the client disagrees and insists that therapy is quite helpful. The client may have a stable pattern of showing up for scheduled meetings, but the provider is concerned because discernable changes are slow and difficult to observe. Providers will of course want to steer clear of implying that the client is a waste of time or too disturbed to be helped. Instead the focus can be on generating options and alternatives to support the client's progress through the stages of change. Case consultation is helpful for stimulating new ideas and directions. In the end, the provider is ultimately responsible for determining whether or not there is sufficient clinical benefit to merit treatment continuation, or if the client might be better served by termination or redirection.

Are We Traveling Together?   To realize the benefits of therapy, the client must first commit to the working relationship and, second, agree to participate in the tasks that will presumably lead to the desired results. If either of these ingredients is missing, client and therapist are not together on the plan and the likelihood of benefit is significantly compromised. This means that the provider must consider termination and in effect tell the client, "You need to make a choice."

The first part of the agreement is commitment to a specific working relationship. Some clients present for treatment in the midst of multiple therapeutic consultations and must sort out these relationships. Proceeding with therapy usually means making a commitment to a specific provider or to a collaborative arrangement, and without that the provider and client are not together on the plan. Multiple providers working with a single client usually work in an integrated manner, each contributing in a specific way as part of a team. For example, it would not be unusual for a client to work with a nurse practitioner for medication management, a psychologist for individual therapy, and a family counselor for marital issues. Working with multiple providers at the same level of intervention (i.e., individual therapy) for the same problem is, however, not typical and potentially counter-productive. An example would be working simultaneously with a psychodynamic therapist and a cognitive-behavioral therapist on problems related to chronic depression. Not only are there likely to be conflicting messages given to the client regarding his or her situation, the client's trust and emotional involvement in either therapy is divided.

Clients are free to consult multiple providers, but they can be encouraged to focus on one therapeutic relationship at a time. The provider must be careful not to discourage the client's autonomy in seeking multiple opinions or alternative providers. As a provider, it is important to discuss the therapeutic issues with the client and try to reduce any confusion or conflict while helping the client to come to a decision that best meets his or her needs (APA, 2002, 10.04). Providers are ethically obligated to facilitate arrangements that help the client to build trust and emotional involvement with a provider, the basic ingredients for effective work.

Sometimes clients seek consultation on the compatibility of a new approach while they are still involved in an established therapy relationship with another provider. The newly consulted provider would of course proceed with sensitivity and caution. Sometimes the client needs assistance in considering whether to continue or terminate with the original provider. Anxiety associated with the idea of "firing" the established therapist creates a quandary for clients who want a different approach or who need to transfer for clinical or practical reasons. Talking this through can help them come to a reasoned decision and work through any communication snags. It might be that redirecting the client back to the established provider is the best option, or it might be that the client remains with the new provider. Although the client has the right to end contact with either provider at any point, it is usually beneficial for the client to have some closing exchange with the discontinued provider, either in a session, with a phone or email message or in a letter, depending on the client's preference. Some may appreciate the added structure of verbal or written communication between the old and new providers, with appropriate consent.

The second part of the agreement is to actively participate in the tasks of treatment. Once the relationship is established, the client might verbally agree to recommended actions and even express enthusiasm and great intention, yet fail to make any of the efforts needed for progress. Perhaps the client actively refuses to make an effort to alter self-defeating behavior and continues to deteriorate despite the provider's best efforts to engage him or her in therapeutic activities. Or the client may have erratic attendance and does not seem to be sufficiently focused to realize any results. Whether or not therapy continues will depend on the negotiated agreement between provider and client. Considering the client's stage of change might be a useful way to adjust the treatment plan and increase the client's involvement. As long as there is some demonstrable benefit in one or more of the benchmarks of progress, the client wants to continue, and it is practically feasible, therapy does not have to terminate.

Many times behavior that appears to be non-compliant is really symptomatic of the actual disorder, and the client will become more engaged if the provider carefully modifies tasks to meet the client at his or her current level of function. However, termination due to lack of client compliance is an option if the client chooses not to make the efforts needed to benefit from a particular approach, even after the level of task demand has been reduced. Perhaps the client is skeptical of the benefits of such small efforts, critical of the therapy and therapist, or highly averse to any discomfort or risk. It may be that the provider's particular style or approach is not a good match for the client.

To respect the client's autonomy and provide adequate informed consent, it is important to review this situation with the client and attempt resolution prior to initiating termination. The prudent clinician will seek case consultation at this point as a reasonable action to ensure an appropriate standard of care. In the case where low benefit is related to the client's lack of necessary effort or active self-harm, the provider may need to be more forthright in outlining expectations for the client's participatory role and setting limits that include termination as a necessary alternative. If the client remains persistently unresponsive, uncooperative or dissatisfied with the therapy or the therapist and no adjustment fulfills their expectations or precipitates any positive movement on the benchmarks of progress, termination with referral to an alternative provider is indicated.

Am I (Still) the Right Provider for the Job?   The provider ultimately has to determine the answer to this question and decide whether to accept a client or continue working with that client. The primary reasons why the provider might withdraw from a professional relationship are because the problem exceeds their skills or range of competence, there is a mismatch in interpersonal style that is interfering with the client's progress, geographic distance is a barrier to adequate service, or there is some form of conflict of interest. The provider must weigh the situation and tell the client, "You need someone else," or "It's too far to be safe or effective," or "I have to decline or withdraw."

It is not always possible to determine in advance if the provider and client are sufficiently matched for problems and skills and interpersonal style. Over the course of therapy, the client's condition might shift or become more complicated than originally thought, to the point that his or her difficulties exceed the provider's clinical limits or capacity to manage. Or it might become evident that the client is not reacting positively to the provider at an interpersonal level and there seems to be a personality mismatch.

For example, some providers are more directive and focused on tasks and homework, while others are more relaxed and flexible about the agenda. Depending on the client's preferences, either style might be ideal for one and irritating to another. The client's progress could be stalled because therapy is stalled at the level of developing an effective working alliance. Interpersonal discomfort creates a barrier to moving forward, and this barrier may be irresolvable. Even though the provider has attempted to share information "up front" about his or her style, it might take some time to determine that compatibility is lacking and that this is an obstacle to progress. Pinpointing the problem as one of mismatch is the provider's responsibility. The provider must maintain authority in setting the limits of his or her professional competence and adaptability. If the client perceives a mismatch, exploration of their expectations may help. Otherwise termination may be indicated.

Geographic distance does not necessarily mean that the provider is the wrong person for the job, but it does add to the cost and other risk considerations. There are several contextual elements to weigh in determining whether it is reasonable to proceed with therapy when it requires the client to commute a significant distance. Distance is relative to the norms of the area, client resources, and the specialized nature of the service. In areas with a low density of providers or a lack of specialized services, there may be no other option but to commute to therapy, maybe an hour or more. In most cases, clients will self-select the service providers who are most convenient or whose location falls within the client's ability to manage via transit time.

There are two types of circumstances where more discerning provider judgment is needed. The first is when there is an already established therapy relationship and the client relocates to a new geographic area. Reluctance of either party to terminate may result in efforts to continue therapy in some abbreviated or truncated fashion. Whether or not this is a reasonable action depends upon several factors, including the client's overall clinical needs, level of functioning, emotional stability, the distance involved, and the availability of alternative resources. More often than not, the client would be better served by establishing a new relationship in the new location.

It may be incumbent on the original provider to firmly insist on termination in order to prompt the client to make this shift. Despite advanced technology, attempting to maintain therapy via long-distance telecommunication or email is fraught with legal, ethical, and clinical risks. The lack of face-to-face interaction blunts the overall impact of the interaction (Nickelson, 1998). The client is less likely to benefit and the risks of incompetent service or other potential harm are increased (Fisher, 2003). In case of emergency, the provider does not have access to local resources and has a serious disadvantage for handling any potential conditions of imminent danger. The legal and regulatory implications of client and therapist being in two different states at the time of contact are murky at best. The therapist could be violating clinical practice laws in the client's state if he or she does not have a current license to practice in that jurisdiction.

Moreover, if the client bears significant travel expense solely to continue with the same provider, this suggests the possibility of an unproductive dependency or even an emotionally and financially exploitive relationship. This is obviously not inevitable, especially if the service is highly specialized, but the possibility should be evaluated.

The second type of situation occurs when the client chooses not to access local providers in the first place and instead seeks services at some significant distance. Reasons for this usually include a concern for privacy, a desire to work with a particular specialist, or a lack of confidence in local resources. These may all be legitimate concerns, but each should be carefully considered in light of other contextual information. A stable client who is well-known in a small town might travel a couple of hours to a larger town on a regular basis, combining business, various health care consultations, and visits with family in the alternate location. Compare this with an unstable client who tends to mistrust all providers and travels great distances in search of someone who will fulfill what are essentially unrealistic expectations. Unstable clients present many risks, and these are multiplied when significant distance is involved. Not the least of these risks is the difficulty of managing an emergency when physical proximity is limited.

There are many possible sources of a conflict of interest, and not all of these can be detected at the outset of therapy. Most often the provider will check these possibilities in the beginning and discuss the potential conflict with the client to assess impact on the objectivity or quality of service. Sometimes conflicts develop during the course of therapy and include other relationships that are also confidential. In this case, the provider must judge the extent of the conflict and, if appropriate, notify the client that he or she must withdraw from their agreement because of a conflict that is confidential in nature. The provider might state that he or she is no longer the right provider for the job due to this conflict as it might affect performance of therapeutic duties.

Are We Out of Time or Money? The client's financial responsibility is one area where an ounce of prevention is worth a pound of cure. Responsible financial behavior should be shaped from the beginning of therapy to prevent the accumulation of an unpaid balance. If there are foreseeable financial circumstances that will limit services, the provider is ethically obligated to discuss this as early as possible and establish an agreement regarding billing arrangements and compensation (APA, 2002, 6.04). Clients frequently need assistance in fully understanding their insurance coverage and the extent to which third parties will cover the cost of services. Usually this means confirming with them the specific number of visits allowed under coverage and ensuring that they understand their financial responsibility for any additional treatment beyond that limit. The client can and should be directly involved in planning how to "budget" the time in therapy given the extent of their third-party coverage. Two key assertions that providers can tactfully advance from the beginning of therapy are that "We need to track the limits of your resources" and "You are responsible for timely payment."

In today's business environment, the provider simply can not effectively practice without being alert to these parameters. Providers who delegate any of their financial business tasks to administrative staff must provide enough supervision to ensure prompt attention to pre-authorization, insurance claims processing, and the collection of aging accounts to minimize any potential termination errors related to financial matters. Some providers explicitly limit their therapy contracts to exclude third-party payments or to shift all responsibility to the client for managing these issues. For those who do participate within the three-party system as a contracted provider, there is the added necessity of tracking the authorization for payment and remaining alert to contract limits and provisions.

The provider also needs to remain alert to changes in the financial parameters and assess the client's agreement with the new terms before continuing with therapy. For example, if maximum insurance benefits have been reached and the client wants to continue, can the client assume financial responsibility for additional service? If the client has a change in insurance plan that shifts more of the cost to the consumer, does he or she understand and accept this arrangement? Can the client provide the expected copayment? Encourage the client to take time to consider and understand all financial obligations and changes to those obligations so that he or she can make responsible decisions without undue pressure or confusion. Be cautious about any effort that could be construed as exploitive, such as persuasive efforts to reduce the client's financial cautions about the costs of therapy. Payment plans may fall into this category. Offering unsecured credit establishes an unethical debtor-creditor relationship that is in conflict with the therapist-client relationship (Ebert, 2006). In addition, waiving the client's copayment is considered a violation of any insurance contract.

If the client does not pay as expected and has an aging balance, it is wise be alert to this situation and investigate its causes. It could be a simple matter of misunderstanding when and how to make payment or not having received an accurate or understandable bill. Sometimes there are contributing marital or family communication problems, as bill payment might be handled by a spouse, parent, or even an accounting service and there is a snag in this process. On the other hand, it may be that the client does not actually intend to pay because he or she is unhappy with the service, felt pressured into therapy, thinks that the provider charges too much, thinks that someone else should or will take care of the bill, or is overwhelmed by debt and going bankrupt. Any of these reasons are very important to identify as soon as possible so that appropriate remedies can be implemented.

Exploitation can also be a two-way street, a point that is often overlooked by benevolent and trusting mental health practitioners. Financial stability has an impact on the provider's personal well-being and ability to help others. Although the principle of beneficence calls for charitable efforts, providers still must deal with their own limits in this respect. Overextending oneself creates both emotional stress and other business and personal risks. When the lack of payment is the precipitant for termination, it is important that the client understands this reason and has a chance to make prompt payment, particularly if the provider intends to implement formal collection proceedings (ACA, 2005, A.11.C; NASW, 1999, 1.16 (c); APA, 2002, 10.10, 6.04 (e)).

Have Our Circumstances Changed?   Practical situations that prompt termination are sometimes referred to as "forced" termination because these circumstances truncate the clinical objective of ending because of emotional and clinical readiness. Circumstances other than finances that prompt termination can span a large range of events, from joyful to benign to tragic. Such situations will vary according to degree of predictability, certainty, salience, and amount of advance notice. Generally these precipitants are personal or professional changes for either provider or client that make it impractical or unfeasible to continue. Anticipated changes such as relocation, shifts in job responsibilities, or family changes can alert the provider to the possibility that termination is on the horizon. Unanticipated changes can occur for either client or provider as well, including sudden changes in health or employment or practice infrastructure. Sometimes the changes that precipitate termination are highly salient and other times so subtle the termination potential slips past notice. The provider needs to remain alert to the possibility that "this situation has changed things."

Although no provider can directly control unexpected events or circumstances, it is important to anticipate changes that might affect the safety, quality, or effectiveness of therapy and to recognize the termination implications. Providers are generally held to a standard of care in which they must anticipate the unexpected and have a general protocol for orderly management of clinical contacts and data in the unlikely but possible event of an emergency or catastrophe, as stipulated by provisions of the HIPAA law. If compromising conditions are brief or temporary, it might be reasonable to interrupt therapy and resume at a later point, if that is appropriate and acceptable to the client. Otherwise, termination may be the best resolution.

It is usually best to inform the client at the earliest possible opportunity of any predictable interruptions because advance warning increases the client's sense of control and choice. If therapy must terminate at a specific point because the therapist will no longer be available, the client has a right to know this. Relocation, maternity leave, an extended vacation (months), or a shift in professional responsibilities might fall into this category. Unpredictable disruptions in the professional's life such as becoming ill, overwhelmed, impaired, or otherwise unable to continue require advance preparations. These will be taken up in Chapter Five. If the interruption is caused by something unexpected in the client's life, the provider can be supportive and respectful of the client's situation and try to be as flexible as possible. For example, the client's elder parents are having difficulties and the client must frequently travel a significant distance to provide assistance, so sessions might be cancelled and rescheduled more often than usual.

If the provider makes an effort to deal with predictable and unpredictable events in a businesslike manner, the client is more apt to follow suit. Rather than using up energy fighting the limits or avoiding the subject, the provider can model a forthright, problem-solving approach. If termination is the best solution, the provider can frame change as an ongoing process and emphasize the client's gains, review the options for resuming therapy at a later point, and consider alternative services, providers, or self-help efforts. Encouragement and positive regard can contribute a great deal toward bringing the client to a point of reasonable understanding or acceptance. If possible, at least one session is devoted to discussion of the termination and the reasons for it. If for some reason the provider cannot conduct this session (e.g., in the hospital), then a qualified colleague should complete this important task of discussing the transition with the client.

Am I Being Manipulated, Threatened, Stalked, or Harassed?   Most providers have little cause to anticipate this reason for termination. The people who seek our help are not expected to have deceptive intent or to pose a threat to our well-being. Yet this is possible. Our consulting room is not a place where we are primed for self-protection. As a matter of course, we usually approach our clients as potential allies. Unless we are treating a specialized population, we have to make a concerted cognitive shift to recognize ominous signs.

If it becomes evident that a client is being dishonest, deceptive, menacing, or otherwise inappropriately intrusive, the provider should spot this as an imminent, "high-risk" termination. Practitioners are *not* expected to endure threats to their own personal safety or professional integrity to continue treatment with a threatening or dishonest client. Managing such a situation takes a toll in terms of emotional and personal energy, potentially compromising the provider's ability to remain effective with *other* clients. Instead, the provider has a right to privacy, respect, and self-protection and to say, "I will not work under these conditions."

If a patient lies or intentionally misrepresents basic information necessary to conducting treatment, such as presenting a false identity or fabricated clinical symptoms, termination may be warranted. The basic trust required for psychotherapy (APA, 2002, Principle B) has been compromised, as the therapist now has significant cause to suspect the patient's motives and treatment has been substantially disrupted. The provider may not be willing or able to participate in a treatment agreement under the true conditions. Because of the potential for colluding in some form of criminal behavior, most therapists or agencies make it a policy to refuse or terminate any patient who is not willing to confirm their identity or who becomes known to be using a false or stolen identity.

Similarly, many therapists would consider the therapeutic alliance significantly compromised if the patient attempts to solicit fraudulent or unprofessional action from the provider. Requesting that the therapist provide false statements such as an inappropriate diagnosis for insurance purposes, billing insurance for missed appointments as if the services were rendered, or making statements of fact that are not true in order to gain disability reimbursement, entry into jobs or military service, child custody or legal advantage are examples of such solicitation. Cooperation with the client's request could result in professional reprimand or other legal charges. Even worse, this unprofessional action is exploitive and harmful to others. If the client attempts use therapy or the therapist to aid in the commission of fraud, the therapist bears the responsibility to refuse such action. If services are obtained for the purpose of commission of a crime, the communication privilege is voided in many states. Soliciting the provider's complicity in criminal behavior is a clear and valid reason to initiate termination.

Providers are specifically empowered to protect themselves and those associated with them personally or through practice (e.g., staff) by terminating therapy with a client who poses a threat or endangerment (ACA, 2005, A.11.C; APA, 2002, 10.10 (b)). This right to termination applies even if the source of the threat is someone associated with the client but not the actual client. If the client should make a retaliatory charge of unethical behavior, the provider has a means of defending such action on the basis of common ethical standards. Termination under these adverse conditions can occur precipitously, possibly without pre-termination counseling or referral, and might require the provider to seek legal protection (APA, 2002, 10.10 (c); 4.05 (b) (3)).

Obviously, there is some ambiguity in what constitutes a threat. Threats can be verbal or physical (words or actions) (Fisher, 2003). The client might deliver a verbal threat in the form of a voice or electronic mail message, or through an action such as following, inappropriately touching, or intentionally damaging property. Any criminal action or suggested criminal action against the provider, the provider's significant others, or people associated with the provider's practice is an endangerment. The criminal action does not have to rise to the level of attempted murder for the provider or the provider's associates to be at risk. Any threat of bodily harm to the provider or any suggestion of using a weapon is an obvious threat of criminal action. Other types of crime also can endanger the provider and those persons associated with his or her practice by compromising the safety and trust of the clinical environment. Presenting at the provider's office at unscheduled times or repeated telephoning of the provider can constitute harassment. Threatening, harassing, or harming other clients or staff is also an endangerment. For example, a client was arrested for credit card fraud after being identified on surveillance videotapes during a shopping spree with credit cards stolen from clinic staff. With felony charges pending for her actions, the client could no longer return for therapy where her victims worked, so therapy was terminated.

In assessing any possible threat, the provider's subjective discomfort and feelings of vulnerability are important signals of potential danger. One's anxiety level can be an important barometer for determining the need to seek consultation and support. Consultation is not only an essential tool for judging whether or not a client's behavior has reached an inappropriate threshold, it is part of a good legal defense whenever the provider's actions may be called into question. Consultation is also an excellent source of emotional support in a trying situation. For behaviors that are inappropriate but not overtly threatening, the provider should set limits with the client and expect immediate compliance. If the client persists or the actions are of a more serious nature, decisive termination could be indicated before the provider loses more control and experiences greater jeopardy (Younggren & Gottlieb, in press). As previously noted, the provider could be subject to reprimand if he or she overreacts to client behavior that is more annoying or inconvenient than truly threatening. But the provider could be seriously harmed if authentic threats are improperly handled.

The threat of civil action against the provider means that the client has terminated therapy. If the client threatens to sue the provider for malpractice or bring civil suit for any other reason, an adversarial relationship has been created. The relationships of legal opponents and therapeutic allies are mutually exclusive. The provider is relieved of any obligation to provide further service, including resolution of the termination. The client's actions have already resolved the termination in a definitive way.

Once serious threats have been made or harmful actions carried out, there really is no other choice but to unilaterally stop contact because therapy is over. No further negotiation should be offered or pursued. Even if things cool down or the dispute is resolved, therapy should not be reconciled. Doing so significantly increases the risk to the provider that some negative outcome will ensue. Continued or resumed contact with a client who has made any sort of threat is a very dangerous and most unwise course of action.

Are There Any Conversational Targets to Help Structure Termination?

Discussion of termination is easiest when it occurs in the context of fluid and spontaneous conversation. Because the topic may not come up spontaneously, it is helpful to think of termination as an agenda item on reserve for strategic openings. In other words, we want to "strike when the iron is hot." As noted in Chapter Three, the intake and informed consent process is the optimal time to begin talking about termination. Progress review points also present natural opportunities to assess termination goals. Termination issues also come up when the client misses, postpones, or repeatedly reschedules appointments. This section proposes conversational targets to facilitate useful discussion of the termination process. This is not meant to be a recipe or set of steps to execute at specified points, but rather some ideas for how to systematically address this important task.

Consider the "T" Word   The word "termination" may be too formal or even harsh to some clients. It is a commonly accepted word for referring to the conclusion of therapy, but it is not absolutely necessary to use this specific word if alternative terms or phrases seem more suitable. The provider might refer to concluding the current work, wrapping up, ending sessions, or even beginning a discontinuation phase. Many learning-based therapists prefer to fade sessions out over the course of increasing intervals of time between contacts, which can be aptly called a phase for discontinuation, maintenance, follow-up, or generalization of learning.

It may be useful to talk about terms with the client, exploring the idiosyncratic meaning associated with different possible phrases (i.e., termination, ending contact, wrap-up, follow-up phase) to understand the client's frame of reference. A discussion of different terms can provide a forum for establishing shared expectations and working out an individual plan. For example, termination is the common word that traditionally has referred to a final conclusion of intensive therapy. Termination still refers to concluding therapy, but endings arrive more quickly today. Wrapping up may mean ending sessions with an option to re-activate at some point. Concluding a segment of care could mean that the maximum number of allowable visits has been completed. Breaking contact implies that someone has been "fired" and there may be some negative feelings involved. Stopping connotes putting on the brakes, while ending signifies an element of closure. As provider and client talk about these different terms, they are also sifting through the different options and developing a common language that will describe their experience.

In managed care situations where treatment plans must be updated in limited segments of time, the discussion may focus on time allowances toward the overall goals. If the provider anticipates that more sessions are needed and will be authorized, then it may be better to use more tentative phrases such as "wrapping up" or "taking a break." For example, the provider might say, "We have two more approved sessions in this authorization of care. We need to decide if I should request an authorization for more visits beyond your next session or whether we are ready to wrap up at this point. Let's talk about that." Although the terms may make no difference to some clients, selective language can soften the perceptions of force or pressure among clients who are sensitive to the frequent review and anxiety associated with third-party oversight.

Create Psychological Order and Productivity   Of the various termination objectives, creating a sense of productivity and psychological order may be the most important. Both provider and client benefit when there is good psychological closure in termination. Closure in this context comes from understanding the reasons for termination, expressing feelings associated with therapy and its ending, and attaching value to the invested effort. At the point of conclusion, it is especially important to draw attention to helpful aspects of the experience and place the work into a broader context that helps the client to understand a coherent overall process. This can begin with a discussion of what the client has accomplished or learned in therapy, from their personal perspective and from the provider's perspective. The provider can offer validation of the client's movement through the various stages of change. For example, the provider may be able to comment on the client's progress from vague emotional discomfort toward developing and initiating a behavioral and emotional commitment to change. It is also helpful to review the reasons why the changes have been meaningful to the client in terms of life impact. This reinforces the functional purpose of changes and the connection to client values.

Productive therapy relationships often include some doubt or ambivalence about the decision to terminate. Providers can increase the sense of order by reviewing the rationale for the decision and validating the client's choice among options. Encouraging clients to ask questions about the reasons for termination enhances their understanding and fulfills the expectations of reasonable, ethical practice. There may be feelings of disappointment, dissatisfaction, or other negative emotion that the client wishes to express. In uncomplicated terminations it is rare to have any significant expression of dissatisfaction. However, it is important to allow an opportunity for the client to express both positive and negative emotions and to provide support for both. Information about the client's minor dissatisfactions or suggestions for improvement is vital to maintaining the quality of one's practice and part of the provider's closure. Often the client's feedback will relate to their overall clinical presentation in some way, so the provider's responses will correspond to these issues. If possible, a schedule of diminishing contact over time will allow both client and provider to adjust to the emotional impact of termination and to attend to any remaining needs or concerns.

Closing Questions for Order and Productivity

- Of what we have done so far, what has been the most meaningful or valuable to you?
- Anything you could have done without?
- Do you have a sense of having learned or accomplished something?
- What do you want to remember?
- How will you continue to use what you have learned?
- Do you feel ready to end therapy sessions?
- Do the reasons for this decision make sense to you?
- Do you have any questions about ending therapy or what happens after therapy is ended?
- Is there anything you want to ask or tell me about your experience with me?
- Is there any feedback you want to give me as a provider?
- How do you think you will look back on our work?
- Are you comfortable with contacting me again if you want to?
- What do you expect from yourself as a result of your involvement in therapy?
- Is there anything that would help you feel more confident about ending therapy at this time?

Make It Personal   Another important component of a positive ending is the sense of a favorable interpersonal connection. This is also part of the psychological closure for client and provider. The time of closing is a particularly relevant opportunity to express positive affect in professionally appropriate way. This might include reflecting on the client's strengths, expressing appreciation for the client's efforts in the face of challenges, and offering some general insight into your personal appraisal of the individual. This leaves an impression on the client of having been known, accepted, and appreciated. Offering negative interpersonal feedback in a closing session is ill-advised, as it may leave the client with the summary impression of having been disliked or rejected all along, perhaps confirming some of their worst fears.

Examples of Positive Interpersonal Comments at Closing

- I'm glad to know you.
- I appreciate your persistence and willingness to take positive emotional risks.
- I'm impressed with your commitment to living.
- I hope that you know I care about you and what happens to you.
- It has been a pleasure and a privilege to work with you.
- You have worked hard and I respect that.

Keep the Usual Limits Clear It is important to keep in mind that termination is a point of elevated risk for professional boundary challenges. Various client actions might flummox the unprepared clinician, particularly gestures of appreciation, affection, or attempts to elicit a more intense personal relationship. Successful management of these risks depends on being consistent with usual and customary limits and alert to the possibility that limit testing could be part of the client's termination agenda. Besides limit testing, it could be that the client is simply misinformed or uninformed about what happens at termination and after therapy. Just because therapy is ending doesn't mean that professional propriety is now dispensable. Nothing should happen that could suggest or promise an alteration of the essential personal and physical boundaries that have already been established. At the same time, closing sessions offer a natural opportunity for sharing positive feelings and reinforcing the client's efforts to reach out and connect. Therefore, clinically relevant and acceptable expressions of appreciation must be taken in context and handled with finesse.

For example, if a typically reserved and inhibited client offers a hand for a handshake or an arm for a hug on his or her way out the door, it would be quite awkward, even punishing, for the provider to shrug away, saying, "We've never made physical contact before, and we're not doing that now." Taken in clinical context, the client's initiative represents a growing capability to be spontaneous and proactive in reaching out. It is very important to affirm this effort with a reinforcing response, allowing the client to depart with a sense of mastery and growth.

On the other hand, the client might say, "So, does this mean we can be friends now, and maybe go out to lunch sometime?" The provider will need to respond with a clarification of the options for follow-up contact in a professional context and speak directly to limits on friendship or any other personal relationship. Tangible gifts also call for a contextual decision about magnitude, cultural relevance, and the potential function of accepting the gift. The expressed feelings can and should always be acknowledged, even if the provider's judgment is to refuse the specific item. Novice clinicians often find these unexpected challenges perplexing, which speaks to the expertise and professional clarity needed for adept handling of therapy boundaries. Examination of the options, discussion with colleagues to increase one's awareness of community norms and standards and familiarity with professional resources are all good ways to establish and maintain boundary management skills (see Zur, 2007).

Reinforce Self-Management as a Lifestyle Once a decision has been made to terminate, it is helpful to reduce the frequency of sessions and increase the time interval between meetings. This creates an opportunity for the client to practice new skills and continue self-directed efforts with decreasing input from the therapist. Termination is gradual and natural, with sessions fading out in frequency over time.

This fading approach helps to reinforce the coping versus mastery objective of therapy. Therapy is intended to guide the client in learning how to solve or prevent certain problems and acquire new skills or responses for use in the context of future living, rather than to fix or cure some psychological or emotional defect. Part of the termination process is to review what has been learned and to generalize and transfer this learning to potential challenges ahead. The client can be prepared to expect new stresses and encouraged to view this as normal and "par for the course." The client might also be encouraged to schedule times for "self therapy," during which he or she carries on a personal dialogue to review issues, do a symptom check, pinpoint problems or struggles, generate solutions or practice activities, anticipate challenges, and schedule the next self-therapy session (Beck, 1995). Such self-management can also include a specific "well-being" agenda of personally selected plans for regular exercise, positive social contacts, pleasure activities, emotional support, creative pursuits, spiritual connection, and physical rest. These positive activities are considered basic to an emotionally stable lifestyle, much the same as healthy eating should be a lifestyle habit and not just a short-term project.

CREATING A RECORD

What Documentation Is Necessary?

If communication is the essence of structuring termination, then documentation is the framework of this structure. A formal professional record of the decisions and actions taken is required to fully complete the process of termination. The record does not necessarily need to be lengthy or overly detailed, but inclusive enough to determine what happened and why. Brief reference to termination can be included in regular progress notes, to reflect the ongoing consideration given and the reasons established for continuing therapy. Other specific procedures of record may also be required as policy in individual clinical settings, such as hospitals, clinics, or service centers.

At the closing meeting, a simple note that establishes the event, reason and outcome is sufficient in most cases. If a closing meeting did not take place, this too can be noted along with the appropriate reason such as client discretion. In uncomplicated cases, the termination statement is brief and to the point. For example, the provider can simply say that termination occurred by mutual agreement because of improvements and client's wish to conserve additional approved visits as an option for later use if needed. Clinically, it is useful to assess the client's overall level of functioning at the point of termination, perhaps using a GAF (Global Assessment of

Functioning) (APA, 2000) score. Specific points of progress that are linked to the initial goals of treatment may be reviewed in brief to further describe the client's status at termination. For example, the client's symptoms of anxiety have dropped significantly from intake and no elevations have occurred despite being exposed to triggering stressors. Any recommendations or referrals that were made are also listed.

Finally, the provider may want to summarize or quote any spontaneous client comments that express satisfaction with the service. If the client says, "You have helped me more than I ever thought was possible," the provider should make explicit note of this pointed statement of propitiation or fulfillment. An objective measure of client satisfaction with service might be included, at the discretion of the provider or agency. This could be a standard questionnaire or checklist that the client completes at or after the final visit. A quick measure could be taken by simply asking the client to provide a verbal global assessment of overall satisfaction (e.g., high, medium, low, or decline to say) to include in the closing progress note.

Further description of the content of discussion or explanation of the action may be needed only in complicated or contentious situations. A more detailed termination note should summarize the provider's efforts to assess the situation and take reasonable professional action, including consultation and initiation of termination. A letter of termination that is sent to the client may be advisable, depending on the circumstances. Even though some sources recommend routine use of a written termination letter as important documentation for risk management (Barnett et al., 2000; Bernstein & Hartsell, 2000), this conservative legal position is debatable unless an adversarial relationship has developed. Providers are encouraged to consult their own legal counsel as well as malpractice carrier for advisement on written termination letters, as mediating factors can be extremely important. Written statements can be easily misconstrued and should be carefully constructed. Termination letters are optional for routine closure but almost always in order with contentious terminations.

In routine terminations where the contract is ending but the relationship does not need to be severed, a formal dissolution letter may be clinically contraindicated, or at least unnecessary. This action could appear to have the impact of admonishing the client to never come back, thus greatly diluting the clinical benefits of the residual psychological attachment that is very helpful to most clients. However, a different, more complex termination might demand actions that contain and discourage the client's maladaptive psychological attachment. For example, the provider might need to establish a unilateral termination by sending a written letter if the client has threatened or stalked them. In such instances, a concise and carefully worded document is needed.

Attention to detail in constructing a termination record is useful for routine follow-up procedures and overall risk management. A good record verifies that an ethically and clinically appropriate termination process has taken place. It also provides an organized source of information if the client requests disclosure to others such as the primary care provider, an insurance carrier, or other outside evaluators such as military recruiters. If the client returns for further sessions, the provider has a quick reminder of the closure process and the client's functional status as a basis of comparison for the new presenting complaints. Finally, having a clear record of the client's clinical status and the provider's actions at termination is indispensable if there are any subsequent challenges to the quality of care.

SUMMARY POINTS FOR APPLIED PRACTICE

1. The current trend toward sequential segments or episodes of therapy demands more attention to termination and more frequent and earlier actions. Providers must be mindful of the risk of prolonged therapy or delinquent termination.

2. Handling termination requires certain skills of knowing when and how to discuss it. Providers need to be able to take the lead and guide this discussion under the best and worst of conditions.

3. Sometimes termination is a stormy, emotionally loaded topic. Totally avoiding the subject will probably not make this problem go away.

4. Traditional cultural expectations about "being in therapy" hold that termination should culminate a long-term intensive relationship. Clients may enter therapy either expecting or fearing this open-ended process and lacking information on when and how termination will happen.

5. Certain therapist beliefs tend to inhibit reasonable action, prolong therapy, or promote procrastination on broaching termination. By the same token, specific beliefs can promote direct discussion and action.

6. Every termination occurs for a reason. Being familiar with typical reasons will aid the recognition and discussion of termination triggers. These reasons include:
    -   We have arrived at our destination.
    -   We are stalled or going the wrong way.
    -   We are not traveling together.
    -   I am not the right person for the job.
    -   We are out of time or money.
    -   Our circumstances have changed.
    -   I am being manipulated, threatened, stalked, or harassed.

7. Avoid becoming an unsecured creditor to the client. Structuring the financial arrangement and shaping behavior at the beginning is the key to avoiding problems related to financial matters.

8. Every provider has a right to privacy, safety, and respect in his or her work. Termination is an option if the client does not meet these conditions.

9. Look for opportunities to explore what termination means to the client. At closing, make it a point to ask questions that will foster a sense of psychological

order and productivity, offer statements that convey positive regard, keep the usual professional boundaries clear, and reinforce self-therapy as a lifestyle.

10.   Closing notes provide an important record of the clinically and ethically appropriate process. These can be brief, including pertinent clinical data, disposition, and information on client satisfaction. Documentation of any potentially volatile situation needs more detail and care in preparation. Termination letters are used at the provider's discretion, but highly advised for acrimonious terminations. Always seek consultation for adversarial conditions.

5

Achieving Closure: Assuring Professional Action

Key Questions Addressed in This Chapter

- Are we ending sessions or ending the relationship?
- How do I know that I've done *enough* for an appropriate termination process?
- When should I insist on termination?
- What if the client refuses termination or becomes hostile?
- What should I do about my personal needs and limits?

DIRECTING THE TERMINATION PROCESS

If abandonment is defined as the provider's failure to take clinically indicated and ethically appropriate steps to end the professional relationship (Younggren & Gottlieb, in press), then providers are clearly charged with the ultimate responsibility the termination process. Every provider needs to have a systematic strategy and be able to establish that reasonable protocol was followed even though terminations can vary widely in terms of reasons and types of communication.

Are We Ending Sessions or Ending the Relationship?

Transitions that mark the end of segments of therapy can be distinguished from transitions that dissolve the therapeutic relationship. Ending scheduled contact does not necessarily mean that the relationship is permanently ended. In fact under most circumstances, an inactive professional relationship remains available for reactivation. Ongoing sessions may be either interrupted or drawn to a close, with future sessions a viable and reasonable option, subject to negotiation of a new contract.

Open versus Closed Termination   Open termination refers to ending the agreement or contract for an episode of care, but not extinguishing the relationship per se. Closed termination is less frequent and involves final closure of any future professional contact between provider and client. Open termination creates a certain "boundary ambiguity" in terms of whether the professional relationship still exists. However, this ambiguity serves the purpose of allowing the client an option to return if needed. The provider's only duty or obligation to the client is to maintain the record and to respond to follow-up requests. Any additional therapy would require a new contract or agreement for specified service.

It may be helpful to refer back to the culture of expectations formed from a health-based standard of care. Most patients expect to return to a doctor from whom they have received previous care if subsequent need develops. The doctor either treats the presenting problem or redirects the patient to someone more suitable for their current needs. For psychotherapy, we might expect the client's default assumption is that the option of returning is open unless the provider communicates explicit limits on further contact.

Specific policy concerning these options should be detailed in the informed consent process and discussed at closure to reduce possible misunderstandings. Providers can describe their role as either similar to a primary care provider that client intermittently consults for a variety of concerns across the lifespan, or the specialist who offers a focused service for a limited range of concerns, or some combination of both. In an agency setting, it might be important to confirm the open policy as pertaining to the agency as a whole, but not necessarily specific providers.

Although an open policy leaves some ambiguity about the status of the professional relationship, it offers maximum support of the client's autonomy for personal decisions about the intensity, duration, and purpose of therapy. The notion of "client-titrated" therapy has been proposed by DiClemente (2003) to highlight the client's pivotal role in directing a self-change process, in which formal intervention plays a contributing and complementary part. The provider's stance in this approach is to remain flexible, provide relevant information to assist the client in making decisions, and generally encourage the client's self-responsibility in using psychotherapy as one of the tools for achieving personal change.

How the provider implements this stance will vary somewhat according to the nature and severity of the client's difficulties and their level of effective self-management. Organized, relatively autonomous clients with mild to moderate difficulties typically need only minor guidance on matters of follow-up contact or returning to therapy. For clients with more severe or chronic problems and/or personality disorders, greater structure is often needed to set clear boundaries and guide the client in choosing appropriate and effective ways to follow-up with the practitioner (see Beck et al., 2004;

Chapter Six of this volume). There is less tolerance for ambiguity about the status of being in or out of therapy among these clients.

In closed termination, the relationship comes to a definitive end. It is expected that the practitioner and client will say a permanent good-bye. This may be more characteristic of intensive or psychodynamic therapy where a primary objective is resolving the transference (Weiner, 1998). However, some psychodynamic and psychoanalytic practitioners accept post-therapy contact and even additional therapy as an indication of therapeutic success (Novick & Novick, 2006) much the same as cognitive behavioral practitioners. For any client or approach, termination is closed when the practitioner will no longer be in practice in the area, is a trainee and will no longer have access to qualified supervision, or a high-risk or threatening relationship has developed and it must be permanently dissolved.

Boundary Management   A desire for follow-up contact is quite natural and appropriate regardless of whether the termination is open or closed. There are several advantages of allowing and even encouraging follow-up contact from the client post-termination, if it is possible to do so without violating any ethical or legal regulations for practice or without fostering unmanageable boundary ambiguity for the client. One advantage is that it may offer an opportunity to intervene early in a relapse or potential relapse. This creates a soft or non-threatening way that the client can be alerted to potential issues without having to wait until distress justifies a return visit to the practitioner. The provider may simply serve as a reminder of certain coping skills and merely thinking about the contact will activate the client's thoughts about what he or she can be doing. Another advantage is that it fosters a sense of positive accomplishment in client and practitioner. By taking the time to briefly update, both can take note of the client's successes and accruing progress, maybe even marvel at his or her resilience, and enjoy the warmth of the familiar contact. As most practitioners know, the process of caring about the client and his or her life does not cease just because the record is in the inactive file.

Clear policies and procedures for handling these follow-up contacts are important in order to control potential boundary ambiguity. Informal contacts can be helpful but must be dealt with properly to avoid confusion or mismanagement. Sometimes the client wants or needs continued contact, but avoids returning to therapy because it is supposed to be finished or complete. Informal contact is the client's attempt to continue therapy but without the limits and responsibilities of the formal relationship. Perhaps returning to therapy is held as some sort of failure because it contradicts the client's self-expectations for competence. Or it may be that the client is making a bid for a personal friendship or even intimate relationship. The client protests that a formal therapy session is not necessary, but still wants to "see" you. This is a signal that something is amiss and further information is needed.

Mild client initiatives such as sending the practitioner a letter of update or making a phone call "just to touch base" are acceptable and routine. These can be supportively acknowledged and noted in the client's treatment record as follow-up information. Numerous letters or contacts or any communication that contains disturbing content is another matter that warrants a strategic clinical response. Invitations for direct personal contact, such as meeting for coffee or a meal, hold a greater risk of confusing professional and personal boundaries. The practitioner must always remain alert to boundary issues and avoid the appearance of impropriety. Such contacts should be conceptualized as continued professional contact and managed in a way that is appropriate to professional rather than personal/social interaction.

Any personal contact following therapy termination should be carefully evaluated for potential exploitation, harm, or disruption of therapy follow-up (see Ebert, 2006). Even though the most highly personal contact, sexual intimacy, might potentially be acceptable if at least two years have elapsed since termination, the provider still bears the burden of protecting the former client from exploitation (APA, 2002,10.08).

The fact remains that it is exceedingly difficult to unlink a new personal relationship from the established professional relationship and the original purpose of therapy, power issues notwithstanding. There are a number of contextual factors to examine including the intensity and duration of therapy, the circumstances of termination, the nature of the personal relationship being entertained, the client's personal history, mental status, and likely response to personal involvement, and whether or not the provider fostered the idea of a personal relationship during the course of therapy. For the vast majority of practitioners and clients, follow-up contacts should be construed as a "tail" phase of therapy, and should be located within the bounds of a professional encounter. Allowing the follow-up contact to become too informal suggests that the provider is fostering a personal relationship during what is still construed as professional contact. Particularly with vulnerable clients, this could be confusing and over stimulating and deter the client from a needed re-involvement in therapy.

Providers working in rural areas or even with certain populations within urban areas do not always have the ability to avoid incidental contacts with clients or to fastidiously limit overlapping relationships (Helbok, Marinelli & Walls, 2006). One strategy for handling such circumstances is to differentiate the therapist role to the extent that one does not enact that role in casual circumstances or when interacting with a client or former client in the context of another role. For example, you would not quiz a socially anxious client on their SUDS level if you run into them at a picnic. Even though one is not interacting as a clinical provider, information about the client must remain protected despite the informality of the situation.

Personal relationships with former clients should be carefully managed if they are considered at all, in the present author's opinion. It is best to maintain a professional reserve when interacting with clients in multiple contexts and avoid deepening unavoidable role overlap. If provider and former client become friends or associates, this means the open policy no longer applies and termination is now closed. This might be very confusing to a former client who sees no problem at the outset with incompatibility of the friend and therapist roles. Trying to resolve this confusion after unexpected problems develop elevates the provider's risk of being accused of professional misconduct, as we can recall from the example of Dr. Kathryn, the provider who started a business with her former client (Chapter Two).

Perhaps the following simple guideline might serve even those dealing with "small community" issues (or community within a community). The guideline is that as long as you are maintaining a clinical record of service to someone, this person should not become your *close* friend, lover or spouse, business partner, work subordinate, or *personal* service provider (e.g., accountant, attorney, masseuse, housekeeper, etc.). This role boundary needs to be particularly tended with long-term clients who have a high likelihood of needing to return to therapy on an intermittent basis. Although the therapist may become quite familiar with the long-term client's total life picture and in doing so become a friendly advisor and role model, this familiarity should not open the door to a reciprocal intimate relationship (Beck et al., 2004). The thicker the clinical file, the firmer the boundary needs to be.

How Do I Know That I Have Done *Enough* for an Appropriate Termination Process?

As a strategic professional action, termination should be based on an identifiable reasoning process. Although terminations vary in how much attention and effort is needed to reach the threshold of "enough" action due to differences among clients, providers, the clinical context, and the dynamics of interaction between these elements, the following six essentials steps can help the provider to assure a thorough and systematic effort.

Protocol for Termination Action: Six Essential Steps

1. Review clinical progress and discuss with client
2. Assess any potential reason for termination and possible client response
3. Identify any compelling legal or ethical obligations
4. Evaluate level of risk exposure, risk management, and need for consultation
5. Discuss termination with the client, provide notification, and pre-termination counseling
6. Establish the disposition and note in the client's record

Review Clinical Progress and Discuss with Client   Termination ideally begins with a progress review and a general assessment of the client's current status. In a prospective termination, the provider starts with information in the client's clinical record. How is the client doing at the present time, is he or she stable, and if so for how long? What clinically significant changes have been realized since beginning therapy? Providers will also want to review the client's clinical history, emotional propensities, coping strategies, and current stress level to assess any specific issues. This is an optimal time to readminister any symptom measures that have been used to track progress, and especially to note the presence or absence of key symptoms such as suicidal ideation, panic attacks, or any imminent risks of harm. In a flexible termination, where the precipitants may come up abruptly or there is little advance notice, the provider will still want to do some brief assessment of progress and current functioning. It is helpful to at least note a GAF (Global Assessment of Functioning) score at the last contact as a clinical reference point.

The next step is to elicit the client's assessment of his or her progress. One option is to ask the client to gather this information for homework between sessions. Another option, particularly if time is limited, is to discuss the benchmarks of progress during a session. Now, provider and client have an important decision to make: whether or not therapy should continue and, if so, to reconfirm the purpose and direction of their work. To make this decision, they can recap their original intentions, whether or not these have been fulfilled, whether progress has been made since the last review, and if there is reason, opportunity, and desire to proceed.

Assess Potential Reasons for Termination and Possible Client Response   Consider each of the questions that pertain to the clinical, ethical, and practical reasons for termination that were detailed in Chapter Four. In thinking about the progress of therapy, we want to know: Are we there yet? Are we stalled or going the wrong way? Are we traveling together? Am I still the right provider for the job? Is the client out of time or money? Have our circumstances changed? Am I being manipulated, threatened, stalked, or harassed? If the answer is yes to any of these probes, the next step is to consider the client's likely reaction to the same question. What do you think the client will do or say in response to each query? A parallel step may also be to seek consultation at this point, if you have any doubt about your assessment of the situation or if the client poses any threat or potential for a contentious response.

It may be evident to the reader that these assessments range from relatively negotiable aspects of therapy productivity (Are we there yet? Are we stalled? Are we together?) to limits that must be maintained by the provider (I am not the right provider; we are out of time; our circumstances have changed; I can't allow this). The negotiable issues allow the provider to accept more influence from the client in formulating his or her opinion, and there is more concurrence in the conclusion. On the other hand, the fiduciary role requires the provider to assume authority for setting certain boundaries rather than seeking the client's input on the location of limits. Some information may be needed from the client, but the limits are by and large non-negotiable and must be set by the provider.

For example, if the reason for termination is completion of goals, the client's preferences will have a significant impact on whether therapy stops or whether therapy continues with new goals. It is not only possible but highly advisable to negotiate a mutual and flexible decision on the achievement of goals or the direction of therapy. However, if the reason for termination is that there is a conflict of interest or the problems are beyond the provider's competence, then the provider must resist persuasive efforts from the client to continue therapy. The client's good faith, positive connection, and sincere need can not erase or alter the ethical and legal boundaries by which the provider must abide.

This distinction between negotiable and non-negotiable issues is important because of the different ways that clients respond when confronted with a non-negotiable conflict. Most clients will have little or no difficulty with the negotiable issues and will appreciate the provider's attention to pursuing results. Sometimes personality patterns or disorders affect the client's response in predictable ways that complicate the process of communication. For example, the dependent client might refuse to assess his or her own progress and instead defer to the provider. On less negotiable issues, client reactions will depend on how disturbing the termination reason is and what strategies they typically use to reduce stress or regain a sense of control. Some will be frustrated or confused and attempt to counter-argue the provider's assertion. Others will be defensively angry and perhaps direct these feelings toward the provider. Some may overreact initially and then calm down and become more cooperative after having a chance to think things over. Hopefully most will use the therapeutic context to express and understand their feelings and work with the provider on an appropriate course of action. Predicting the client's emotional response and allowing the client an opportunity to react and work through these feelings is an important part of the termination process and itself an opportunity for further growth. At the same time, it is crucial for the provider to retain control over matters of professional responsibility.

Identify Any Compelling Legal or Ethical Obligations   Any decision regarding the termination of therapy services should be made in the context of understanding legal limits or ethical obligation. Specifically, are there any legal or ethical parameters that either compel or prevent termination? Two primary areas of legal concern are the laws governing professional practice and the laws that stipulate any professional duties of the provider.

Clinicians who provide therapy in violation of professional practice laws do so at considerable personal risk. For example, if the provider does not possess an appropriate license for the practice of psychotherapy or counseling that is valid and in good standing with the state where the services are being delivered, he or she is violating the law. During the course of training and career development, there may be periods of transition when the provider continues working at a clinical placement after completing a formal practicum, or is obtaining post-doctoral experience necessary for independent practice. These working conditions must fully conform to the relevant practice laws and include qualified supervision for services delivered. Employment in an agency setting by itself may not meet these conditions, as some states and professions require a provisional or temporary license and registration of a designated supervisor with the state regulatory board. If mandated conditions are not met, the provider is legally compelled to terminate therapy and provide appropriate transfer information. For instance, Tina, the trainee described in Chapter One, was about to complete her practicum placement, and she wanted to continue working with her clients. However, she lacked the specific supervision needed to practice as a trainee, and she was not yet licensed for independent practice. Despite the interest held by Tina and her clients in continuing, Tina had legally compelling reasons to terminate their work.

There are few legal mandates concerning termination, perhaps because it is important to not to impose too much legal constraint where a high degree of clinical discretion is needed. However, laws that stipulate a duty to protect the public from imminent harm to self or others create a legal reason to delay termination, at least until that duty has been sufficiently discharged. The treatment continuation may be brief or limited, but support is available until either imminence of harm has subsided or alternative protection such as hospitalization has been established. The notion of client abandonment is often thought to be a legal constraint on termination. It is but primarily as an obligation to conduct termination in a professional manner. As noted elsewhere in this text, abandonment is not legally well defined or specified in a particular law. It has been operationally defined as the absence of a clinically and ethically appropriate termination process (Younggren & Gottlieb, in press). Thus, barring any threat of imminent harm, the legal obligation may favor termination, as the failure to end therapy when it is clinically or ethically appropriate can be a dereliction of professional duty.

Are There Ethically Compelling Reasons to Delay Termination? We have already discussed the fact that providers are compelled by ethical obligation to limit therapy under certain conditions. Here we are concerned with ethical reasons *not* to initiate termination. This question is apt to cover more "gray area" with significant differences of opinion on what constitutes compelling. What is compelling in one clinical situation with a given client may not be compelling in another. Clinicians will also hold differences of opinion on the necessity of continuing treatment because their personal judgments are influenced by varying heuristics.

Providers are ethically compelled against termination for capricious or exploitive reasons. For example, psychologists are expressly prohibited from termination for the purpose of pursuing sexual intimacy with a relative or significant other of a current therapy client (APA, 2002, 10.06). They are also ethically compelled to delay termination until they can provide a clinically appropriate process. For instance, a provider may become overwhelmed or impaired and need to terminate or transfer some or all of their clients. This must still be handled in an orderly fashion, whether by the primary clinician or a qualified colleague. It would be unwise and unethical for the provider to respond to stress by impulsively terminating every client who happens to show up on a given (bad) day.

The question of whether to continue working with a client who falls at the edges of one's competence is a possible, and fairly frequent, conundrum. Most providers hold an ethical and moral commitment to serve those who are in clear need but, for various reasons, would otherwise not be served. This does not refer to situations where the client would not be served because of unwillingness or lack of persistence in obtaining alternative services or providers. In the interest of fair access to treatment, providers may have latitude to deliver services at the boundaries of their competence when more appropriate services are not available, provided they take reasonable steps to build competence and protect the client from harm (APA, 2002, 2.01). They also have the latitude to provide services in an emergency in order to ensure that services are not denied, but should discontinue as soon as the emergency ends or appropriate service becomes available (APA, 2002, 2.02). If the choice is made to continue treatment because of an ethical obligation to provide service, this also obligates the professional to takes steps to ensure the competence of service and to encourage the use of the most appropriate resources.

Clinical Example of Delayed Termination. Consider the following clinical example of a situation where the provider felt ethically compelled to continue treatment to reduce the client's risk of harm to himself or others, despite the lack of any specific imminent threats. During the course of therapy, Dr. Brown learned that his client, Sam, had a significant sexual preoccupation with children. Sam had never acted upon any of his fantasies, and he wanted help in keeping this boundary. Sam's original complaint was generalized anxiety and panic attacks, and he had made considerable progress with these issues. Dr. Brown had limited experience in working with pedophilia, but there was not a more qualified, available provider in the area. Part of Sam's reason for not initially disclosing the sexual issue was his experience of being disdained and dismissed by two previous therapists who found pedophilia morally repugnant. It was very difficult to risk trusting Dr. Brown, and he was against the idea of transfer to another provider. Termination would be a reasonable course of action given Dr. Brown's limited skill set, but at the same time Sam was making progress by confiding his serious problem and working on the goal of preventing criminal behavior. Given the overall potential risks associated with Sam's disengagement from any sort of treatment, Dr. Brown felt ethically compelled to continue therapy, despite the current primary problem being at the edges of his competence. Part of Dr. Brown's ongoing work with Sam included study and consultation on the treatment of pedophilia.

Evaluate Level of Risk Exposure, Risk Management, and Need for Consultation No termination is completely risk-free, although most risks can be sufficiently managed, especially when approached with forethought and strategic effort. Different aspects of an adverse outcome can arise in clinical, emotional, administrative, and professional domains. The measure of any of these risks can range from mere inconvenience to major fiasco. A combination of risks may also be more than just a simple sum as a single risk may escalate the magnitude of the other risks in an exponential way.

It is somewhat hazardous to consider any termination a minor risk, yet some risks clearly need more vigilance and strategic management on the part of the provider. A useful heuristic for evaluating overall practice risks is offered by Bennett and colleagues (2006). In this formula, the overall risk is calculated as a function of the interaction between client risk factors, context risk factors, and disciplinary consequences, as mediated by the degrees of freedom provided by individual therapist factors (skills, strengths, experience, and emotional capacity). The formula can be stated another way as: Overall Risk = (Client × Context × Discipline Consequence) ÷ Therapist Factors. Overall risk can thus be conceptualized on a continuum of potential for adverse outcomes relative to the provider's capacity for mediating those risks. This formula is useful in evaluating termination risks and the degrees of freedom for managing those risks.

Client Risk Factors. A primary area of concern for both provider and client is the impact of termination on the client's functional status. Will the client deteriorate without the benefit of ongoing psychological intervention? Will a return of symptoms precipitate other problems? The answers to such questions will depend on several factors such as the overall severity of the client's problems, the gains already made, external supports, and the client's ability to deploy specific coping skills and manage stress.

Even when the reason for termination is the achievement of initial goals, there are emotional risks such as feeling a sense of loss or discomfort in the termination process. The emotional distress with goal attainment is usually minimal, quick to pass, and easily offset by positive feelings of accomplishment. However, a somewhat bigger emotional risk associated with goal attainment might be the potential feelings of failure triggered by a subsequent return of symptoms. Unless the client is prepared to expect this occurrence, and to regard it as normal, the usual response is to think of being "back to square one" and to become demoralized about previous efforts (see Chapter Six for more discussion of termination with chronic and recurrent conditions).

Being a poor participant in their own care elevates the client's risks for termination difficulties. Clients who expect therapy to be a passive experience and who do not exercise their capacity to assume responsibility for self-management are more apt to be psychologically dependent on the provider, resistant or confused about their role in better functioning, and dissatisfied with the idea of termination. This client may perceive psychotherapy as a medical intervention that depends entirely on the ministrations of a skilled provider. Rather than viewing psychotherapy as a participatory learning process with a highly flexible, individual time structure intended to prepare the client to continue self-help efforts once formal consultation has been discontinued, this client expects clinician assistance on call or in perpetuity.

Clients who are stuck in a passive position may be prone to feeling deprived or mistreated by the provider, and they may misconstrue appropriate termination actions as some form of misconduct or incompetence. When the issue of progress and sufficient participation is raised, the provider may become a target for the client's defensive anger. The client may blame the provider for poor progress, triggering apprehension about the client's probability of complaining to the community or the licensing board, adversely implicating the professional's integrity. The best management for this risk is engaging the client in a process of active participation from the beginning and revisiting the issue as the interaction progresses and the client's level of engagement becomes more apparent.

Context Risks.   Termination can be emotionally stressful, especially when it eclipses the potential completion of goals. Both provider and client may be saddened by the lost opportunity and foreshortened relationship. When the termination is precipitated by the provider's positive life events, the client may experience envy, resentment, and anger related to a sense of personal abandonment. When termination is triggered by positive changes in the client's life, the provider is likely to be glad for the good turn of events but perhaps uneasy about the stability of the client's internal changes.

Circumstances that bear a negative element also increase the risk of emotional distress. Clients are apt to be disappointed, discouraged and perhaps even offended if the provider has to withdraw due to skill limitations, conflict of interest, or other administrative reasons. Financial limitations are often frustrating for all involved. Clients may be very unhappy with the realities of seeking services in a lower cost setting, where there are often long waits for service and less choice among providers. Providers typically can only provide pro bono or fee-reduced services to a limited number of clients. An external third party may become the target of vexation, whether it is the managed care entity that implements contract limitations or simply "the system" that is so complex and seemingly unfair. Unfortunately, the provider sometimes becomes the proximal target of anger if he or she is perceived as intentionally withholding, depriving, or unfairly discriminating.

Most of these affective discomforts can be addressed with a combination of emotional validation and problem-focused coping strategies. Providers can offer understanding, support, and guidance toward adaptive and functional responses to these challenging situations. Angry clients can be given an opportunity to express their concerns and test their perceptions, which will provide resolution in many cases. With clients who are reluctant to deal with emotional discomfort, it is useful to emphasize the importance of having at least one (or more) termination session so that some shared processing of feelings can take place.

Administrative and Professional Disciplinary Risks.   Administrative or professional risks associated with termination are apt to be located in how the termination is handled rather than the simple fact of its occurrence. When the provider carries out the termination in a professional manner, his or her risk of censure for professional misconduct is greatly diminished. The essential steps listed here are intended as a general guide for establishing that one has followed a professional protocol. This is not foolproof insurance against disciplinary action as complaints can be precipitated by client or context factors despite the provider's best efforts to prevent them (Hjelt, 2007).

Individual Provider Risk Factors.   Providers who are under stress and feeling burned out are at greater risk for skewed perceptions and clouded judgment concerning termination. Hubris about one's competence and command of the clinical interaction is also a significant risk factor. Together these can pave the way into a situation one sincerely hopes to get out of. The potential for termination troubles is magnified when the provider becomes tired and careless, detached from caring about clients or over-involved with their demands, surly about the worth of clinical efforts, unrealistic about what he or she can or should handle, and unwilling to tap into support resources or set limits.

Provider risks relate not only to overall state with regard to work, but the particular style of coping as well. Self-assessment is an important start in sizing up your professional risks. First, check your ability to realistically self-monitor problematic issues. Do you think that trouble happens only to other, less competent people and therefore believe you have no particular need for coping or risk management efforts? Are you likely to seek consultation or personal help only when negative consequences are evident or things get "bad enough?" Do you know what types of situations might make you more vulnerable to problems or boundary violations? Are you aware of your current level of stress and what is contributing to it?

Next, check your skill level for coping with stress. Does your current pattern of coping decrease or elevate your emotional and professional risks? For example, are you avoiding termination issues with clients? Are you in the habit of working ridiculous hours and trying to be all things to all clients and then complaining about your workload, managed care limits, and unmotivated clients? Do you believe that no one can really help you with your stress? Do you try to reduce stress through impractical strategies, such as excessive rumination about clients or obsessing over the clinical record, instead of seeking consultation or practical solutions? Are you a martyr to your job to the extent that there is no time for exercise, leisure, or having a life beyond your practice? Are you personally or professionally isolated? Do you depend on your contact with clients for social interaction or emotional intimacy? Do you rely on negative coping strategies for relief, such as smoking, alcohol dependence, overeating, Internet preoccupations, and so on? High stress and low coping add to the provider's vulnerability for risks of error in matters of clinical management such as termination (Bennett et al., 2006). Recognition and self-awareness is the key to taking the next step toward mediating these risks and maintaining a better quality of clinical performance.

Consultation may not be needed for each and every termination, unless the provider's scope of practice requires this for their particular level of licensure. On the other hand, every provider needs consultation sometimes. A high level of self-regulation is required of mental health providers, and this can be thought of as a participatory process. The highest level of self-regulation includes tapping the resources of a qualified outside perspective. Thus, consultation on terminations should become a routine part of our general plan for clinical consultation and quality assurance. Usually this consultation would target complex terminations, but it can be useful to periodically review standard practices as well. Regular consultation increases the provider's capacity for mediating risk and managing stress.

Clinical Example of Risk Evaluation.   Theo was moving to another city for a job promotion. His functional status was greatly improved from baseline, although he still had occasional bouts of worried preoccupation in response to specific triggers. His participation was excellent, and he readily assumed responsibility for reviewing and evaluating various coping strategies. During the course of therapy, he developed an action agenda for stress management that included a more relaxed lifestyle and other preventive efforts. Theo's client risk factors at termination were low.

The context of a termination precipitated by a personal move created some stress, but the primary risk was in not having access to an established consulting relationship in his new location. So his therapist encouraged him to contact a primary care physician in his new city and offered the names of two potential therapists to contact as needed. In this case, termination was appropriate, and there was little risk associated with its action. Failure to terminate Theo would have elevated the overall risks in terms of contextual and disciplinary factors. The client might have not taken as much responsibility to establish local consulting relationships if he still relied on contact with the former provider. Trying to conduct long-distance therapy might have caused the quality of care to fall below acceptable levels and thus increase the risk of formal discipline for negligence and perhaps violation of state licensure laws. This provider also lowered his personal risk level by maintaining strong self-care habits that helped him to keep his client relationships in proper perspective and promoted good decision-making and willingness to let clients go when it was appropriate to do so.

Discuss Termination with the Client; Provide Notification and Pre-Termination Counseling It is important to provide clients with information on circumstances that might impact the continuity of therapy, as we have discussed. When termination or interruption of service can be anticipated, the responsible provider notifies clients promptly (NASW, 1999, 1.16 (e)). Any anticipated circumstances that create specific time limits or predictable interruptions known at the time of intake are included in the informed consent process (APA, 2002, 3.10; 10.01 (a) and (c)). This includes advisement on the limits associated with managed care contracts. Otherwise, clinical considerations are the primary basis for the timing of termination. The provider generally wants to ensure the most effective use of available time and to budget time for handling termination concerns, without allowing the idea of termination to preempt the focus on essential clinical concerns. It is important that the provider allows the client an opportunity to assimilate information, explore emotional implications, and become a participant in the process of termination.

Generally, pre-termination counseling will occur over the course of one to three sessions that mark the end of a particular segment of therapy. There are two main objectives for this pre-termination discussion. The first objective is to discuss the circumstances and to evaluate the client's needs, preferences, and options, with an assessment of risks and benefits of the primary options. The second objective is to provide a forum for the client to express his or her feelings, to be understood, and to receive any helpful feedback or practical information to facilitate the transition. Many of the strategies discussed in Chapter Four about talking with the client can be used in this closing session or sessions. If the client has precipitated the termination, he or she can be invited and encouraged to attend a transition session but is not obligated to do so. There may be times when client actions or the third-party payer's limits preclude pre-termination counseling (APA, 2002, 10.10 (c)). Encouraging participation in a termination session is generally useful, but extreme or repeated efforts to contact the client are not required. The level and nature of the client's pathology is important in determining how much follow-up effort is needed. This is a decision that involves reasonable clinical judgment in a given context.

Establish the Disposition and Note in the Client's Record Disposition can be established following the pre-termination consultation and the gathering of any additional information that might affect the termination decision. Notes on the termination discussion are entered into the client's record, with an indication of the closing outcome. Any further follow-up telephone contacts should also be noted, as well as possible written correspondence. The record must also be made available if the client requests a copy or wants to have information forwarded to other providers. Creating an adequate record of each step is an opportunity for the provider to reflect on the work and draw a sense of closure as well as a basic professional risk management strategy. If the client or any other providers ever have questions about what transpired, the record will reflect the degree of professional integrity that was maintained.

MANAGING RISKS

All providers have a right and a responsibility to promote and protect the safety, quality, and effectiveness of the services they deliver and the conditions under which they work. Without adequate protection, the risks of ineffective, unethical, or potentially dangerous conditions are elevated. Any circumstance that compromises these conditions should prompt a systematic assessment of whether adjustments can be made or if termination might better serve the principles of beneficence and nonmaleficence. This includes providers' right to protect their own well-being and competence with safe and effective working conditions. Working conditions can be construed broadly to include physical facilities and location, overall workload and compensation structure, level and type of responsibilities, and interpersonal relationships of respect, integrity, and support.

When Should I Insist on Termination?

Therapy has to stop when it is not safe, ethical, or reasonably practical to continue. It is up to the provider to ensure that these basic conditions are met for both the client and the provider as a prerequisite for service delivery. Therapy can not proceed if there is risk that the client might be harmed, exploited, subject to incompetent, ineffective, or unnecessary service, or impractical arrangements that increase the possibility of other risks. Therapy also should not proceed if the provider might be harmed, exploited, degraded, or professionally compromised. Providers are expected to recognize when these basic conditions are in jeopardy and take initiative to rectify the situation. This means that the provider might have to refuse to continue, even if the client does not agree or the provider's employer objects. Careful evaluation is important in addressing such matters, so providers are advised to include a clinical consultation as part of their strategy. A thoughtfully and deliberately constructed decision will help the provider to remain confident and steadfast in implementing that decision, especially if the going gets tough.

If termination is necessary and the client needs and wants continued service, providers must "make reasonable efforts to provide for orderly and appropriate resolution of responsibility for client care" (APA, 2002, 10.09) and "suggest alternative service providers as appropriate" (APA, 2002, 10.10). Usually this means that the provider helps the client review options and possible choices but refrains from taking direct responsibility for client decisions and actions.

Situations where termination occurs at the provider's discretion can be ripe for misunderstanding or conflict. Providers are not obligated to continue therapy in untenable conditions or to locate a pleasing substitute for the client who is unhappy about the termination or the alternative choices. Instead, the situation can be approached in a systematic, reasoned way that emphasizes the client's capacity to make choices. For example, referral back to a managed care plan for information on the selection of another in-network provider could be considered both reasonable and appropriate (Younggren & Gottlieb, in press). The provider does not have to be cold, inflexible, or insensitive, but it is important to remain firm once a decision has been made. Being inconsistent about the limits or conditions for continuing therapy implies that the provider does not exercise an appropriate degree of control over his or her professional actions.

Example A: Dr. Greene worked with the oncology clinic in a large hospital providing psychological services to patients and their family members affected by cancer. Because space was tight in the clinic, especially on certain days, the administrator wanted Dr. Greene to conduct therapy in a hallway alcove that lacked both visual and auditory enclosure. Dr. Greene determined that this would compromise the safety and effectiveness of his therapeutic consultations. He refused to provide services under these conditions, despite pressure from the administrator and medical director. Without access to private office space, he asserted that he would have to terminate and refer the clients who could only come in on the specific clinic days in question. With this firm position, Dr. Greene was able to obtain the necessary office space and did not have to terminate any clients for this reason.

Example B: Dr. Gray was considering the appropriateness of initiating termination with her verbally abusive, hostile client who was making no progress, did not cooperate with the tasks of therapy, and engaged in sexual harassment (trying to hand her condoms in the session and asking her to help "practice" their use). After consulting with two qualified colleagues, she reviewed the problem behavior and lack of therapy progress with the client and made clear what she expected the client to do (and not do) to continue therapy and avoid termination. The client failed to respond to these directives and persisted with the unproductive and hostile behavior. Dr. Gray then told the client that, due to this lack of appropriate response, therapy would have to terminate. She offered the client a termination session, which he scheduled but failed to attend.

In the record, Dr. Gray made note of the behaviors that formed the reasons for termination (lack of benefit, specific threatening and uncooperative behaviors), the clinical consultations, the limits that were discussed with the client, the client's response, the notification and offer of a termination session, and the client's failure to show for the appointment that he scheduled. Dr. Gray also sent a follow-up letter that confirmed the termination on the basis of client behavior that was incompatible with safe and effective therapy with a corresponding lack of benefit. In the letter, she also noted her attempts to resolve the problem by providing notice of the termination plan as well as the date and time of the scheduled termination session that the client did not attend.

What If the Client Refuses Termination or Becomes Hostile?

Feelings of ambivalence about ending therapy are not unusual, but occasionally these rise to a level of strong opposition and persistent efforts to continue the relationship or retaliatory behavior. The client who angrily or defiantly refuses to accept the termination may be the most difficult of all. Sometimes these reactions are brief and can be mediated with a supportive but firm therapist stance. Talking through the circumstances in a session or two may yield a more cooperative response.

On the other hand, it may become clear that the client is escalating and the provider should take additional efforts to protect him or herself, including the possibility of legal protection. In any case, the provider must stand firm on the decision to end therapy or risk further loss of control. The best results clinically, professionally, and personally require that one makes the effort to obtain consultation rather than attempting to meet this challenge in isolation. Each high-risk situation is unique and should be approached carefully, with thoughtful consideration of the client's issues, the current context, and the overall intent of the therapy. More information on clinical strategies to prevent these risks is provided in Chapter Six. Let's return to the example of Dr. Gray's termination of her verbally abusive, hostile client to consider some further developments.

Several months after their last visit, the client phoned Dr. Gray requesting an appointment to resume therapy. When she explained that therapy was terminated and would not resume, the client cursed and called her a vulgar name. Dr. Gray replied, "I need to end this conversation now." "Good-bye." And she hung up the phone. A few hours later, the client left a vulgar phone message. Dr. Gray noted both phone calls, including his statements (verbatim) in his record, but she did not respond to the communication.

A few months later, Dr. Gray received notice that the client had filed a complaint of wrongful termination and client abandonment with the state licensing board. Although this was a distressing experience, Dr. Gray was prepared to effectively cope with the challenge. She began by obtaining legal counsel to assist in her response to the board's disciplinary investigation. Upon review of the facts of the case, the complaint against Dr. Gray was dismissed as unsubstantiated by evidence. Dr. Gray's case record for the client memorialized the steps that she took to complete a clinically and ethically appropriate process of termination, providing powerful evidence that a reasonable standard of care was delivered.

What Should I Do about My Personal Needs and Limits?

Hopefully, every provider has an adequate and even abundant personal life that will at various times impact his or her practice. Sometimes it is a matter of keeping one's personal life private and separate from practice, and sometimes it is a matter of adjusting or changing one's practice to accommodate the events and developments of one's personal life. Therapists move, change jobs, get promoted, bear children, get sick, make career changes, retire, and eventually die. Along the path of those developments, they also reside within a community where they go about living a personal life, forming significant attachments, pursuing hobbies and interests, and relating with others in multiple contexts. The intersection between the provider's personal and professional lives is a point where a number of termination issues can arise.

Conflict of interest. A conflict of interest may develop during the course of treatment when non-compatible relationships develop with an individual client out of sheer coincidence. For example, the client buys a lovely home that happens to be in your neighborhood. Or the client's spouse lands a new job where your spouse is a direct supervisor. Or maybe the client shows up at the yoga class that you attend. These developments can not be ignored or dismissed. Client and therapist need to discuss the circumstances and issues and forge some sort of agreement on how to handle the conflict, including the possibility of termination. When considering options, the provider will want to take into account the nature and duration of the therapy, the intensity of the secondary relationship, the stability of the client, and the potential for any exploitation or disruption of the therapy, and the relative threat to confidentiality that might be caused by simultaneous relationships. Sometimes these events are purposeful attempts by the client to cross boundaries and infiltrate your personal life. This is not just a coincidence to be resolved, but a high-risk interpersonal situation that has just stepped up in intensity and requires a careful plan for management.

If the conflict can not be resolved or the relationships kept sufficiently separate, it is likely that therapy needs to be terminated or transferred to a new provider. Living in the same neighborhood with a stable client whom you will rarely see is probably not a problem, but living next door to a significantly impaired client is not feasible. Spouses in a supervisory relationship at work are not likely to quit their respective jobs so that therapy can continue. Yoga class, on the other hand, is a fairly incidental contact of the sort encountered on a frequent basis by those practicing in tighter communities. Other factors, such as the client's emotional stability and capacity for tolerating this contact, would influence a case-by-case decision. Although multiple relationships may be unavoidable, care should be taken in determining whether it is advisable to continue psychotherapy given such circumstances (see Younggren & Gottlieb, 2004). There may be plenty of times that the provider can go on living his or her life without substantially altering personal choices on where to live, eat, play, or shop, but a few times when either the provider has to give something up or therapy has to terminate. This is a contextual decision that should be made wisely and with deliberation.

Relocation. When a therapist moves or relocates a practice, provisions should be made to either complete therapy or transfer clients while making sure to provide adequate notice and avoid abruptly ending. Whether clients transfer with the therapist will depend on individual circumstances and options available. First, the provider needs to establish if it is feasible to accept the client at the new practice location. Clients have the right to leave one location and obtain service elsewhere, as clinics or group practices do not "own" the clients. However, the client might not fall into the practice profile of the new setting or it might not be feasible to accept their transfer. It is the client's choice to either conclude therapy or to continue with another provider, depending on relative need for further treatment versus the effort of starting anew.

For example, suppose Dr. Sprout left her job at the medical center and opened a private practice. Her client, Mrs. Root, might simply follow her to the new office, without interruption to their work. However, if Dr. Sprout was no longer accepting Mrs. Root's insurance plan in her private practice, Mrs. Root would have to decide whether she wanted to stay within her insurance network or continue with Dr. Sprout as a self-pay client. But if Dr. Sprout moved from Minnesota to Mississippi, it would not be feasible to continue working with Mrs. Root at all. If Dr. Sprout stayed in town, but closed her private office to take a job at the Veteran's Administration Medical Center, Mrs. Root could transfer only if she qualified to receive services at the VA clinic.

Therapists are advised to check for any specific state or local rules or regulations of practice that stipulate steps for relocating or closing practice, such as providing notice to former patients. It may be that some form of public statement is required, such as an advisement posted at the clinic or in a newspaper. The intent of such provisions is not to create an onerous task for the therapist of personally tracking down every inactive client but rather to allow the client the courtesy of being informed, particularly about how to access treatment records. In psychotherapy, we also want to provide a sense of closure and understandable explanation for the action to discourage any distorted misinterpretations that the patient might develop in the absence of such explanation (see APA, 2002, 10.10 (c)). Despite whatever the client may think, the provider is not trying to slip away under cover of darkness to avoid the burden of saying good-bye.

Provider absence. Eventually, every therapist will end his or her practice. Hopefully, that will occur in a gradual and planned manner that allows clients sufficient opportunity to complete therapy at a reasonable pace. Predictable, defined absences, such as an extended leave for the purpose of study or travel, a sabbatical of sorts, can be handled much like a retirement or relocation, with a gradual winding down and redirection of clients.

Things don't always proceed according to plan, however, and all clinicians must allow for the possibility of their own absence due to circumstances, sometimes arising abruptly, that significantly interrupt or precipitously end their practice. Current standards require that provisions are made either via one's will or as stipulated in a business associates agreement to name a qualified professional who can handle the closing of practice, transfer of patients, and orderly management of confidential records in the event of the therapist becoming indisposed by fortuitous death, illness, relocation, or compromising circumstances (APA, 2002, 3.12; 10.09). Just as it is wise planning to establish a contingent guardian for one's children, it is important to have a qualified contingent professional to oversee the orderly termination of a practice in the event that the clinician is not be able to carry this out.

Providers in an agency or group practice will most likely establish this agreement within their employment setting. Those working more independently or in solo practice need to take additional steps to establish a designated person for this essential task. It is important to clarify terms of the agreement with the designated person to minimize any potential confusion or distress for clients. For example, therapists can not exercise "ownership" over clients. If someone returns to practice after a hiatus, the client is free to choose to return to the original therapist or continue with the clinician who provided interim services.

Things are not always clear cut with regard to situations where a provider is compelled to reduce his or her practice or turn it over to another professional, either on a temporary or permanent basis. The feasibility of being able to offer competent service needs to be weighed against the level of care needed and the scope of one's practice. A range of options may be available for reducing or restricting one's practice, which could mean terminating some patients or services while continuing with others. To illustrate, consider the following examples of providers dealing with different sorts of challenges that are impacting their ability to practice.

- Dr. Aaron has long-term complications from diabetes and has to undergo kidney dialysis three times per week, as well as monitor his activity level and avoid contact with those who might carry contagious illnesses.
- Dr. Betty is in her first trimester of uncomplicated pregnancy, but is unsure about whether she and her husband want to hire out infant care or provide full-time parent care once the baby is delivered.
- Dr. Carlos is an only child and sole care manager for his elderly parents who both require help as they alternate between a nursing home and assisted living. In addition, Dr. Carlos has been experiencing extreme fatigue, which he attributes to the stress of his parents' needs. Unfortunately, Dr. Carlos finds out that he is suffering from serious complications of Crohn's disease. He is hospitalized in the intensive care unit and told he will need multiple surgeries at unpredictable intervals, with extended hospital stays and a long course of recovery.
- Dr. Diane is a horseback-riding enthusiast who is thrown from her horse on a trail ride. She suffers a head injury with extended loss of consciousness and several broken ribs and is hospitalized for several days.
- Dr. Ellen reaches a professional crescendo when she learns that her research grant proposal has been funded, she has just agreed to advise three extra graduate students beyond her already full cohort while a colleague is on sabbatical, she has just been elected to an office in her professional association, she has committed to chair two symposia at an international conference, her spouse just signed a consulting agreement that will requires extensive out-of-town travel so her family responsibilities will increase, and referrals are flooding into her practice because of a recent news story on her area of practice.

What should each of these therapists do, if anything, about their clinical practice? Should clients be terminated or transferred? If so, when and what sort of termination process is needed?

These are all situations where the therapist might reasonably initiate termination of treatment. Providers are not superhuman and their needs and limits constitute "legitimate" reasons for termination to protect the quality of care. Some situations require assistance from another provider, while others can be handled by the original provider. In any situation, it is imperative to have a contingent provider and consultant available. One person could serve in both of these capacities, or the provider might tap multiple resources. Determining the threshold when termination should occur may be somewhat negotiable, depending on the circumstances.

Some patients will move toward ending treatment if the current provider will no longer be available at all, others will readily accept transfer, and others may take a "wait and see" position before accepting a transfer.

Of the therapist scenarios described above, Dr. Carlos and Dr. Ellen each closed their clinical practice in response to their circumstances. Dr. Carlos, the Crohn's patient, was going to be unavailable to see clients for a prolonged and undefined period due to extensive medical problems. Added to this medical situation was the ongoing situation with his parents, as their needs didn't go away just because he was ill. Just covering the basics was absorbing all of his mental and physical energy, with no predictable resolution in sight. Dr. Carlos had a solo clinical practice, so a designated colleague took possession of the clinical records and assisted him in the process of contacting current clients to explain the circumstances and help each one make a decision regarding further care. Dr. Carlos happened to be hospitalized at the same time as one of his clients, although on different floors (medical versus psychiatric), and they completed a pleasant and satisfying face-to-face termination session in this unlikely context.

Although Dr. Ellen greatly enjoyed her clinical practice, she had to reassess her overall academic, clinical, and personal responsibilities. There were simply not enough hours in the day to meet her role obligations. Sheer overwork was compromising her ability to provide effective service. She tried for a time to juggle her schedule to allow for continuing practice, but soon realized that even if she was physically present, she did not have the energy to be sufficiently mentally and emotionally present for her clients. She closed her practice more slowly than Dr. Carlos, first by redirecting all new referrals and then informing current clients of her practice closure with 8 weeks notice. Because her practice was quite small and limited in scope, it was reasonable to attempt closure within this time frame. All of her clients were able to complete therapy, with one exception: This client had long-standing problems and wanted to transfer to an established, full-time community provider who had broader availability.

Dr. Aaron, the provider with diabetes complications, continued practice at the community mental health agency where he was able to specifically limit his hours, and where alternative providers were readily available in the event of a worsening of his medical condition. He was also diligent in his self-care, doing what he could to protect his clients from unplanned interruptions or termination due to his absence.

Dr. Betty continued practicing throughout the duration of her pregnancy, and made individual arrangements with each client for the interruption of her delivery and maternity leave. She also established a back-up plan similar to that of Dr. Carlos for the possible transfer of her clients should she experience any unexpected medical complications and be rendered immediately unavailable.

Dr. Betty informed all new clients of her pregnancy, and did not accept any new referrals beginning one month prior to her due date. During her maternity leave, she decided to return to practice on a limited basis and to assess her family and work situation over a longer period of time. She arranged part-time office hours for continuing clients only, and did not accept new referrals until she had a clear plan for practice. Within six months of her return to work, all of her patients had completed treatment and she accepted a part-time position restricted to psychological evaluations so that she could provide the majority of her children's care yet remain professionally active. During this decision-making process, she had many conversations with her colleague, Dr. Belinda, who had also returned to practice after having a baby. Dr. Belinda followed a different path, resuming her clinical caseload right away, with day care and back-up babysitters. Both agreed that it was not the life change that dictated how one should go about practice, but rather a personal choice about the scope of one's practice.

Thankfully, Dr. Diane, the horseback rider, had a rapid recovery without any long-term deficits, not even a fear of getting back on the horse. Her assistant cancelled all of her appointments for the duration of her brief hospitalization, but no decisions were made until the extent of her medical condition was known. As a provider in independent practice, she too had a designated colleague who was ready to help her assistant with client management in the event she was suddenly unable to practice. Prior to returning to practice, she was medically evaluated for any cognitive or physical impairment that could impact her overall competence to practice.

Personal biases. An overdeveloped work ethic can be dangerous in clinical practice, as we can see from the examples of medical challenges faced by providers. Although most therapists have a sincere desire to help others, no one possesses all of the skills needed to treat all of the clients all of the time. Every practitioner needs to recognize his or her psychosocial limits, and be prepared to work within those limits. Although it is unethical to allow social and culture prejudices to affect one's work (APA, 2002, Principle E), providers are also compelled to take appropriate measures to "limit, suspend, or terminate their work-related duties" when personal problems may interfere with adequate performance (APA, 2002, 2.06 (b)). In addition, as previously noted, the provider must ensure that services are competent and effective. Unflattering as it may be, the reality is that the provider might have personal biases toward certain populations of clients or types of problems. Or the provider may be inadequately prepared to address the needs and concerns of specific populations. To fully conform to ethical standards, the provider must be aware of such biases and limits and take appropriate action. This might mean that therapy should be terminated because the clinician can not provide service at the level of competence to which the client is entitled. In a sense, therapy with this provider is not an emotionally safe experience for the client. Without knowing why, the client might be subject to subtle or overt debasement or generally sub-par treatment.

Eliminating personal biases is an ethical aspiration that often requires persistent, conscious effort (APA, 2003; Fiske, 1998). At the level of required professional standards, providers must be aware of negative or pejorative attitudes and respectfully protect the client from any damaging impact. If fair treatment is not likely, then one's first obligation is to decline certain referrals. For example, a therapist whose sibling had been sexually molested by a member of the clergy found it impossible to work effectively with highly religious clients of the same faith. Personal biases can present a significant risk to the integrity of treatment and require the provider to take appropriate protective measures including declining or referring clients with whom an effective working relationship is unlikely.

When dealing with socio-cultural stereotypes, it is possible that the provider might come to recognize biases during the course of treatment if the client activates assumptions and reactions associated with a dormant schema. For instance, the provider recognizes his or her own negative automatic thoughts as a link back to personal socio-economic stereotypes of "arrogant rich people" or "backward, racist Southerners." Sometimes these biases can be mediated if the provider makes a concerted effort to change his or her beliefs and modify his or her behavior. Whether this is possible will depend on how deeply the beliefs are held, how closely linked they are with the provider's identity, how extensively these ideas have been reinforced by the culture at large, and how motivated the provider is about changing this particular cluster of ideas (Beck, Freeman, Davis, & Associates, 2004).

When termination is indicated because the therapist is unable or unwilling to adjust his or her beliefs or effectively serve the patient's best interest, care must be taken to communicate only the message of provider limitations. The reason for the termination is that the provider is not the right person for the job due to insufficient skills. This message should be delivered with utmost tact and care taken to redirect the client to more productive resources. Self-control is crucial, as all clients must be treated in a humane and sensitive manner, no matter how virulent the provider's reaction may be. There is no personal bias that ever justifies a disrespectful termination, without a semblance of help in locating alternative resources. For example, Dr. Brown's client Sam, described earlier in this chapter, reported the experience of being called a pervert and literally ordered out of a therapist's office when he revealed his problem with pedophilia.

Thus, for many reasons, the juncture of personal and professional characteristics, roles, and responsibilities is a place where many termination issues emerge and demand thoughtful consideration and professionally responsible action.

SUMMARY POINTS FOR APPLIED PRACTICE

1. Most termination ends the current contract without necessarily dissolving the professional relationship. If termination is to end the professional relationship, this final closure should be explicit.

2. Providers need a clear strategy or policy for handling contacts from clients after termination. Being systematic will reduce clinical and ethical risks.

3. Brief guidance on follow-up recommendations and procedures is apt to be enough for clients who are generally organized and have mild to moderate difficulties. Those with more severe disturbances and/or personality disorders may need explicit structure on post-therapy contact and appropriate avenues for re-engaging in further therapy.

4. Personal contact following termination is a choice that elevates provider risks and should be handled with caution.

5. The vast majority of provider-client contact after termination is part of a "tail" phase of therapy and should be construed as a professional encounter. Think deliberately about the risks associated with professional encounters in a casual setting or with a casual attitude.

6. Following a systematic set of steps will help to ensure an adequate termination process, no matter how quickly termination comes up. As a general guide, six points to cover include: (a) current status and GAF, (b) the reason for termination, (c) legal and ethical duties (d) risks and benefits of termination, (e) pre-termination notice and discussion, and (f) clinical record. Pre-termination notice and counseling is possible only if the client cooperates. An adequate record of termination is one that will let the reader see that systematic reasoning was followed and termination was clinically and ethically appropriate. Take the time to do this even if you are busy or don't want to bother.

7. Humility has its benefits. Providers must be willing to let go if they can't help, if the client pushes their worst "bias buttons," if the client is dissatisfied or wants to stop, or if it is necessary for self-protection. Try to find an effective approach that engages the client, or to modify personal shortcomings, but if this does not yield results, be ready to quit.

8. Sometimes the provider must insist on termination. Client refusal or hostility should not stop this decision from moving forward if the provider has thoughtfully determined that termination is appropriate. Use consultants to help you get through this difficult process.

9. Life is about more than doing therapy. Provider needs and developmental changes will sometimes precipitate therapy termination.

10. Figure out a plan for who will tend to the matters of your practice if you are suddenly unable to show up for work.

6

Adapting Termination to Client Needs: A Consumer-Oriented Perspective

Key Questions Addressed in This Chapter

- Does the client's cultural background or social environment impact termination?
- How do Axis II personality disorders affect the termination strategy?
- What about termination when clients have chronic or co-morbid disorders?
- Does life stage or health status affect termination needs?
- How can I handle practical concerns about time, convenience, and money?

SOCIOCULTURAL CONTEXT

As a consumer of services, every client must make cost-to-benefit judgments about seeking and continuing therapy. Personal needs and resources play a very direct part in these judgments. Providers can increase the likelihood of a positive termination by taking an empathically based consumer-oriented approach when helping clients with decisions about starting, continuing, or ending therapy. The client's consumer needs are considered here in terms of four domains: cultural and social context, clinical needs, developmental/health status, and practical concerns. Each of these domains is relevant to decisions about an appropriate point of termination and potential needs for follow-up care.

Does the Client's Cultural Background or Social Environment Affect Termination?

Culturally Competent Therapy   The fit between the client's cultural needs and the provider's ability to respond in a culturally competent manner has significant implications for positive termination. First, there is the issue of the provider's ability to appropriately understand and respond to the client at a cultural level. When the practitioner demonstrates awareness, knowledge, and skill in working with culturally salient issues (APA, 1993, 2002; Hansen et al., 2000; La Roche & Maxie, 2003), the client is more likely to trust the provider and expect that therapy will be beneficial. When therapy is not consistent with the client's cultural expectations or there is a mismatch of culture with the practitioner, the risk of client harm or termination without benefit is elevated. This may be particularly important in the early stage of therapy when rapport and the working relationship are being established. It is also relevant to the overall plan for therapy including judgments about termination. Providers hold a responsibility to ascertain whether the client's concerns and needs fall within the scope of their cultural competence. They must assess the cultural fit early in therapy and determine with the client the appropriateness of the match.

At any point during therapy, there is the risk that recommendations that are dissonant with the client's cultural beliefs, norms, expectations, and practices will hurt rapport and diminish the level of benefit. The client may think, "This provider does not understand me or my world and does not know how to help me" or "This therapy must not be for me." Providers have an ethical obligation (APA, 2002, 2.01 (b)) to obtain training, experience, consultation, or supervision on cultural factors that may be essential to competent service, including age, gender, gender identity, race, national origin, religion, sexual orientation, disability, language, or socioeconomic status. They must not only grasp the client's worldview, they must reach into the client's cultural framework to understand the prevailing forces that shape the client's cultural identity and how those relate to possible sources of conflict and potential solutions (Freeman, Felgoise & Davis, 2008). Otherwise, the ethically appropriate course of action is to terminate the service with an appropriate referral.

Personal Social Support   Personal social support is a component of cultural context that can have a moderating effect on the client's participation in therapy, depending on the attitudes and influence of those close to the client. Fortunate clients have friends and family who validate the effort and value of therapy. This positive social support encourages the client's overall progress toward a predictable termination. Significant others show concern and interest without being intrusive and they might offer helpful observations and suggestions. They might even serve a facilitating role when asked to do so, for example in assisting exposure exercises or other self-help assignments. Supportive others also can help the client develop realistic expectations for therapy. Their helpful and caring stance directly contributes to the client's overall resilience and recovery.

On the other hand, some clients have significant others who antagonize and complicate their therapeutic progress. In short, they contribute to the client's problems. Significant others who are bothered, frustrated, or impatient with the client's problems sometimes send them to therapy on orders to "get it fixed." They might then "meddle" in the therapy, grilling the client about the content of sessions or assigning goals and topics for sessions. Or they might chide the client for gullible behavior in "going to see all of those quack head doctors," demeaning the effort and dismissing the client's progress. It is important to assess whether the client is subject to these sorts of pressures and to discuss it in therapy if possible. The emotional conflicts triggered by these messages could worsen the client's condition, especially among those who are already depressed. If not addressed, this emotional cost might lead the client toward abrupt, unilateral, or early termination. When clients are dealing with high social stress, it is helpful to take a non-pejorative stance, encourage the client's efforts, and be flexible about possible solutions or accommodations.

Isolation   Clients who have few social resources or who experience persistent isolation may be more vulnerable to dependence on the therapy relationship. Their problems might include an unrewarding or sparse social environment and personal skill deficits. For those who want and need more social contact, therapy is hugely beneficial because it reduces painful loneliness and provides a close connection with someone else in the world. It may also provide a crucial opportunity for altering maladaptive interpersonal beliefs and behaviors. The risk, however, is that reliance on the provider as the sole source of emotional support may lead both to believe that therapy must continue at any cost. It is possible that isolated therapists might become dependent on their clients for social contact as well. This reduces their ability to remain objective about the client's needs and can reinforce beliefs that prolong therapy or foster client dependence. Providers can reduce their risk of social dependence on clients through involvement in professional and social networks and activities.

Working toward termination with lonely and fragile clients can be a difficult and uncertain task. Progress may be stalemated at a certain plateau yet the client thinks that continued meetings are essential. Attempts to discuss termination goals might trigger deterioration. Socially isolated clients who form a positive alliance with the provider are predictably reluctant to end treatment, but for different reasons. Sometimes the client is clearly benefiting from the alliance by using it for stabilizing functions such as reality-testing their perceptions, activating coping skills, managing the stresses of an unpredictable or negative environment, or dealing with pervasive problems of Axis II traits or disorders. However, there are times when the isolated client stabilizes at a non-productive level, complacent in a passive role, perhaps misusing therapy as an outlet for chronic complaining while avoiding the emotional risks and stresses of active change. Unless the provider diligently maintains a clinical focus on developing a realistic range of social support, there is a risk that therapy will drift toward being habitual and overly social in tone.

Not all socially isolated clients want to prolong therapy. Clients with schizoid or paranoid personality or those with elevated suspicions and perceptions of danger do not view relationships as a source of support (Beck, Freeman, Davis, & Associates, 2004). They are likely to doubt the benefit of therapy, wrestle with the cost-to-benefit assessment on a session-by-session basis, terminate early, or disappear without warning. However, if they do form a positive alliance with the provider, they too may have difficulties in ending contact with one of the few persons they consider trustworthy.

Strategies for positive management of termination issues related to personality traits and Axis II characteristics are considered in more detail in the next section on clinical needs.

CLINICAL NEEDS

When the client's symptoms have improved, it may appear that further services are no longer needed and termination is the appropriate disposition. But not all terminations are so clear-cut. Embedded in every potential termination is the question of whether treatment could and should be continued. Would further therapy maximize the client's functioning or have an impact on his or her ability to maintain improvements and avoid relapses or other problems? If the client wants to continue therapy, what is the clinical necessity? Although it is difficult to answer this question on a strictly empirical basis, it is widely recognized that clinically significant and lasting improvement involves multiple levels of change (Prochaska & Norcross, 2003). When symptoms have remitted, it may be useful to focus on other issues pertinent to the client's long-term stability and overall functioning. This is particularly true when the client's level of psychopathology is more severe or persistent over time and there is notable psychosocial stress or nominal psychosocial support. Here we will consider client personality and coping style (Axis II issues), chronic or recurrent Axis I conditions, and individual psychosocial development and health status in terms of appropriate and useful termination strategies.

How Do Axis II Personality Disorders Affect the Termination Strategy?

Terminations will not all look alike or follow a standard process. Even with a good basic strategy, every therapist will encounter terminations that do not proceed as expected. Sometimes communications are less than optimal and decisions are not mutually agreeable. Variations and snags in termination can result from many different interacting forces including the client's personality style and typical ways of coping with stress, the provider's vulnerabilities, the situational constraints, the duration and benefit of therapy, and the reasons for termination. These are complex terminations and they require heightened attention, energy, skill and strategy.

Given that Axis II disorders are associated with Axis I conditions about 50 percent of the time (van Veltzen & Emmelkamp, 1996), it seems sensible to include personality factors when developing an individualized termination plan. Difficulties and potential conflicts may be minimized by adapting the termination strategy to the proclivities of the client's personality profile and interpersonal schema.

Many clients can talk about when and how to end therapy in a collaborative way without extreme emotions or conflicts about the disposition. Termination is something that is expected and desired when appropriate, although it is not a major preoccupation. The feeling between provider and client may be quite amiable as they discuss the future of their relationship and work together. There may be some wistful feelings about loss and separation, but these are usually balanced by satisfaction in the work accomplished or resolution to draw the contract to a close. The client is able to grasp a rationale for the transition without becoming enraged or oppositional. There is some relief about drawing closure, appreciation of the benefits, and gratitude for the personal care. Many clients are able to form realistic judgments about the process of change and the relative contribution of therapist support and guidance.

In contrast, some clients hold beliefs that distinctly alter this prototypic communication and the feelings and actions associated with it. These are the clients for whom termination is a "hot" topic. The subject of termination and the client's feelings about it either may be exceptionally difficult to broach or a repetitive concern that seems unaffected by reasonable discussion. Various schemas distort the otherwise ordinary communications about termination, triggering the client's intense emotions and maladaptive interpretations. Potential emotional reactions include heightened anxiety, helplessness, sadness and dysphoria, or disappointment, resistance, anger, and even abandonment rage. These idiosyncratic reactions usually serve some functional purpose: to escape anticipated rejection, avoid perceived danger, compensate for helplessness, maintain proximity to a source of perceived power, or attain personal power and control.

Providers may also experience heightened emotional distress in dealing with the stress of these challenging reactions. Being regarded as unfair, intrusive, malevolent, controlling, gullible, mean, perfect, all powerful, rejecting, irresponsible, or dominating while intending to be just the opposite is emotionally taxing. Difficulties at either end of the duration spectrum can be demoralizing or draining, when clients either quit too soon or hold on too tightly without the benefit of progress. These conditions are more stressful than termination-as-usual because of the need for extra scrutiny of one's efforts, the elevated risk of adverse events, the limited degree of one's impact with usual efforts, and the emotional dissonance associated with ending. Thus, it is crucial for providers to have a systematic way of understanding and dealing with complex terminations that includes personal self-care and professional self-protection.

Adapting Termination for Axis II Personality Disorders   From a cognitive behavioral perspective, the client's personality is linked to self-regulatory schemas that filter experiences and activate predominant patterns of affective, cognitive, and behavioral responses (Beck, Freeman, Davis & Associates, 2004). Personality disorders occur when certain patterns of appraisal, emotion, and behavior are overdeveloped while other patterns that would provide balance or attenuation are non-preferred and underdeveloped. For example, the Avoidant Personality Disorder involves overdeveloped schema for self-inhibition and underdeveloped schema for self-assertion. Particular patterns are thought to arise from a combination of innate predisposition and biological responsiveness that is further elaborated and shaped by learning processes of modeling, identification, direct instruction, positive reinforcement, and escape conditioning. Counterbalancing patterns are not primed by predisposition and are subsequently neglected, directly discouraged, or simply unknown in the developmental learning process. Central to the prevailing pattern is an internal communication framework consisting of self-concepts, self-monitoring, self-appraisal, self-evaluation, and self-instructions that form the self-regulating schema that integrate and give meaning to experience.

The result is a schema-based personality structure that systematically organizes how a person uses data about themselves and others. Biases in the schema-control system, especially in exaggerated negative or positive self-concepts, may be a crucial link that leads from a personality type to a personality disorder (Beck et al., 2004). When Axis I clinical syndromes develop, these add to the dysfunctional bias in information processing, often reinforcing the basic schematic structure. Overdeveloped beliefs about the self and the world are major points of reference that give the personality disorders their distinctive characteristics and distinguish them from normal personality structure. Within each personality disorder, certain beliefs and strategies are predominant and form a characteristic profile. Prototypic schema content for each personality can be assessed via various means, including the Personality Beliefs Questionnaire (PBQ) (Beck & Beck, 1991; Beck et al., 2001), a self-report measure designed to map directly on to Axis II disorders.

When termination is considered from this schema perspective, a new understanding of complex and challenging client responses begins to emerge. Maladaptive beliefs about the provider, the process of therapy, and termination vary according to the predominant client schemas, distorting the process of termination communications, interfering with positive planning and resolution, and elevating the risk of adverse outcomes. Although this formulation has not been studied extensively to date, recent clinical investigation has linked poorer outcome in depression treatment to the presence of maladaptive avoidant and paranoid beliefs (Kuyken, Kurzer, DeRubeis, Beck, & Brown, 2001). This negative effect on outcome is thought to be a result of prevailing beliefs that produce self-instructions that pull the client away from productive involvement in therapy collaboration.

A schema-based conceptualization can be useful in formulating individualized termination strategies for clients with Axis II features. The primary objectives of this conceptualization are to effectively manage the length and productivity of therapy, to maximize collaboration at points of transition, and to minimize maladaptive conflicts or adverse events at disposition. Both ends of the spectrum of treatment length are targeted: early termination and prolonged therapy. A schema conceptualization is most helpful when developed early in therapy, but its accuracy should be tested and revised as the client progresses and new information is gathered. A consistent and valid formulation of key schema often takes time to compile, even though those schemas have an impact on therapy from the first meeting.

Clients do not necessarily have to meet full criteria of a specific personality category for the schema conceptualization to be relevant to the termination strategy. Few clients represent a "pure" category, without some overlap within a cluster of disorders or even across clusters. A composite of dimensional features of the client's cognitive personality profile can help to distinguish the variations within specific diagnostic categories and inform clinical decisions (Beck et al., 2004) such as termination. The disorders of each cluster are discussed here as they might present in a pure form to illustrate the prototypic features. In practice we might expect more unique blends of features in varying degrees that correspond to a composite cognitive profile or system of self-regulating beliefs.

Cluster A Personality Disorders   Cluster A personality disorders include paranoid, schizoid, and schizotypal patterns. Persons with Cluster A personality disorders have odd, eccentric, or unusual features of thought, affect, or behavior (APA, 2000). Early experiences of bullying, rejection, and abuse are often linked with the characteristic self-protective strategies of Cluster A syndromes (Beck et al., 2004). Although the overdeveloped strategies range from vigilance and attack to autonomy and isolation, the common purpose is to reduce interpersonal vulnerability and organize information about their experiences internally and in relating with the world. Underdeveloped strategies include trust, intimacy, reciprocity, and serenity.

Table 6.1 Adapting Termination to Personality Style

Personality Style	View of Provider	Beliefs about Therapy & Termination	Problematic Termination Behavior	Suggested Termination Strategy
Paranoid	Manipulative Discriminatory Exploitive motives	"Watch out for therapy traps. Their scheme is to keep me coming back so they can make money."	Suspicious; Doubts value; May accuse provider of unfairness or discrimination; Terminates early or stays too guarded to benefit	Address trust openly; Be willing to earn trust; Re-evaluate short-term contracts; Request termination discussion
Schizoid	Unimportant Intrusive	"Therapy is a bother. There is little point in continuing."	Passive and detached about commitment; May respond to soft follow-up but be unresponsive to repeated efforts	Offer brief contracts with clear terms; Reconfirm continuation
Schizotypal	Judgmental Threatening Controlling	"The therapist will think I am odd and try to make me fit in." "I need to be careful and not expose too much."	Uncomfortable; Hesitant about disclosure; Brief contacts, then disappears	Empathize with client's discomfort and offer support; Help client evaluate reasons to continue or not on a session-by-session basis; Emphasize interpersonal safety and client-centered goals
Anti-Social	Gullible An easy mark	"Therapy is a tool to get what I want. I'm entitled to work the system because I'm smart enough to get away with it."	Abrupt, unemotional departure; May threaten provider for personal advantage	Take self-protective precautions; Avoid billing; Refuse to comply with deceptive practices; Keep careful records
Borderline	Powerful Perfect Rejecting Mean	"I need therapy to cope." "I can't control myself. You have to help me."	Overwhelmed; Frightened; Abandonment rage; Self-damage to reduce tension; Dramatic pleas for help	Validate client's distress concerning access to provider's support; Assess collaboration and establish realistic expectations at the outset; Use consultation for trouble-shooting; Set and keep limits

Histrionic	Validating Entertained	"I need the therapist to think I am impressive and charming. Termination must mean I am boring and not worth the time."	Feels wounded or angry; May be dramatic with tears, temper tantrums, or suicidal gestures	Empathize with emotional distress and validate the relationship; Cite specific reasons for termination; Use advance deliberation so termination is not sudden
Narcissistic	Important and powerful but in a subordinate role; Idealized	"Therapy is mainly for weak, marginal people, but the best therapists understand the special needs of exceptional people."	Expects special accommodations; May become angry and condescending if not appeased; Elevated risk of suicide or homicide	Keep clear limits for scope of competence and policy; Avoid power struggles; Assess client satisfaction with methods; Monitor potential for crisis
Passive-Aggressive	Dominating Controlling	"You can't make me change. I will do things my own way. I can't stand rules. What if I want to change my mind?"	Complains but makes little use of recommendations; Resentful about progress evaluation; Immobilized by reluctance to let go of options	Review and follow the limits as a matter of procedure; Emphasize client autonomy and control in setting the pace of change and goals for therapy
Dependent	Powerful Supportive Competent	"I would be lost without therapy." "Don't abandon me."	Confused and disorganized; Fearful of separation; Forms new problems to keep therapy going	Empathize with reactions to loss; Foster resilience and a gradual approach to termination as a process of discovery; Taper sessions
Avoidant	Critical Rejecting Superior	"Therapy is very stressful. I think my therapist wants to get rid of me."	Anxious over-anticipation; Pre-emptive or abrupt departure; Even if over-anticipation decreases, active planning may be avoided	Approach termination gently but proactively as a practical task; Emphasize support, mutual negotiation and the client's pivotal role in making decisions
Obsessive Compulsive	Potentially incompetent Irresponsible	"Therapy should give me the right answers. It should end only if my problems are fixed for good"	Critical of ambiguity; Frustrated in search for completion; Reluctant to draw closure	Set a time frame for progress evaluation; Acknowledge uncertainty as part of termination; Link termination goals to increases in underdeveloped strategies

The paranoid client basically believes that people are dangerous. Therefore, it is necessary to be on guard all the time to protect against being exploited, demeaned, manipulated, or used to another's advantage. Therapy may be perceived as an entrapment, where the provider's main motive is personal or institutional gain, often financial, apparently without concern for the client's best interests. Because of persistent mistrust, paranoid individuals are unlikely to come to therapy and unlikely to stay very long. Entry into therapy may be precipitated by a crisis where the client feels persecuted by circumstances yet doubtful about the benefit of therapy. The paranoid client has a very low tolerance for ambiguous situations and may be vulnerable to focusing on narrow, stereotyped solutions.

Although the paranoid client may act respectful and perhaps even stiffly formal, he or she can also be critical, non-congenial, and guarded about self-disclosure. Friendly overtures can trigger this client's suspicions about hidden motives. Efforts to collaborate are met with aloof, uncooperative, and even argumentative reactions. To the paranoid client, the provider is untrustworthy until proven otherwise. The provider basically has to earn the benefit of the doubt, for it definitely will not be easily given. There is an elevated potential for adverse outcomes of the litigious sort, depending on the client's perceptions of malintent. It is helpful to check the client's history for evidence of a pattern of bitter estrangements and legal entanglements.

Fortunately, the tendency to collect evidence and evaluate the provider may allow some access to the client's schema. If any working alliance develops with the paranoid client, it is usually through a series of tests, overt and covert, of the provider's trustworthiness. Rather than trying to coax the client into trusting or disputing the merits of the client's suspicions, the provider openly encourages the client's evaluation (Beck et al., 2004). With the paranoid client, the provider makes a special point of recognizing that trust is something to be earned through experience and not just given because it is expected. Therapy is regarded as only *potentially* useful until proven otherwise. There are risks that it might not work and it should be discontinued if it does not produce some benefits. The provider can appeal to the client's value of justice by asking the client for a fair opportunity to earn their trust and evaluate the potential benefits of therapy.

The agreement to work together can include a plan for periodic re-evaluation, which might be presented as an effort to protect the client from the risks of unproductive therapy. Termination remains the client's option at any point, and it is helpful to explicitly acknowledge the client's fundamental right to control what happens. However, as a primary participant, the provider wants to have an opportunity to anticipate and properly prepare for termination, so the client's cooperation in discussing his or her decision is requested.

Schizoid and schizotypal individuals may need a similar strategy of short-term agreements and frequent re-evaluations of the ongoing purpose and benefit of therapy. Also unusual or eccentric, their pattern of relating with self and world varies somewhat from the paranoid client. The schizoid client basically believes that plenty of space and privacy from others is essential. Life is better and more enjoyable when one is left alone, free and independent from others. Closeness with others brings anticipations of emotional disappointment, harm, or burdensome responsibility, so interpersonal commitments are minimized. Detached from caring about what others think, this client tends to neglect the simple social reciprocities that others use to build relationships, further distancing those around them. With a view of others as intrusive and demanding, their main behavioral strategy is to get away and stay away from others.

Poorly functioning schizoid clients appear to be loners who are caught up in their solo pursuits to the point that they are unkempt, unapproachable, or disconnected from normal social routines and networks. Compensatory skills or strengths may help the schizoid person achieve a higher level of functioning, particularly if they can strike an adaptive fit with personal and vocational roles that allow much autonomy. These schizoid clients are more pleasant but unobtrusive, self-possessed, and enviously "laid-back," content to live mainly in a world of ideation and some degree of fantasy, but touchy or even rude about intrusions. Higher functioning schizoid clients may have some personal relationships, albeit rather distant or limited ones. Once a tolerable connection is established, the schizoid client is likely to drift along in the relationship status quo, blandly unresponsive to conflict as long as there is a safe retreat position. Compared to the paranoid client, it may be easier to get along with the schizoid client, but it is still difficult to get close.

Therapy is apt to be viewed through the same lens of detachment that filters other interpersonal experiences of the schizoid client, where the provider is construed as potentially intrusive and demanding, particularly when probing for affective information or trying to establish a relationship. Therapy must be linked to objectives that are relevant to the client's priority of autonomy and freedom from interpersonal duress. Without this, the schizoid client may not see any point in coming back.

In dealing with termination matters, it is useful to keep in mind the self-protective function of this client's overdeveloped schema for autonomy and isolation. It is quite likely that the schizoid client has learned to stay isolated because of a history of experience in which he or she was diminished in comparison with others and treated in ways that were unkind, unhelpful, and damaging (Beck et al., 2004). Thus, even though the client might seem cold or indifferent, he or she might be more attached than it appears and sensitive to potential criticism or overwhelming demands. If the schizoid client has to miss or cancel an appointment, disengagement is the client's default safety position, and calling back to reschedule is apt to be neglected. If contact is lost, it can be particularly helpful to follow up and invite the client's return through mild efforts such as a phone call to touch base or demonstrate interest and availability. However, if the client is more decidedly detached and plans not to continue in therapy, repeated calls or letters are not likely to elicit a response. Multiple efforts at contact may be interpreted by this client as intrusive, confirming their perception that others will invade their space and infringe on their freedom or require too much of them.

Also concerned with self-protection, the schizotypal client tends to be anxiously concerned about social interactions, often with a distinctly superstitious or paranoid trend. The cognitive patterns of this client are more frankly odd or unusual, with ideas of reference, perceptual illusions, and belief in clairvoyance, telepathy, and supernatural forces. Their peculiar affect and behavior is connected to a self-protective vigilance of these magical forces and events. Of note is the likelihood of significant social anxiety that persists despite familiarity (APA, 2000). The schizotypal client basically believes that he or she is somehow different from others. This client also believes that their unusual ideas and talents will attract the interest of others, yet they intensely fear being humiliated or rejected as odd or weird. Thus, the basic strategy is to stay to themselves, attentive to their sensory "gifts" and attuned to signs of malevolent attention from others.

In contrast to the criticism and doubts of the paranoid client or the passive emotional distance of the schizoid client, the schizotypal client is anxious, restless, and quick to dart away. The provider can easily be construed as a threatening figure that will misunderstand and try to mold the client toward conventional thinking and homogenize their personality. Thus, the schizotypal client is also very tentative and careful about contact and self-disclosure. Their decision to continue in therapy needs to be frequently discussed in terms of reasons to continue or not continue, possibly as often as each session (see Beck et al., 2004 for more illustration).

Any discussion of participating in therapy is not complete without similar consideration of the client's reasons not to participate in therapy. Including both sides of the decision helps to emphasize the schizotypal client's autonomy and avoid any sense of coercion. In addition to gently guiding decisions about participation, the provider hopes to create an emotionally safe environment by demonstrating interest and willingness to consider the client's ideas and accepting the client's right to unique self-determination as long as there is no threat of imminent danger. Client-centered goals for termination can be emphasized.

Overall, the primary termination challenge with Cluster A Personality Disorders is the initial involvement and participation in therapy. Even if the client is distressed and motivation for relief is high, characteristic sensitivity to interpersonal risk forms a significant barrier to the therapeutic alliance and makes the client vulnerable to reactive termination. Given the same opportunity to work with a caring provider, the paranoid client is skeptically challenging, the schizoid client is reserved and distant, and the schizotypal client is anxiously guarded, each concerned in a different way with self-protection. If the provider can avoid tipping the trust balance in an unfavorable direction early on, the client might continue with therapy.

Clients with paranoid, schizoid, or schizotypal disorders may all respond best to mild but persistent encouragement to proceed with small segments of therapy, even as small as one- or two-session sessions, with concrete goals that introduce greater flexibility into the predominant, overdeveloped schema. The client's right to self-determination and ultimate control over termination is emphasized to reduce the high risks of reactive termination. If this philosophy is emphasized from the beginning, it will also help mediate potential problems of dependence and fears of rejection that might emerge in more extended therapy.

Cluster B Personality Disorders   Cluster B personality disorders include the antisocial, borderline, histrionic, and narcissistic patterns. Persons with Cluster B personality disorders are described as dramatic, emotional, or erratic (APA, 2000). Passive-aggressive personality is also considered here as a distinct syndrome of clinical relevance even though it has been removed from the established list of personality disorders and is currently listed in a provisional category. Passive-aggressive personality is similar to the emotionally intense and erratic Cluster B in its description as impulsive, quixotic, and driven by negativistic emotion (Millon & Davis, 1996). In addition to its unique elements, the passive-aggressive pattern blends features of the narcissistic personality (Fossatti et al., 2000) with passive dependent and avoidant strategies, overlapping some with Cluster C traits.

Clients with Cluster B disorders are prone to mood dependence. They are motivated by emotion, and their thoughts and actions are highly fused. Although the beliefs of this cluster differ in content, all have overdeveloped strategies of interpersonal dominance, from self-aggrandizement and dramatic expression to passive resistance and a variety of tactics for rule manipulation. Underdeveloped strategies include self-control, systematization, assertiveness, empathy, and social cooperation. Maladaptive patterns of relating predictably clash with aspects of the therapy relationship that call upon these underdeveloped strategies. Tactics of rule manipulation can play havoc with the therapist's efforts to maintain proper therapeutic boundaries, including negotiating termination as a boundary.

The antisocial client basically believes that others are weak and meant to be taken. The world is viewed as a predatory place where people will get you if you don't get them first. Antisocial clients also believe that one should grab any opportunity to get what you want and do whatever is necessary to get it. To the antisocial client, it is not really important to keep promises, honor debts, or play by the rules. Lying and cheating are acceptable as long as you can get away with it. Their overdeveloped strategies of exploiting and preying on others operate without the constraints of empathy or social responsibility. The antisocial client's self-instructions often include the belief that they have been treated unfairly and are thus entitled to get their fair share by whatever means they can.

Clients with an antisocial personality usually approach therapy as a tool for achieving some personal objective or to gain some personal advantage, but rarely is their objective to become a more conscientious or empathic person. This client is simply exercising a sense of entitlement to use the system to get something they want or feel they deserve. The gains being pursued by the client will depend on what circumstances precipitated the entry into therapy. Perhaps the client wants to manipulate a favorable impression from the provider to help him or her get out of trouble (legal), regain certain privileges (e.g., parole, child custody or visitation, family support), assemble evidence of damages (to win a lawsuit), or gain access to an opportunity (fitness for a job).

Any of these objectives can be a legitimate reason to consult a mental health professional. It is the use of deception that distinguishes the antisocial client from one who honestly wants help in resolving a problem. For example, Ms. A. wants to understand how she lost control of her life, what mistakes she made, and how to be a better parent to regain visitation and possibly custody of her children. Ms. B., on the other hand, tries to seduce the provider into accepting her hard luck story about an unfair life and a biased system. Ms. B. will make sudden demands for written testimonials that are urgently needed, and use anger, hysterics, or even threats of violence if the provider balks. She has no interest in self-understanding or change. She simply wants to get the provider to write a letter on her behalf so that she can regain custody of her children. A primary motive behind her pursuit of custody may be to use child support as a source of personal income.

Antisocial clients present significant financial and professional risks to providers. This client may exploit the provider in unexpected (but not unpredictable) ways simply because the opportunity is there. Allowing the antisocial client to accumulate an unpaid bill is a clear mistake, as the client will abruptly depart and fail to make expected payments. Attempts to contact the client or to collect the unpaid bill will go unheeded. That is unless the client surmises that counter-attack might be worth something, in which case the provider might be subject to legal actions such as a malpractice complaint or report of misconduct to a licensure board. It does not matter that there likely is no real basis for these actions, as the intent is manipulation rather than justice. The goal may be to threaten and intimidate the provider into submitting to their demands, to directly exploit cash from the provider's malpractice insurance coverage, to extort a personal settlement by making threats against the provider's license to practice, or simply to steal services from the provider and hang on to their own cash.

With antisocial clients, the most likely errors in termination are that of omission: not considering it soon enough or failing to be sufficiently authoritative in implementing the decision and the process. If the provider assumes an unguarded supportive stance, this gives the client precisely the right conditions to aggressively pursue his or her advantage. Termination may need to be enacted swiftly and decisively in response to client actions or threats. Prolonged and unproductive therapy is not usually a problem, but it could occur if the client is motivated to carry out an extensive set-up or grooming phase as part of an exploitive plan. The provider can proactively manage termination challenges by recognizing the personality pattern early and remaining cognizant of the risks associated with it. This is an alert to take extra precautions in terms of explicit payment expectations (e.g., no billing; payment due in full at each visit), clear policy on written statements or testimony, prudent office practices (keep things locked up; don't be alone with this client), and extra careful record keeping (to defend your actions if accused of impropriety).

The borderline client is apt to be perceived as one of the most difficult clients to successfully guide through termination and indeed is somewhat difficult to conceptualize in terms of distinctive schema. The profile of specific thought content of the borderline client appears to blend some of the beliefs characteristic of dependent, paranoid, and avoidant personality (Butler et al., 2002). The borderline client basically believes they are helpless, needy, and weak and must have someone available at all times for support and protection. At the same time, they can not trust other people and believe they must remain guarded. Unpleasant feelings pose an ever-present threat as they are predicted to escalate and get out of control.

To the borderline client, the provider can be both a powerful hero and a heartless villain. Internal beliefs about personal weakness, incompetence, and unlovability leave the borderline client constantly fearful of rejection or abandonment and clinging to therapy as essential for basic functioning. The borderline client strongly believes that he or she can not cope as other people do, so discussion of termination can trigger a multitude of fears, causing the client to become emotionally overwhelmed and disorganized. Threats of a dramatic or punitive response to termination, such as suicide or lawsuit, may be the client's attempt to end the intolerable emotional arousal and maintain a vital source of support.

There are several termination issues that are useful to address with everyone at the outset of therapy, but especially important with the borderline client. The first is to assess in the first few sessions whether or not the client will be able to develop trust and collaboration with this particular therapist. Trust can be enhanced by fostering realistic perceptions and expectations of the provider from the very beginning. The second is to ensure that the limits of the therapist's availability or the length of proposed therapy are clearly structured from the outset. Any specific constraints can be spelled out at this time, helping the client to establish realistic expectations for limits that may be encountered along the way. The third is to clarify the provider's termination policy, including various conditions and reasons for termination. This transparency reduces ambiguity, provides good informed consent, and encourages self-responsibility in the client.

Although not foolproof by any means, effective therapy is probably the best tool for reducing and managing termination challenges with borderline clients. Given that the needs of the client might extend in perpetuity, it may be most helpful to plan a structured break or "vacation" (Linehan, 1993) from ongoing therapy. This provides an opportunity to re-evaluate client progress, reduces the risk of therapy becoming prolonged, and fosters an emphasis on the client's autonomy and coping skills. This break can be planned well in advance in most circumstances, thus reducing the client's sense of vulnerability to personal rejection and increasing predictability of the event. Dramatic threats and self-destructive actions that characterize the maladaptive coping tactics of the borderline may arise as special challenges to termination, particularly if termination is sudden, unclear to the client, or related to a lack of progress. If this occurs, the provider is well advised to include consultation in their termination planning and to develop a risk-management plan. Issues of risk management and termination challenges are discussed in more detail in Chapters five and seven.

Histrionic clients believe that unless they entertain or impress people, they are nothing. The histrionic client anticipates that others won't like them unless they keep them engaged with compelling stories. Dazzling or amusing others is the way to get what you want and distract from your weaknesses. The attention of others is needed in order to be happy. Thus, strategies for gaining attention through dramatic expressiveness and exhibitionism are overdeveloped and strategies for retreating from attention by restraint, organization, and contemplation are underdeveloped.

In termination with the histrionic client, it is helpful to focus on the reasons for termination and make it clear that the decision is unrelated to the client's personal likeability. Given this client's sensitivity to the loss of attention, it is important to warmly affirm the underlying relationship throughout therapy and especially at termination. Advance deliberations that frame the termination as a predictable and understandable event can mediate the client's tendency to construe the provider's actions as boredom and loss of interest.

The narcissistic client's self-regulating schemas are organized around the basic belief that "I am special." This client also believes that since they are so superior, they are entitled to special treatment and privileges. They may present in a very social manner, assuming that the provider recognizes their special qualities and will give them whatever they want. What they want is flattery, admiration, and assistance in expanding their accumulation of wealth, attractiveness, brilliance, power, and competitive status. What they also want is protection from stresses that threaten to destabilize their inflated self-esteem and trigger intolerable thoughts of inferiority and feelings of shame. Overdeveloped strategies of self-aggrandizement stand in stark contrast to underdeveloped strategies of self-restraint, empathy, and broad social identification or social reciprocity.

Because the narcissistic client believes that only people as brilliant as they can understand them, the provider is apt to be selected on the basis of fitting this profile of superlatives and "bests." Although ordinary therapy is construed as something mainly for weak and marginal people, the narcissistic belief system allows that there are certain providers with special expertise who can deal with the particular needs of exceptional people. If the narcissistic client is not impressed by the provider's prestige and acumen, he or she will drop out early, disappointed that the provider is not so special after all. On the other hand, if the client idealizes the provider as top rank, he or she may attempt to bully or manipulate the provider into keeping them as a client, even if it is a clearly inappropriate match.

From the beginning of therapy, the provider will want to avoid power struggles and remain sensitive to the narcissistic client's propensity to protect their positive self-image of strength and superiority. Termination is not apt to be especially conflicted unless there is some threat to self-esteem involved. Narcissistic clients will not like being held to the same policies and procedures as others, and tend to expect special exceptions to be made for them. They may quit therapy angrily if the provider refuses to grant an exception, no matter how nicely the refusal is couched. If the provider must raise the issue of termination for lack of progress, it must be done quite tactfully. The narcissistic client is hypersensitive to being the subject of critical examination and quick to react to any suggestion of failure or inadequacy. Providers might deal with this by focusing a progress evaluation on the suitability of the therapy and effectiveness of its methods in producing results that are satisfactory to the client. For example, if a therapy goal is to reduce family conflicts, periodic assessments can focus on the client's satisfaction with the results he or she is achieving.

Providers should note that narcissism is a marker for readiness to behave aggressively toward others (Baumeister, Bushman & Campbell, 2000), risk of violence against family members (Dutton & Hart, 1992), and a notable characteristic among violent criminals (Baumeister, 2001). Thus, there may be an elevated risk of crisis termination by suicide, homicide, or other violent action by the narcissistic client. The potential for imminent danger should be monitored, particularly during periods of high stress, depressed mood, or when combined with other violence risk factors (e.g., age, gender, history, means, etc.) (see Oordt et al., 2005, and Sommers-Flanagan & Sommers-Flanagan, 1999).

Passive-aggressive clients basically believe that they must protect their autonomy and remain free of control. They also believe that they can rely on special status to meet their needs and achieve their goals. Key features of passive-aggressive personality (PAPD) incorporate elements of narcissism, dependency, and negativism blended together in unique ways. First, there is a preoccupation with self-centered concerns combined with a passive behavioral style. This client thinks mostly about their desires but does little to constructively achieve self-satisfaction. They hold an optimistic view of self, but a relatively negative view of the world. Second, a passive style makes this client more dependent on others, but the dependence is marked by grandiosity and personal entitlement, with less of the obsequious caretaking and submissive features of a dependent personality. The client with PAPD may have audacious expectations of what others should do for them and yet see little to no obligation to fulfill their own responsibilities or show gratitude. Their passivity encourages a dominant response in others, to which they respond with resentment and self-pity because this is a direct blow to their pride and self-direction. They can be exploitive, unreliable, and apparently immune to the feelings and frustrations of others, but present an attitude of agreement, cooperation, and all good intentions.

This blend of beliefs and strategies seems to produce characteristic distortions in relationships with authority and the normal balance between dependence and self-assertion. Authority figures (which may include spouses and significant others) are viewed as powerful and controlling but flawed figures that must be manipulated to produce special treatment and privileges for the client. Rules are regarded as arbitrary, stifling of freedom, and unnecessary if one is special. External demands such as deadlines, productivity, or social cooperation are viewed as a personal affront. Expectations for performance or compliance trigger considerable resentment and defiance, which is suppressed or covertly expressed through cynicism, disdain, and irksome behavior such as forgetting, stalling, or obstructing and demoralizing others. Performance expectations are perceived as oppressive and intolerable, but direct opposition is too dangerous because it would risk the dependent relationships.

Passive-aggressive clients are likely to perceive the provider like other authority figures: as intrusive, domineering, demanding, and withholding. Narcissistic clients think they *are* the authority while passive-aggressive clients view themselves as *victims* of authority (Beck et al., 2004). Overdeveloped strategies include avoidance, surface submissiveness, evasiveness, stubbornness, negativism, and passive exception to customs or expectations. Underdeveloped strategies include assertiveness, cooperativeness, generosity, reciprocation, empathy, and responsibility for self-satisfaction. The imbalance of these self-regulating patterns and their negative consequences may not internally register as a significant problem, even as the client becomes enveloped in a spiral of self-defeat. Instead the client is preoccupied with excuses and irritations with trivial external issues. Significant problems of alcohol abuse, interpersonal strife, verbal aggression, emotional storms, impulsivity, and manipulative behavior have been associated with PAPD (Small et al., 1970).

One of the most significant termination challenges with the passive-aggressive client is determining whether or not further progress or benefit is likely or even possible. The passive-aggressive client may express sincere interest in change, but something always seems to foil their efforts so that the net result is minimal if any progress. The client complains of not having a sufficient chance, yet in truth the chance was there but the client did not take it. Sometimes immobilization is due to rumination and the tendency to put off decisions, choosing inaction over action. Caught on the two horns of an unsolvable dilemma, the passive-aggressive client fails to act out of reluctance to give up any freedom of choice and the entitled belief that someone else should do the work. It is as though all options have to be indefinitely preserved, if only out of resistance to external pressures toward effort from which they should be exempt. Even mild expectations for effort or progress may trigger stubbornness and subterfuge. Observable progress is apt to occur in fits and starts over a fairly long-term course, if it occurs at all.

Termination with the passive-aggressive client may be difficult, particularly if participation in therapy is directly tied to some secondary gain (special status). The client might insist that therapy is very useful, yet show no clear benefits. Raising the issue of termination might produce a brief response of marginal cooperation, barely enough to justify continuing. It may be helpful to work with specified time segments and emphasize the client's autonomy in choosing the pace, direction of change, and goals of therapy. Setting out specific behavioral goals for the client should be avoided as this triggers reactance. Some evidence of progress is needed to continue therapy given the realities of the "system," but it is up to the client to choose what progress to make and how fast to make it. If the client wishes to continue therapy, the provider must make a clinical decision as to whether this is a feasible and potentially effective alternative.

Cluster C Personality Disorder   Cluster C includes the Avoidant, Dependent and Obsessive-Compulsive Personality Disorders, which are characterized by prominent anxious and fearful features (APA, 2000). The patterns of beliefs and behaviors of this cluster tend to be associated with early experiences that emphasized the sovereignty of authority and the need for certainty, perfection, social conformity, and emotional control. Overdeveloped strategies include excessive self-inhibition in the form of avoidance, help seeking, clinging, threat monitoring or fault-finding, excessive caretaking, restraint, and risk aversion. Underdeveloped strategies include self-expression, assertion, spontaneity, gregariousness, self-sufficiency, mobility, or playfulness. Clients with Cluster C patterns of schema are usually unlikely to terminate early, as long as the therapist is sufficiently empathic, supportive, and authoritative. However, prolonged therapy is a distinct possibility as such clients may be prone to passive dependence or chronic contemplation.

Avoidant clients basically view themselves as socially inadequate or inferior and vulnerable to being hurt by the judgments of others. Other people are seen as powerful, superior, and potentially critical or demeaning. Given the strong view of themselves as socially inept or undesirable and the view of others as indifferent or rejecting, avoidant clients construe social or work situations as circumstances that threaten to expose their perceived weaknesses.

An important aspect of the avoidant client's cognitive profile is the beliefs that relate to affect. The avoidant client believes that they can not tolerate unpleasant feelings and that unpleasant feelings will escalate and get out of control. The way to control unpleasant feelings is to avoid unpleasant situations at all costs. Thus, the avoidant client habitually escapes or avoids affectively arousing experiences. They are vigilant to the potential for discomfort in a variety of situations, much like the paranoid client, but the threat is associated with their internal arousal in response to perceived external evaluation. Overdeveloped strategies include avoidance of affect and stress, threat monitoring, risk-aversion, self-inhibition, and restraint. Underdeveloped strategies include self-assertion, gregariousness, trust, and risk taking.

Avoidant clients can easily misread or misunderstand the interpersonal cues when interacting with the provider, as they are highly sensitive to scrutiny and the potential for disapproval and rejection. This prompts a "flight" response of self-protection to preempt being scolded, scorned, or cast aside by the authoritative clinician. The avoidant client's sensitivity to interpersonal threat and the anxiety it causes can make the issue of termination a veritable constant, one that may have to be considered often, to prevent an abrupt or incomplete termination.

At the same time, it may be very difficult to engage the avoidant client in developing a pro-active termination plan. The very idea of termination may trigger associations with rejection and more affective arousal. Their tendency is to avoid the arousal, so the provider will need to be tactful but matter-of-fact and persistent. It may be useful to address termination as a practical task that is not difficult, but does require collaboration and advance planning. Communicating warmth and support of the client's progress is essential, as is reassuring the client that he or she has a pivotal role in treatment planning and termination decisions. The provider is benevolent and responsible for guiding termination negotiations, but not capricious or critical in issuing arbitrary dismissals from therapy.

Dependent clients basically view themselves as needy, weak, and helpless when left on their own. The dependent client believes that he or she needs somebody available at all times to help carry out what they need to do or in case something bad happens. Overdeveloped strategies include submissiveness, help seeking, hesitance, clinging, and cultivation of subordinate caretaker roles. Being in therapy makes the client feel safe, as long as the provider is nurturing, non-demanding, and available. Underdeveloped strategies include competence, self-sufficiency, mobility, and assertiveness.

The dependent client is prone to misinterpret the idea of termination as a threat to his or her very functional existence because the provider represents necessary support. Talk of time limits and possible termination may trigger high anxiety and even panic over loss of contact with the provider. The dependent client is apt to have the most fears of abandonment, relapse, and catastrophe. Borderline clients also show these fears, which may be related to an overlap with specific dependent beliefs about being needy, weak, helpless, and reliant on a caretaker (Butler et al., 2002). Indeed, the dependent client may be vulnerable to helplessness and depressive collapse if termination is abrupt and there is little time to adjust to the transition. It is hard for this client to believe in his or her own self-sufficiency or take the steps necessary to build self-confidence.

There are several strategies to help the dependent client deal with the task of termination. A strongly empathic stance is particularly important when approaching termination with any of the anxious and fearful clients. For dependent clients, specific fears and concerns about independent functioning can be mapped out and tested. Active strategies are useful in countering the dependent client's tendency toward passivity, hesitance and chronic contemplation without action. Fears about relapse and catastrophe can be addressed by developing a relapse prevention plan or a resilience agenda (see below). Actual termination can be organized around an extended "fading" process during which the client gathers information on his or her ability to manage stress and use coping skills during successively longer intervals between sessions. Finally, the post-therapy phase can be framed as an open follow up, if possible, where the client contacts the provider for "booster" consultations as needed. One of the tasks of the fading process is for the client to develop confidence in their personal competence, strength, and ability to use self-help and assertive communication.

Clients with obsessive-compulsive personality disorder basically believe they must do a perfect job on everything. They feel compelled to the highest standards at all times. The potential for failure or inadequacy looms large in their view of self. Flaws, defects, or mistakes are intolerable because any sign of imperfection is viewed as a failure to meet expected standards. This client may despair of ever achieving a sense of satisfaction from meeting expectations or doing well enough. Thus, the client with OCPD attempts to travel the one-dimensional path of doing everything right, at the highest level, missing nothing. Overdeveloped strategies include inflexible rules, constant critical evaluation and fault-monitoring, over-responsibility, tight fusion with expectations, and punishment. Underdeveloped strategies include spontaneity, casual attachments, hedonism, forgiveness, and tolerance of uncertainty, impermanence, or imperfection.

Of all clients with Axis I or II problems, the client with OCPD may have the most difficulty finding an endpoint in therapy. Highly uncomfortable with ambiguity, this client wants reassurance that therapy has "fixed" their problems. They may be most troubled by the lack of objective standards for knowing how much therapy is "enough." Clients with OCPD tend to view the standards of others as irresponsible or overly slack, and the provider is no exception. When confronted with the task of constructing a reasonable endpoint to a segment of work in therapy, the client may challenge the adequacy of the provider's efforts. There is some elevated risk of adverse events with an obsessive-compulsive personality as the client may feel compelled to report the provider's perceived irresponsibility to someone in greater authority. This might trigger a complaint to the provider's supervisor or perhaps to a licensing board.

Talking about termination raises the OCPD client's anxiety about impermanence, imperfection, and the enigmatic aspects of normal living. Client doubts can easily trigger the provider's own anxieties about responsibility and competence. As a result, one might get caught in a prolonged and conflicted termination, in which the provider strives to assure the client of adequate protection from emotional and behavioral vulnerabilities. Instead, the central issues in ending may be to acknowledge the presence of some doubt and uncertainty and avoid chronic contemplation. At a practical level, it may be useful to set time boundaries as points of re-evaluation and target the growth of underdeveloped strategies (e.g., spontaneity, casual solutions, and tolerance of uncertainty) as possible termination goals.

Clients who fall within the Axis II spectrum differ in their respective needs for clinical management of termination, as illustrated by this overall conceptual framework. Understanding the client's particular cognitive profile and basic strategies associated with it early in treatment can enable the provider to develop effective, targeted strategies for navigating termination. Provider actions can either escalate or help to contain potential problems. If early termination is avoided, the course of therapy for clients with Axis II problems is still uncertain at best and likely to be longer than non–co-morbid Axis I treatment. Therapy can be extended in time as long as it is practical, safe for both provider and client, and productive in terms of general goals for Axis II problems. Possible goals include (a) supporting the client's adaptive fit with his or her social and vocational environment, (b) modifying the beliefs and behaviors that reinforce or maintain the overdeveloped beliefs and strategies, and (c) activating and reinforcing the underdeveloped beliefs and strategies.

What about Termination When Clients Have Chronic or Co-Morbid Disorder?

Many illnesses persist over a long duration (e.g., two years as specified for Major Depressive Episode-Chronic or Dysthymic Disorder) (APA, 2000), with a course that varies from chronic but fluctuating to chronic and continuous with possible progressive deterioration (e.g., schizophrenia, anorexia nervosa, bulimia nervosa, substance abuse and dependence, panic disorder with agoraphobia, generalized anxiety disorder, social anxiety disorder, post-traumatic stress disorder–chronic and personality disorder). With a chronic and potentially progressive course, it is much more difficult to determine how long therapy should last or when termination is appropriate.

The possibility of having more than one chronic clinical disorder appears to be greater than 50 percent (Merikangas & Kalaydjian, 2007), which worsens the course of the disorder, complicates treatment, and makes it even more difficult to estimate a reasonable point of termination. As a general rule, clients diagnosed with co-morbid disorders can be expected to respond more slowly and need more time in treatment than those with only one symptomatic disorder, particularly when personality disorder is the co-morbid condition (Jakobsons et al., 2007; Marchand, Goyer, Dupuis & Mainguy, 1998; Pilkonis & Frank, 1988). Estimates of the co-occurrence of Axis I symptomatic disorders and Axis II personality disorders suggest that approximately 50 percent is common (Persons, Burns & Perloff, 1988; van Velzen & Emmelkamp, 1996). Clients with a co-morbid personality disorder may also terminate prematurely (Sanderson, Beck & McGinn, 1994) and have more variable treatment results (Beck et al., 2004).

Providers differ in their perspective on whether treatment of chronic, recurrent and co-morbid psychiatric disorders even has an endpoint. Some may consider termination only as an externally forced event, as the client with a chronic disorder really needs non-terminating follow-up. Others may view recovery not only as a possibility but as a goal that catalyzes the healing process. On one hand, chronicity and severity seem to indicate the need for continuous care and monitoring. On the other hand, it is possible that this disease perspective fosters pessimism that exacerbates the illness and impedes recovery by implying that the condition is unchangeable and hopeless (O'Connor, 2001).

An optimistic perspective endorsed by the consumer-survivor recovery movement asserts that people with psychiatric disabilities can and will recover (Carpenter, 2002; Rodgers, Norell, Roll & Dyck, 2007).

From this perspective, recovery primarily means that the consumer takes increased responsibility for achieving self-management, with the support and hope shared by family, professionals, friends, and community resources (Carpenter, 2002). There is no presumption that the illness will disappear or no longer require any treatment or management, but there is hope for symptom remission and recovery of personal functioning. Positive goals are pursued in the context of learning how to live with a mental illness (Smith, 2000).

Certain types of interventions are designed specifically for resolving symptoms as quickly as possible and developing skills of self-management that can diminish the rate or intensity of future problems, if not entirely prevent possible recurrence. There is growing evidence that cognitive-behavioral therapy (CBT) can produce these effects for a number of chronic and severe disorders in the anxiety and depression spectrum (Hollon, Stewart & Strunk, 2006). Closer consideration of the mechanisms of these effects indicates that tactics of a compensatory nature, when practiced over time, contribute to changes in the client's characteristic tendencies in processing and acting on information. In other words, CBT is designed to help the client learn the skills of recovery and resilience through effective self-regulatory practices.

Recover and Resilience Perspective The recovery perspective begins in an obvious place, with the recognition that many people with psychiatric problems can and do recover (Anthony, 1993; Hollon et al., 2006; Rodgers et al., 2007). When recovery is expected, the provider is more likely to focus on the client's strengths and to promote the elements of resilience associated with sustained improvement. Resilience is variously defined as "the ability to thrive, mature and increase competence in the face of adverse circumstances" (Gordon, 1996, p. 1);); "the capacity for successful adaptation, positive functioning, or competence despite high risk, chronic stress, or prolonged or severe trauma" (Henry, 1999, p. 521); or the ability to readily recover from illness, depression, and adversity (Abrams, 2001).

This capacity for resilience appears to consist of learned strategies that can be developed at any time and under a variety of circumstances throughout the life cycle (Glicken, 2006). One can become a more resilient person by learning how to think and behave like a resilient person. Resilient people develop positive characteristics and tend to experience more positive emotions that buffer the impact of stress (Duckworth, Steen & Seligman, 2005). Resilient people also tend to seek mentors and support systems to help them achieve or develop their ongoing "self-righting" abilities (Glicken, 2006, p. 231). Various characteristics of resilience can be found among people who successfully cope with problems such as substance dependence, major depression, schizophrenia, post-traumatic stress, and disabling or life-threatening physical illnesses (Glicken, 2006).

Recovery assumes that the professional relationship is a partnership between client and provider that serves the purpose of helping the client develop and maintain the capacity for self-righting, self-management, positive traits, and positive emotions. The provider's role is that of mentor and participant in a multidimensional system that supports client's self-directed recovery efforts. Psychotherapy is a participatory learning process in which provider and client may work together briefly on a focused issue, or they may have a long-term relationship. Over time, their contact might be continuous, or it might be intermittent with periods of more intensive work. There is no single point of termination other than that determined by the client's current needs for achieving, sustaining, or restoring effective and stable functioning. As a mentor and support person, the provider looks for opportunities to model, instruct, and reinforce the skills and strategies that contribute to the client's strengths and resilience. Attachment to the provider is encouraged and the relationship between provider and client is regarded as a cornerstone in the client's recovery efforts (Drake, Merrens & Lynde, 2005).

The concept of resilience is particularly relevant to interventions for clients with chronic, recurring, or co-morbid disorders. Throughout the process of moving from symptom reduction to readiness for termination, providers want to help clients recognize and develop a positive coping perspective. Becoming less extreme is important in developing realistic and proximal goals for improved functioning. Unrealistic optimism is a form of "overshooting" the goal, which produces an elevated risk of relapse (Hollon et al., 2006). Less wishful thinking about an idealized life and more tedious reality checking is often the most appropriate goal. Resilience is an attractive yet prudent way to frame a positive coping perspective where termination is a possible goal.

With a resilience perspective, not only can the client learn to handle the stresses that could produce relapse, he or she becomes oriented to the idea of leading with strengths. Disease management and recovery perspectives have some distinct differences in the focus of clinical attention. A disease management perspective encourages clients to focus on monitoring signs of distress and dysfunction so that a preplanned set of illness management strategies can be mobilized. Unfortunately, this can foster hyper vigilance toward symptom return and anxiety about the adequacy of the clinical tools. When experiencing a mood such as mild dysphoria, the following internal sequence of thought might be typical. "Uh oh, I might be getting sick again. What if I can't handle it this time? Maybe therapy didn't work well enough. I must be some sort of treatment failure."

On the other hand, a recovery perspective encourages the client to focus on the development of mediating strengths and to recognize signs of distress as opportunities to apply those strengths in response to a challenge. Recovery is not the absence of any distress, but it is an active process of coping with stressors and symptoms. Thus, the client may be more likely to activate internal communications that directly mediate the negative affect rather than activating illness appraisals. The internal dialogue following mild dysphoria might be very different when the focus is on understanding and coping with the triggering factors. For example, the client might think, "Being rejected is a tough experience. No surprise I'm feeling down. How does a resilient person react to this? What strengths might help me bounce back? I need to try some things and see what helps."

A spinal cord metaphor may be useful in explaining the concept of resilience to the client. A healthy spine is what allows us to stand up straight and move in various ways, from simply sitting and walking to dancing the waltz or hitting a hole-in-one golf shot. To be healthy, the spine needs strong muscles to support it and adequate padding between the individual vertebral bones. This padding is provided by the intervertebral disks. Psychological resilience can be likened to the muscles and disks of the spinal column. Without adequate padding or muscle tone, the vertebral bones collapse and collide, sliding out of place and clacking together, causing pain, loss of stature and disruption of movement. This state can be likened to the client who lacks sufficient resilience to handle life's chances and challenges. Without the padding and strength that comes from resilience, problems can clack together and collapse into one another, causing anguish, impaired problem-solving, and psychic stenosis.

Tools of Resilience   The skills of resilience and recovery can be developed with the use of any or all of the following strategies. These ideas are drawn from a summary of resilience research and practical applications offered by Glicken (2006). Resilience tools can be combined with additional tactics for risk management and relapse prevention that are specific to the client's disorder. For example, the recovering substance abuser makes it a point to stay away from high-risk, triggering environments or enters them only with adequate support, and the recovering depressed client makes it a point to regularly schedule pleasant activities. Efforts to develop resilience are not merely palliative tasks designed as a distraction from intractable illness, but are actual tools of remediation.

- Do an "asset review" to identify positive behaviors that build success and competence in various areas of living. What are the client's capabilities? What strengths are evident in the problems that he or she has successfully solved or the accomplishments achieved? Better still, teach the client some ways to recognize and develop personal assets and strengths (see Duckworth et al., 2005; Frisch, 2006). Encouraging strengths is vital to optimistic and hopeful perspective, no matter how complex the problem, how long it has been around, or how difficult it is to resolve. Persistence, effort, and willingness to try new and emotionally challenging things are all aspects of resilience that are strengths when moderated by appropriate judgment and context. A review of these strengths throughout therapy, at termination and at various points in follow-up or subsequent episodes of care, can reinforce the client's belief in his or her ability to recover.

- Assess any beliefs the client may have about their illness as a perpetual and hopeless condition and target these for direct intervention (O'Connor, 2001). Potential beliefs might include high expectations for continuous distress ("I will never really feel any better"), low expectations for change ("My condition is chronic and beyond improvement"), or fear of the idea of recovery ("It's foolish or even dangerous to think that I could get well"). Providers can suggest alternative constructions that stimulate more active coping strategies to see if it makes any difference.

  For example, the provider might propose the idea "If I change what I do, it might change how I feel." Or the provider might suggest the possibility that "If I change how I think, it might change what I feel and do." The provider can then offer to help the client to evaluate the merit of these ideas as they apply to his or her situation. Other beliefs about the rate and extent of change may be important in fostering patience, persistence, and appropriate expectations for recovery. Such beliefs are exemplified by the notion that "A journey of a thousand miles begins with a single step." The client's capacity for resilience may be limited by serious trauma or extensive debilitation and may take time, effort, and support to grow stronger.

- Elicit and support the client's dreams, hopes, aspirations, and desires. These are hidden motivators that foster hope, even in times of trial and despair. Building dreams about something is a strategy that resilient people use to generate energy and motivation, even though practical constraints exist. Giving some attention to desires and aspirations helps to balance the realities of limitations, impairments, and loss of functioning that may be attributable to the illness. For example, the client may not be able to sustain typical full-time employment because of persistent symptoms and functional limitations. Instead of focusing only on what has been lost or can't be done, the client can still explore other dreams, hopes, and ideas for productive activity.

- Promote contact with others as a way to gain new information and develop social ties. This can include self-help and support groups, but should be broadly construed to include any type of social contact. The potential benefit in these contacts is to develop acquaintances, friendships, and emotionally satisfying connections with a community, to offer oneself as a resource to others, and to stimulate new thinking. Selecting the nature and type of social contact should be the client's prerogative, as this is a highly personal choice and will vary significantly with cultural and personality preferences. Encourage the client to be curious about others and inquisitive (in socially appropriate ways) of the ways others accomplish their success in living.

- Endorse the use of creative activities as a source of stimulation of imagination, potential social connection, feelings of pleasure and mastery, and as a general outlet for self-expression. Creative pursuits are not just something to fill time, but rather a purposeful effort to develop internal resilience. Some options include reading, writing, painting, woodworking, collecting, gardening, flower arranging, decorating, building/construction, dancing, bodybuilding, photography, crafting, cooking, sewing, repairing, baking, remodeling, racing, singing and playing or appreciating music, gaming, planning events or travel, playing sports or attending sporting events, artistic performances/showings, or cultural/ethnic festivals, and play in general.

- Encourage philosophical or spiritual practices or traditions as an element of resilience. Spirituality can be broadly defined as a subjective experience that involves an internal focus on one's personal value and worth and an external focus on connecting to a life force greater than our individual selves (Nezu & Nezu, 2003). The greater life force might be found in a relationship with God, a Higher Power, Allah, or nature and universal energy. One can connect with spiritual beliefs, traditions, and practices either within a community or on one's own, but this should be an individually defined choice (Frisch, 2006).

  Providers might assist the client in exploring spiritual goals and values and connecting with a larger life force, as this is often directly relevant to clinical conditions, especially depression and suicidality. Clients can be encouraged to pursue some form of regular activity, such as religious or meditative practices, that reinforce an internal sense of worth and a feeling of connection with life. Some people prefer formally structured activities such as attending services, doing mission outreach, listening to sermons, reading spiritual literature, singing hymns, saying prayers, and being a member of a congregation. Others prefer less structured, more autonomous activities such as reflection, retreat, attending to the natural world, spending time with animals, enacting cultural practices (e.g., family traditions or community rituals), reading philosophy, or doing general volunteer work. Many people enjoy a combination of these various activities.

- Guide the client toward a present and future orientation. Intrusive, traumatic memories, of course, need an appropriate treatment strategy. Resolution of regrets, mistakes, and missed opportunities (Freeman & DeWolf, 1989) as well as resentments and grudges (Kassinove & Tafrate, 2002; Nezu & Nezu, 2003) might be useful part of the client's therapy agenda. As a general strategy for building resilience and readiness for termination, the provider can assist the client in integrating positive memories to build self-esteem, improve life satisfaction, and focus on the task of moving on with life (King & Hicks, 2007; Singer, 2005).

- End with a beginning in mind. There is an old saying that "whenever a door closes, a window opens." Often this aphorism is invoked to activate hope in the face of loss, but it can also prompt a sense of purpose and direction at a time of transition, such as therapy termination. Therapy may begin with the problem list, but it ends with the resilience agenda. This agenda can be linked to the client's strengths, dreams, and aspirations, and broken down into specific behavioral targets, considering the client's stage of life development and health.

  For example, the client might make a list of 10 things he or she will begin (or continue) to work on independently at the close of therapy. Each of these actions is likened to the padding that the intervertebral disks provide in the spinal column and the muscles that hold the spine in place. Adequate padding will keep the client's problems from collapsing upon one another and causing psychic stenosis. Sufficient muscle strength will support the bones and padding and allow for better quality movement through life. Consider the following example of a resilience agenda that was developed as part of the process of termination.

Wanda's Resilience Agenda

1. Walk a mile most days. Build up to being able to walk three miles. Finish with at least five minutes of mindful stretching and breathing.
2. Plant an herb and flower garden.
3. Sign up for and attend an Italian cooking class.
4. Work on planning my dream trip to Italy.
5. Feed, water, and tickle my social life. At least once per week make plans to eat with someone, have drinks or coffee, make contact by phone or e-mail, or do something enjoyable with someone.
6. Attend a meditation retreat and find volunteer work.

Ending with some form of agenda helps to reinforce the idea that the provider believes in the client's capability, resourcefulness, and capacity to be responsible for doing well on their own. This does not necessarily mean that the client must "go it alone." Rather it means that the client is in charge of selecting goals, resources, and mentors to assist in their self-directed recovery.

DEVELOPMENTAL AND HEALTH-RELATED NEEDS

How Does Life Stage or Health Status Affect Termination Needs?

In the example of Wanda and the resilience agenda just described, what age would you estimate for her? What health status? What about her primary developmental tasks? More to the point, would any of these factors have an impact on her clinical needs at termination?

Developmental Perspective   Matters of life and health play a significant role in the client's needs for starting or concluding therapy. As people move through life, the challenges associated with maintaining a continuous subjective sense of identity while encountering and resolving primary psychosocial tasks (Erikson, 1963, 1968) are often the precipitants of help-seeking (Freeman, Felgoise & Davis, 2008). Considering Erikson's (1968) conceptualization of identity as consisting of three interacting domains – biological, psychological, and socio-cultural – it is easy to see how disruption in any of these realms can impact the continuity of character as perceived by self and others. Kroger's (2007) assessment of Erikson's optimal identity development "involves finding social roles and niches within the larger community that provide a good "fit" for one's biological and psychological capacities and interests" (p. 8). Although this begins in mid- to late adolescence, reformulations of the various tasks of identity development continue throughout the life span as one experiences changes in biological, psychological, and social domains. The central task of adolescence, identity versus role confusion (trouble with identity-defining commitments) serves as a building block for the tasks of adult life (intimacy vs. isolation, generativity vs. stagnation, and integrity vs. despair), and it reworks the tasks of earlier development (trust vs. mistrust, autonomy vs. doubt and shame, initiative vs. guilt, and industry vs. inferiority).

Thus, people frequently pursue psychological intervention to resolve symptoms that may be triggered by the biopsychosocial demands for identity change and re-stabilization, a state described by Erikson (1968) as an *identity crisis*. Life changes, transitions, and circumstances disrupt the known and familiar and create demands for new and perhaps unwanted roles. For example, the demands of shifting from high school to college, or into new parenthood, or from physically vigorous to medically fragile all require assuming a new role, a new position in relationship to others, and a new way of thinking about oneself and one's responsibilities and priorities. This can create an internal sense of turmoil, uncertainty, and disorganization or alienation from oneself. Presenting complaints in therapy often include the explicit statement: "I'm not myself anymore."

Naturally, the client's therapy goals usually include the desire to "Get my old self back" or "To get my new self moving." As providers we know that the old self is in a state of transformation, and the new self is in a state of formation. It is the sense of integration and confidence in a reformulated self that we hope to restore. The skill-building efforts and emotional support of therapy typically resonate with the matters of psychosocial development encountered for the first time or troublesome issues revisited. Can people be trusted? Am I capable on my own? Can I control myself? What are my interests and strengths, and what are those worth to the world around me? What is my role and status in life now? Who loves and cares about me? What else can I do in life? Did I make the right choices? How do I best prepare for the future? As we explore these questions, we aspire to help our clients understand their current psychological needs, interests, and personality style, their current physical attributes and capacities, and their prevailing social opportunities for fulfilling these capacities and interests.

At termination, the provider may want to evaluate how effectively the primary developmental issues have been addressed. The success of this resolution will impact what sort of additional support or follow up the client may need, if any. This depends in no small part on the nature of the developmental stress that precipitated the contact and the kind of resolution that was possible. Even though symptoms may have largely remitted, it could be important to extend the treatment contract to include the goal of resolving the developmental tasks and restoring subjective integration of identity and self-regulation, hopefully by tapping into the client's baseline strengths and helping them to build resilience. In the client's terms, we want to help them get their sense of self back, to feel comfortable in their skin again, and to feel a renewed energy, confidence, and hope.

Clinical Example A: Recovery and Developmental Readjustment. Wanda, the client noted above, entered therapy at age 49 due to recurrent depression, chronic post-traumatic stress disorder, chronic pain, and generalized anxiety disorder. About 18 months prior to being referred for therapy, she had been physically injured in a hostage situation where she worked, suffering damage to her back, neck, shoulder, and a broken arm. The psychological trauma was as significant as the physical injuries, as she had been set up and betrayed by a trusted co-worker. In the aftermath, she also felt betrayed by the administrative handling of the incident investigation, and especially by the unsympathetic and suspicious manner of a particular supervisor whom she had considered a personal friend. Recently, she had been diagnosed with rheumatoid arthritis, which was unrelated to the effects of her injuries but which added to her pain-management challenges.

Wanda was divorced with one grown son, unemployed and living on government-based disability income, preoccupied with managing chronic pain, and trying to function in the face of persistent and pervasive psychological and physical distress. She had a history of depressive episodes and had always been a "worrier." Prior to the trauma, though, she had been trusting, somewhat outgoing, and could recall happy periods and positive relationships in her life. Since the incident, she had become more isolated and depressed, repeating wistfully, "I just wish I could have my old life back." Money was tight; she lived alone in subsidized housing and was frequently overwhelmed by fears of physical attack from malevolent people around her (with some realistic basis), worsening pain, social catastrophe (evil forces and the war), medical maltreatment, loss of her meager resources (unstable social services), and stressful social demands from her family.

Wanda developed a good relationship with the provider and participated in an extended course of therapy (more than 50 sessions). Her symptoms began to diminish as she reworked issues of *trust* (Can I trust the person behind me in the check-out line at the discount store not to pull a gun on me or grab me?), *control* (What can I do to manage this pain?), *industry* (It's not my fault that I can no longer work like I used to; I'm not a bum; I do the work that I can), and *intimacy* (My family really loves me and wants me around; I can assert my needs to make it more pleasant) that had all been affected by her trauma and changes in health status.

Wanda had lost her connection with any useful or appealing social role and, as a result, struggled a great deal with her sense of *identity*. Her tendency to dwell on the past absorbed much of her energy and interfered with focusing on the present or future. In her depressed mood, she ruminated about past mistakes, such as the error of taking the job where she was injured. She located her most successful and important identity in the past, as she bemoaned being divorced, her child now grown, and her tasks as a wife and mother finished. Her physical self-image was diminished by aging, injury, illness, and pain, and that made her hopeless about the possibility of any new intimate partnerships. "Who wants a crippled old lady over 50, always in pain, can't really do much of anything fun anymore," she wondered. "Besides, I don't think it's safe to trust men anyway." So she avoided thinking about the present and future because it seemed so hopeless.

Working on *generativity* helped her to move beyond this plateau as she explored various dreams, aspirations, and options to build energy, enthusiasm, and a sense of purpose in life. She was encouraged by the task of reviewing strengths that had served her well earlier in life, such as her interest in people and overall kindness, her persistence, and her previous willingness to try new things. Exploring ways that she could tap into her creative interests was also a great help to her. As noted in her resilience agenda, Wanda enjoyed cooking, growing and using herbs and flowers, and shopping for bargains that she collected for gift-giving occasions and rituals. She liked to cook special recipes to contribute to family dinners and to bring small trinkets for her nieces and nephews that she'd found at the dollar store. Eventually she found two part-time volunteer jobs that she enjoyed. One was distributing movies to the families and children at the Children's Hospital once per week, and the other was being a tutor with an adult literacy program. Both options helped to restore her sense that there were people she could trust in the world and that she had something to offer, in spite of her own physical challenges.

Wanda continued in intermittent follow-up therapy as support for her efforts to create and sustain her "new normal." She came for a session every few months, and increased the frequency when she needed additional support. Her symptoms of depression diminished, anxiety was confined to specific situational triggers, and pain was reasonably well managed. To maintain her recovery, she used a variety of resources, including reaching out to her therapist for emotional support, encouragement, reminders of the positive perspective, and new ideas on ways to cope. The provider's last contacts with Wanda focused on the satisfactions she felt at the end of her life (*integrity*), when at age 58 she developed ovarian cancer and died a few months after her diagnosis.

Clinical Example B: Recovery and Developmental Fulfillment.   After several years of recurring cycles of Bipolar Disorder, Nancy achieved extended symptom remission through medication, psychotherapy, and life-style management. She continued a regimen of medication but terminated regular therapy, following up occasionally for specific stress management consultations (e.g., once per year or so). Her life was busy and satisfying, her work was going well (*industry*), and her relationships with family and friends were good (*trust; intimacy*). However, she was disappointed that her dream of marriage and children had not been fulfilled, and she believed that, at the age of 41, her window of opportunity was pretty well closed (*isolation; role loss*). Her history of illness was a particular sensitivity and the main reason, she believed, that this possibility was lost forever. "Even if I found a guy that I liked at this point, who is going to want someone with all this psychiatric baggage?" (*shame; inferiority*).

Nancy's active efforts to build social ties and connection through a community volunteer job (*resilience*) led to meeting Tom. To her surprise, Tom was a great guy who offered stability and levity, tremendous love for her, and a chance to fulfill her unfulfilled life dreams. Even though Tom knew all about her psychiatric history, he held her in the highest regard and declared her company as his good fortune. Tom and Nancy fell in love and were considering marriage. Before she could proceed, Nancy had to rework some concerns with *inferiority* and *identity* that were triggered by the differences between her real love and the fantasized ideal that she had carried around for years. Tom was not wealthy or famous, so marriage to him meant that she would stay in her job, still have to balance a budget, and remain in the same social circles. However, one of her strengths was insight into the emotional sources of her concerns: the financial instability of her family during her years growing up and the social stigma she had internalized because of that and her illness. For years, her compensatory tactic was to dream of marrying a rich, important man so that she would feel internally whole, secure, and worthwhile in the eyes of society. The quality of their *intimacy*, however, inspired her *trust* and willingness to relinquish the fantasy in favor of a real life commitment (*identity*).

Tom and Nancy were married in a lovely ceremony at a historic mansion. The bride, radiant in her traditional white gown whimsically paired with sparkling ruby red slippers, was surrounded by family, friends, a beaming groom, and two adoring stepdaughters. Later that year, Nancy sent a holiday card that included photos from the wedding and a picture of their newly established, cozy family home in the suburbs. Nancy continued intermittent follow-up contacts with the therapist for consultation on dealing with various issues associated with her new role and identity, such as managing the balance of work and family and deciding whether or not to attempt biological parenthood. Her story of recovery is essentially that through creativity, reaching out to others, willingness to take risks, persistence, and insight she lived happily ever after in the life that she feared her illness would prevent. The end of her therapy is an ongoing process, as she continues to build the skills of resilience.

PRACTICAL CONCERNS

How Can I Handle Practical Concerns about Time, Convenience, and Money?

Time, convenience of access, and money are pragmatic issues for all clients. Client decisions about therapy are affected by the combined extent of their resources in each of these areas and their level of motivation for therapy. Highly motivated clients might easily resolve practical challenges but only to the extent allowed by the range of their resources. Ambivalent clients may be most open to problem solving and support in resolving their practical concerns, but they are vulnerable to letting such issues become stumbling blocks. For the truly reluctant client, barriers of time, convenience, or money provide a handy rationale for their decision to opt out, despite the possibilities for resolving their concerns. The provider's task is to help remove barriers, reduce unnecessary or premature termination, and facilitate client continuation when indicated without crossing the line into forcing or manipulating the client. A sensitive, tactful, and flexible discussion of time, convenience, and money can be essential in negotiating this task.

Clients need sufficient resources to effectively engage in a process of change (DiClemente, 2006). Thus, it is important to assess the client's goals and resources of time, access, and financial support at the beginning of therapy to see how well these match. If there is a significant discrepancy between the client's expectations and his or her resources that adjustments can not reconcile, it may be best to limit or stop the effort. Proceeding with therapy without the resources to satisfy the client's expectations can be likened to traveling out on a bridge that does not reach the other side (Younggren & Gottlieb, in press), which is ill advised.

Time and Convenience   "With my schedule, I'm not sure how I will be able to make regular therapy appointments or deal with all the traffic and parking." Available time and personal convenience affect the client's perceptions of his or her ability to make use of therapy. If the client already has high demands on his or her time, added tasks will raise the stress level. Making and keeping appointments, getting away from work or home obligations, negotiating the travel involved in getting to the practitioner's office, making up for missed work or arranging for childcare, and finding time and energy to complete homework are all part of the costs of therapy. The client will measure these costs against the expected benefit and their assessment of whether or not professional help is needed.

A flexible, open approach to therapy termination demonstrates respect and understanding of these circumstances. Practitioners may be able to accommodate the client's schedule or help the client set goals that are within reach of his or her available resources. Or, if a time crunch is going to improve in the near future, the client may wish to postpone therapy until more time is available. For example, a change in work or family circumstance may be anticipated in the near future when a project is completed or the children return to school. The provider can suggest that therapy be temporarily discontinued and resumed when conditions are more amenable or with an alternate provider located closer to the client's home, work, or school. Of course, this recommendation assumes that the client is reasonably stable and the problem is not urgent or imminently life threatening. Otherwise, therapy is likely to be more productive when the client can reasonably devote sufficient time to the process and when the convenience costs do not overtax resources. The provider who takes an understanding and collaborative stance demonstrates respect for the client and fosters the client's sense of being accepted and in control of the process.

Finances and Managed Care   In day-to-day practice, the clinical needs, preferences, and progress of each client must be reconciled with available financial resources. All therapy has a cost, even if the client pays nothing directly out of pocket. Regardless of the level of financial remuneration, resources of practitioner time and administrative or facility overhead are used every time therapy is delivered. Sometimes the client or someone who financially supports the client covers these costs. More often, costs are shared. The client provides a partial payment and the remaining costs are subsidized by a third party, such as commercial health insurance, government health insurance, or research funded by the government or corporate entities. Practitioners and facilities also subsidize care when they accept insurance discounts, offer sliding scales, assume unreimbursed charges that may never be collected, or provide free services.

Sharing of costs helps to broaden the spectrum of access to services. However, it also creates the need for some agreement on how resources will be used and how costs can be contained and distributed. Therapy may have to be administered in brief segments due to financial constraints and the need for oversight. Therapy that is mostly or entirely funded by government or other public sources is usually limited to the fewest number of sessions with the greatest administrative scrutiny. For example, a publicly funded agency might have a guideline of limiting therapy to 12 sessions with further continuation contingent upon urgency of need and appropriateness of service.

When therapy is subsidized by private sources such as employers via contracts with insurance carriers, resources tend to be a bit more liberal. Streamlined outpatient therapy might be partially funded at a discounted rate for up to 25 or 30 sessions, sometimes with a management review for each segment of 8 or 10 sessions. A deluxe insurance contract might cover up to 50 subsidized outpatient visits at a discounted rate with minimal management review. As they have evolved over the past two decades, the various procedures for sharing costs and managing care have become routine for most providers of direct services.

When dealing with subsidized or managed care, providers are working at the juncture where public value meets private concern. This precipitates some inevitable tensions in justifying the need for services and in reconciling the client's needs and desires with limited resources. Some of the most challenging terminations essentially require the provider to explain and implement the boundaries of the cost-sharing system. Providers are not in a position to renegotiate the clients' benefits as these are set by the third party. Unfortunately, it may be that the client does not really understand the limits of their particular options until they are sitting in your office. This is why it is imperative that the provider preempt the shock of a sudden termination whenever possible by assessing available financial resources at the outset of therapy and attempting to make sure that the client understands these parameters and their implications.

Clients with low income, unstable employment, or otherwise limited resources are apt to be most dependent on highly subsidized care. These clients may also have the most severe problems and the greatest degree of ongoing life stress. Clients with greater financial resources typically have more options in terms of length and type of therapy. Not only are their insurance benefits apt to be more extensive, but they may also have more degrees of freedom to directly pay for services beyond subsidized benefits. In any of these circumstances, the key termination strategy is to collaborate with the client in choosing treatment goals that are within range of his or her resources. If there can only be 12 or 20 sessions, then treatment goals can be targeted toward what can be achieved in that length of time. If therapy might extend beyond that time frame, then additional goals might be considered.

Ethical practitioners want to provide the most benefit at the least cost to every client and the overall system. There is no ethical or professional expectation that clinicians should provide therapy upon demand, but there is the expectation that services are limited to those needed by the client. When making decisions about offering reduced fees or free care, they are guided by ethical aspirations toward fairness in access to service for all who need it. Often this means limiting free or reduced fee services to those with definite need and no access to other reimbursable options. Clients who have insurance benefits but simply choose not to use them would typically be denied a fee waiver. Some managed care contracts may disallow free continuation of care beyond authorization because of the expectation that providers only provide necessary care. If the care was proven to be necessary, the insurance carrier would authorize it. Providers are generally expected to take an active role in helping clients understand available options, set priorities among competing demands, and develop a plan for working efficiently within those limits. Steps that help to maximize benefits include steering the client toward methods most likely to be helpful, keeping track of the number of sessions as needed and verifying client agreement with pertinent contingencies, such as personal liability for costs beyond a certain point. Good use of smaller segments of therapy can be encouraged by orienting the client toward a positive perspective on the value of incremental effort and resolving large problems through a successive accumulation of small changes across time. In addition, it is important to remember the value of a warm, caring, and respectful relationship as fundamental to efficient and effective therapy. Wise providers recognize that it is possible to offer such a relationship within a limited scope of therapy and strive to do so.

SUMMARY POINTS FOR APPLIED PRACTICE

1. When making termination decisions, attempt to balance consideration of the client's cultural, social, clinical and developmental, and practical needs with available resources.

2. Be sure you are capable of understanding and responding effectively to salient aspects of the client's cultural identity. If not, termination and referral is appropriate.

3. If the client's personal support system is antagonistic to therapy, he or she may need help in managing this emotional cost. Otherwise, the client may worsen or abruptly drop out of therapy, carrying a burden of unnecessary guilt.

4. For clients with few social resources and a higher need of social support, it is important to maintain a clinical focus and good professional boundaries in the continuing relationship. Encourage the best possible adaptations beyond therapy and remain alert to the potential for client over-dependence.

5. Many challenges in the expected termination process may be a function of particular personality styles or disorders. Conceptualizing a cognitive profile of a client's beliefs about the provider, therapy, and termination can help predict some of the likely challenges. Termination strategies can follow directly from this conceptualization, reducing the risks of conflicts, emotional stress, or other adverse reactions to termination.

6. Among clients with Cluster A Personality Disorders, termination challenges tend to focus on prevention of early termination. Among clients with Cluster B Personality Disorders, termination challenges frequently involve matters of limits and boundaries. For clients with Cluster C Personality Disorders, the termination challenges may center on the client's ability to function confidently and effectively without the provider's direct support.

7. Chronic, recurrent, and co-morbid conditions present significant challenges to termination decisions. One option is to attempt continuous care whenever feasible. Another option is to emphasize the possibilities of resilience and recovery. The resilience/recovery perspective builds on a notion of sufficient support but does not assume that continuous care is the sole option. Recovery means that the client assumes increased responsibility for achieving self-management,

and that the provider serves as a support to this process. The duration and intensity of contact with the provider is determined by the overall balance of the client's needs, the scope of resources available, and the client's preferences.

8. Resilience is the antidote to psychic stenosis. Resilience is a set of learned skills that contribute to the client's ability to bounce back from illness, stress, and trauma. Therapy with clients who have chronic, recurrent, or co-morbid conditions can be conceptualized as a partnership designed to mentor the client in the skills and attributes of a resilient person. The provider's partnership is only one component of a broad system of support, and this partnership has limits. However, if the client is oriented toward acquiring and practicing resilience, he or she will recognize many opportunities for reinforcing and developing these vital skills.

9. Issues of biopsychosocial development provide a fundamental context for understanding the client's progress and ultimate readiness for termination. The appropriate point of termination for any disorder will always vary to some extent because each client is a different, whole person with unique developmental strengths, needs, and cultural resources.

10. Practical matters are important to a successful therapy experience and a good termination. Make sure the time, cost, and convenience of proposed therapy are compatible with the client's resources. If adjustments are not possible or agreeable, this is a valid reason to redirect the client to other providers or resources.

7

Provider Challenges

Key Issues Addressed in This Chapter

- I am not sure that we talk enough about termination.
- I worry that this client will never be able to terminate therapy.
- I can't seem to satisfy this client.
- My client has disappeared and does not return my call.
- I've just been fired.
- My client has suddenly died.
- I can not seem to let go.
- I think I mishandled termination.
- I have lost control of the therapy relationship and don't know how to terminate.
- I'm feeling burned out. How can I get my enthusiasm back?

TERMINATION DISSONANCE

Termination is one of the most important boundaries in therapy, yet we often take for granted its easy management. From terminations that are highly satisfying to those that are downright disturbing, the provider's emotional experience receives scant, if any, attention. Counter-transference is the term traditionally used to describe the provider's emotional reactions to the process of therapy. Although the model of therapy used here is learning-based and does not conceptualize transference in the same way as other dynamic models, we nevertheless appreciate that both client and provider bring a set of interpersonal response biases into the therapeutic relationship. As various termination scenarios unfold, the provider experiences a range of personal emotional reactions that might be called "counter-transference." Being able to recognize, understand, and regulate one's own emotional reactions to termination is a fundamental applied skill that is necessary for effective work. Perhaps the window of opportunity for sealing success or souring one's efforts might be found in the ways that providers deal with these emotional experiences. In this chapter, several matters of therapist counter-transference are considered, some very common and some much less frequent.

Objectivity is an indispensable tool for basing termination on sound reasons rather than the sway of difficult emotions or client persuasion. Objectivity in this context implies an awareness and ability to appraise one's own feelings and reactions as a functional component of the communication process. We don't just calculate a formula and send out a notice of termination. Nor do we operate casually, responding to whims and fleeting impulses. In this relationship, we carry a fiduciary duty to the client and an obligation to protect and maintain our personal and professional integrity and stability in each judgment we make.

When considering termination, we deliberate, assess our feelings, decide to take action or not, and reassess our feelings. Do we feel confident, certain, or clear about the next steps to take? Or do we feel hesitant, concerned, unsure, frustrated, worried, startled, anxious, guilty, confused, demoralized, or detached? If we feel any of these unsettled emotions, does that mean that we have somehow erred and need to implement corrective action? Such emotional reactions deserve attention as a rich source of information about the particular termination, as a guidepost for evaluating one's professional actions, and as a barometer of one's state of resilience and emotional competence.

I Am Not Sure That We Are Talking Enough about Termination

With all the focus on planning and strategy, one might become concerned about devoting enough time and attention to the task of termination. Before assuming that you should be doing more, it is important to assess whether or not this is really a problem. How much is "enough"? We have already discussed the trials of bringing this subject into focus and the nuances of our reticence (Chapter Four). If you are neglecting to address termination in the initial informed consent, this can be rectified by updating your forms and procedures. Otherwise, once therapy has begun, it is unlikely that there will normally be any more than brief discussion of termination until the first and subsequent progress reviews. Each time that termination is addressed, it is helpful to make note of it in the client's record. This is evidence that the provider attended to this fundamental task, involved the client in developing a reasonable course of action and maintained an appropriate standard of care.

More forethought on termination in early sessions is needed only if there are indications that complex termination might become an issue (Chapter Six). Otherwise, the focus is on building the therapeutic alliance and its appropriate direction, which will hopefully reduce the risk of early termination. The exceptions to this occur with clients who are in the pre-contemplation stage of change and are not ready to progress beyond the first few sessions, with clients who do not feel a compatible rapport with the provider and may transfer within the first few sessions, or with clients who enter therapy imminently ready to change and are able to rapidly complete their objectives and thus terminate appropriately within the first dozen meetings. After the initial discussion and informed consent review, the provider's attention is usually focused on being alert to early termination potential and attempting to respond to that in the most appropriate way.

As therapy proceeds, termination requires deliberate attention primarily if particular circumstantial reasons precipitate it (Chapter Four). If the provider talks about termination too much during this working portion of therapy, the client might feel unduly pressured or misconstrue this as an intention to dispose of them. Talking too little about termination, however, creates the false impression that therapy can and will proceed without limits or that the client is entitled to unending service. Avoiding talk of termination altogether can raise the client's anxiety about being trapped in therapy that never ends or foster the wishful assumption that the therapist is permanently available. Therapy that proceeds with no consideration of potential termination may lack focus or attention to client responsibility. It can also subtly reinforce an unproductive pessimism about the client's possibility of improvement and recovery. If the provider feels immobilized and unable to bring up the topic of termination, this is an indication of the need for consultation to review the case conceptualization and assess whether personal issues might be impinging on the provider's actions.

Clients who are functionally well organized and pursuing focused goals usually do fine with minimal advance planning for termination. It could be quite satisfactory to discuss their improvements in one session, and then to draw things to a close within one or two more sessions. Once the improvement is noted, this client may execute a flexible termination without returning for the closing discussion, perhaps canceling the wrap-up visit. This may not reflect a reluctance to deal with termination as much as it reflects the client's satisfaction and restored sense of competence and self-efficacy. If therapy has been established as a consulting resource to which they can return at their discretion, then there is little compelling need to further process their feelings and say goodbye. The client may feel that time and convenience costs exceed the benefits of what appear to be mainly formalities. From the client's point of view, termination is merely a matter of deciding that they have received enough help. Any discomfort the provider feels may be a function of the notion that extensive discussion, processing, and saying goodbye are a necessary part of every termination, and that he or she is risking substandard professional performance by not "getting" the client to come in for a termination session or to uncover feelings of sadness over the separation.

One simple way to assess the question of whether or not termination has been discussed "enough" is to estimate how much discussion this particular client might need at this particular point in time. Some need very little discussion to settle the matter without conflict. Others need quite a bit of discussion to address potentially maladaptive reactions. Conflicted clients are likely to avoid the subject, and may need gentle but persistent prompting and support for their autonomy. Acutely disturbed or volatile clients may not be able to discuss termination productively at all and need the provider's authoritative management of limits and boundaries. Depending on the nature of one's practice, it may be that most clients need only a modest amount of strategically chosen termination discussion to help them feel comfortable and empowered in reaching closure.

I Worry That This Client Will Never Be Able to Terminate Therapy

If therapy feels like a forever assignment, the first question to ask is "Why does it continue?" This will help to distinguish therapy with a distinct purpose from therapy that continues but lacks realistic goals. Explore the question of what you think would happen if therapy were discontinued very soon. This can offer clues to the personal emotional reactions that might be affecting your approach to termination. Suppose you are apprehensive that the client would become discouraged and hopeless about the future and be harmed by the loss of regular sessions. You don't want to take any risks until you are certain that the client's problems are "fixed" and he or she will not need to return. This suggests that your core beliefs or schemas reflect Demanding Standards (Leahy, 2007a) for your professional work. When this schema is operative, the provider may be prone to focus too little on the client's responsibility for acquiring and using skills of resilience and too much on using his or her competence as a curative element. There are risks in the client staying too comfortable and depending on the provider's strength. It may be less taxing in the short run but frustrating in the long run.

Perhaps you are worried that the client's life will go into a tailspin if therapy is discontinued (catastrophizing). Maybe you fear that termination is tantamount to abandonment and your professional reputation will be destroyed (ruination fears). For some providers, the acts of worrying, checking, and staying close are important ways to demonstrate affiliation and caring, so that they and the client feel secure. This is a merging of positive beliefs about worry with relationship schemas about value, caretaking, and self worth (worry bonding). The conditional beliefs stipulate that, if someone is important to you, you should express that by taking care of them and worrying about them. Worry is assumed to be a form of care taking that helps the designee stay safe. So the very act of worrying about the client is a schema-driven tactic to show that you care and want to help them stay safe. If you value and help others, they will appreciate and value you. Valuing, caring, and worrying about others are thus ways to ensure one's own security and sense of worth.

Beliefs associated with the schema for worry and bonding can play a role in interminable therapy. To tease this apart, it may be useful to ask yourself a few questions. Do you think that bringing up termination will make you seem cold or uncaring to the client? Do you think that the client needs for you to worry about them? Do you think that if the client did terminate, you would worry even more about the client's well-being? A sequence of interlocking assumptions and conditional beliefs might go something like this: "Worrying will help you (client) stay safe and show you that I care. If I just tell you I care, you won't feel as well-protected as you do when I worry about you." On the other hand, "If I bring up the idea of termination, I will seem cold or uncaring and this will hurt you." Or it may be that "I don't want to consider termination because I would worry too much about you." Perhaps it even feels dangerous to stop worrying about the client.

Worrying about the client can reinforce a mutual care-taking dynamic, where the client must stay in therapy to reduce your tension and worry. You want to keep checking on their well-being as a means of reducing your worry. Perhaps the client comes to depend on you to signal the cessation of worry. Excessive worry can interfere with the client's progress toward recovery and independence, and it reinforces the tendency to use worry as a way to communicate positive affiliation for client and provider. Understanding our own thoughts and beliefs can give us rapid access to constructive understanding of the emotional impasses in our work and the techniques to solve them (Leahy, 2003; 2007b).

The next question is "What would it take for this client to be able to terminate therapy?" This is a question first for the provider's reflection and second to spark discussion that might infuse new energy and productive direction into the therapy. It may come to light that the client does not see his or her potential to terminate or understand the role of collaborator in the task of making decisions about termination. Perhaps the focus has been exclusively on demonstrating the need for continuing therapy (i.e., what symptoms do I still have) to the relative neglect of increasing self-management or resilience skills (what can I do effectively on my own). It may be that the client has a reasonable base of skills, but needs to practice greater independence in deploying those skills. Research on the protective functions of cognitive behavior therapy suggests that at first conscious efforts to think and behave differently are required, but over time there is a shift in the proclivities and ways that information is automatically processed that stabilize this new level of functioning (Hollon, et al., 2006). Finally, termination readiness might be increased by considering developmental issues and readjustments (as discussed in Chapter Six).

Worry that the client may never terminate could also reflect a very different perspective, that of caring *too little* for the client. Perhaps the provider feels that therapy is interminable because they dislike working with this client and wish that they could end the work as soon as possible. This is a form of interference or impasse in the therapeutic alliance that may be resolvable if the provider can determine the source of dislike and develop a plan for coping or remediation. It may also be a function of therapist burnout, particularly if the provider is experiencing these feelings about more than one client or clients in general. Two provider issues that may be triggering the dislike are (a) skill limits for dealing with the client's problems and (b) conflict and sensitivity to the particular nature of the client's problems. Clinicians may find that consultation is useful for sorting this out and arriving at a reasoned plan for either improving the situation or terminating the therapy because the provider is not the right person for the job.

A constructive view of the future is an important barometer of the vitality of therapy and its potential progress. Becoming stuck in a perennially repetitive or aversive process is certainly frustrating and is a significant challenge. This does not necessarily signify that therapy will never end or that it should end promptly, only that it is potentially over because it seems to be going nowhere productive. Looking inward to our thoughts and beliefs can often provide key information about the impasse and how to solve it. With this useful information, provider and client have a better chance of finding a renewed sense of direction and purpose or the means for consolidating and ending their contact.

I Can't Seem to Satisfy This Client

It is easiest to end therapy when goals have been met, the client feels satisfied and empowered, and the therapist feels a sense of mastery in his or her work. It is much harder to end therapy when there is disappointment over what could not be accomplished ("We should have been able to do more"), frustration with the amount of effort invested in trying to satisfy the client ("I tried and tried and nothing worked"), regret over sunk costs ("I should have seen this sooner"), relief for the end of a stressful interaction ("At least it's over"), anxiety about the implications of client dissatisfaction ("I hope I don't get sued or anything"), or self-punishment ("I should not have let this happen").

The vexation of an unsatisfied client can strike deep into a provider's view of themselves as a competent and worthwhile clinician. Most providers will try to retain the client and make every effort to assuage the client's prevailing concerns. Clinically, this is a reasonable way to proceed, if one can build a working conceptualization that effectively targets the clinical and interpersonal reasons for the dissatisfaction. Otherwise, the risks of prolonging an unproductive therapy are elevated when the source of the dissatisfaction is not clear or the result of a poor therapeutic alliance. Problems in the therapeutic alliance are particularly common among clients with personality disorders, as one might expect as a function of the disorder itself.

Being persistent and adaptable is by and large a strength that serves the mental health clinician quite well in the work of treating a variety of behavioral and emotional disorders. Every client is different and very few of their problems will vanish in one or two easy steps. However, these traits can become liabilities when the provider is embroiled in a struggle to prove his or her worth to a client who will not be pleased. If the client's complaints persist and can not be resolved, it is certainly reasonable and potentially necessary to propose termination on the basis of incompatibility (Chapter Four, "I am not the right person for the job."). This is not failure as much as it is a battle where it is more productive not to try to win.

In dealing with the emotional stress of this type of termination, it can help to evaluate your potential to learn from the experience rather than become trapped in self-recrimination or negative comparisons (Demanding Standards again). For example, one does not want too hold tightly to ideas such as "I should have done a better job," or "Dr. Perfect doesn't have these problems; he has only satisfied clients." Instead, you can first check the potential validity of the dissatisfaction. Do the complaints "ring true" in any way, perhaps reiterating something you recognize in yourself or your situation that sometimes irritates other clients? For example, *are* you a bit too breezy in your attitude at times? Does the traffic and parking around your office border on ridiculous at times? The complaints may or may not be resolvable, but the client might have pinpointed some realistic concerns that could affect the satisfaction of other clients as well.

It also helps to form some clinical hypotheses about the client's behavior. What makes the client choose to attack you with these concerns? Is it because you deserve to be attacked? Of course that is not so. The client is trying to communicate something, and this is the form chosen. So what might that indicate? It could mean that the client has learned that complaining pays off with better service, more attention, and a feeling of control. Or it could mean that the client is having trouble forming a bond with you, for any number of reasons that are hard to understand and articulate. Maybe you resemble the sister who tormented their childhood. Or you are nothing like dear Dr. Perfect, the therapist they used to see. Some clients come to therapy with a condensed image of miraculous therapy and a provocative therapist that is based on media glamorization. The real thing just isn't dazzling or quick enough for them.

The real puzzler is the all-too-common pattern of the client who asks for concrete suggestions, ignores the provider's recommendations and even overtly rejects and trivializes the methods, and then complains about a lack of results. Actually, this is not so puzzling after all. One explanation can be found in the same reason why people declare that diets don't work or there are no good men (women) left. Crafting a solution or a change takes effort and may involve discomfort. The end result may be only an approximation of the grand changes envisioned by the client. This is not compatible with the expectation that change is something that happens by external forces, a painless automatic transformation into one's fantasy ideal, rather than an action that is constructed or accrued bit by bit over time to achieve realistic goals. It is just too tedious and ordinary to think that everything counts, even small efforts and obvious ideas. The client may be stuck on hectoring you on *your* limitations because it is safer than letting both of you take a good look at their limitations and try to do something about them.

SUDDEN OR CRISIS TERMINATIONS

Sometimes termination is startling and even downright shocking to the provider. Like any undesirable event that happens without warning, it can produce feelings of confusion and distress and leave one worried and wondering about what to do next.

My Client Has Disappeared and Does Not Return My Calls

If a client does not follow through with rescheduling or fails to show for an appointment and does not return your calls, it is possible that he or she has terminated without specific notice. This oblique termination is indirect and unsettling in its ambiguity. Therapist emotional responses to client disappearance can run the gamut from frustration and annoyance to concern and worry or surprise, bewilderment, embarrassment, even relief or some combination of feelings. It is often useful to seek more information on the client's intention and to attempt a closing consultation. However, the client's actions may preclude this if he or she simply does not respond to reasonable inquiry. In addition, there may be times that the provider deems it best to await the client's initiative in following up.

Failure to return can be interpreted in the overall context of the client's history, progress, current issues, and recent developments. For example, an established client may have a pattern of stopping whenever current pressure is alleviated yet predictably returning if stresses escalate or symptoms return. Many clients offer an implied or indirect message of termination that encapsulates their simultaneous intention to discontinue immediate meetings but wish to retain the option to return if needed. For example, the client might cancel due to immediate circumstances and indicate an intention to call for rescheduling at an indeterminate future time. In an established relationship, the client's communication can be understood in the context of how the relationship has worked over time. The *style* may be abrupt and indicative of a need for better communication skills, but it does not have to precipitate a crisis for the provider.

The experience of having a client unexpectedly disappear without cancellation or response to attempts to contact them tends to be more disturbing and difficult to resolve. The lack of closure can provoke the clinician's fears and self-recriminations. "What went wrong? What did I miss? What if something bad has happened?" What's more, it is difficult to know if there is anything else one can do to achieve better resolution.

Providers need to have some means of achieving closure with this dangling relationship. There is no need to panic or fear the most dreadful situation or to go to extraordinary lengths to make contact, unless you have just cause to predict specific danger. Providers can use their discretion in selecting a course of action on a case-by-case basis. Some clients might respond positively to a prompt, some will not care much either way, and some do not want to be re-contacted. If a follow-up contact seems appropriate, it may be sufficient to simply call and leave a message, inviting the client to re-contact you at their discretion. Possible messages might be something like the following: *"I haven't heard from you and wanted to follow up. If you want to reschedule, please feel free to call me at your convenience."* Some clients will call fairly soon to reschedule, perhaps with a circumstantial explanation or an admission of ambivalence or symptomatic immobilization. Others will call just to check back and let you know they feel ready to stop for now. Some clients may follow up weeks, months, or even years later. Some will never call again.

The client's right to choose a course of action is strictly respected at all times, and pressuring a client to return to therapy should be avoided, although the provider can express interest and concern for the client's well-being. Clinical discretion is important in determining the right amount of follow-up effort based on the client, the circumstances, and the severity of the client's problems (Bennett et al., 2006). There is no standard formula to follow because situations can vary substantially. The provider has to find the appropriate balance between reasonable and caring efforts and what could be construed as unnecessary, intrusive or inappropriate efforts. At some point, it can be concluded that the *client* has abandoned therapy.

All phone calls related to oblique termination should be documented in the client's file to establish a record of the provider's efforts to follow-up. Providers who conduct these communications via email can save a copy of the correspondence in the client's file. Sending a formal letter of case closure to clients who have obliquely terminated is an option, but not absolutely necessary. Some agencies may have a policy that requires formal termination notice because clients who return after abandoning therapy are either refused service or required to re-enter the waiting list as a new client. In other circumstances where this requirement does not apply, the provider needs to weigh the potential impact of a formal termination letter. Although one may have conscientious intentions, the functional impact on the client could be more negative than positive. The client could feel embarrassed or scolded for missing therapy. They might resent the provider's controlling stance and feel deprived of the opportunity to resolve ambivalence on their own terms. They could interpret the letter to mean that the therapist is "breaking up" with them and if there was an opportunity to return, it is now closed. However, in high-risk situations where the client clearly left in anger or the provider is explicitly terminating the therapy relationship and the client opposes this plan, a formal letter is warranted. Providers in such circumstances are encouraged to seek appropriate professional and legal consultation before executing any written documents.

Providers should have a general policy on what they can reasonably tolerate in terms of repeated cancellations and rescheduling. There are many reasons that clients fail to attend sessions and most providers strive to be humane and considerate of the clientele they serve. At the same time, the provider must balance being adaptable with the necessity of running a practice and keeping a schedule, and the need to ensure that therapy is providing some benefit. The general termination policy can reflect a non-pejorative stance that respects the client's right to terminate without notice, allows some provision for returning to therapy if appropriate, sets expectations for the client's responsibility to make and keep appointments, offers assistance with accessing other resources and follows a consistent plan for disposition. Provider emotional reactions to unprocessed departure are apt to be less disruptive if one recognizes that it happens and, although it may be frustrating or disappointing, it can be handled in a routine way.

I've Just Been Fired

There are two types of precipitous terminations that might be imposed on the provider. One is when your employment contract is discontinued, and you must make termination arrangements for an entire caseload, sometimes with little advance notice. The other is when the client abruptly fires you, which may or may not be a contentious situation.

Employment Termination   Release from employment might come as a shock, or it might have been anticipated as the signals accumulated. In this context, there are four tasks that need particular attention in addition to the six essential steps for termination. The additional tasks for crisis termination are (a) deal with your own crisis, (b) protect clients from negative impact, (c) clarify your obligations, and (d) move on. Recall that the six essential steps for termination are (a) review and discuss progress;

(b) pinpoint the reasons and potential client concerns; (c) identify legal and ethical obligations; (d) evaluate risk exposure, risk management, and need for consultation; (e) provide notification and pre-termination counseling; and (f) establish disposition and note in the record.

Elements of your own crisis will obviously follow the circumstances of your personal situation. However, given that loss of employment is a fairly universal stressor, it is understandable to feel some degree of shock, embarrassment, anger over forced changes, worry about one's professional reputation, concern about future opportunities, anxiety about income, or distress over organizational issues, politics, and quality of care. Maybe the job loss is a relief and a blessing in disguise, but most people don't greet this news with a euphoric "hallelujah." At least not at first they don't. So take time to recognize and validate your own feelings, regroup, and mobilize whatever support and coping resources you need.

Dealing adequately with your own emotional reactions is a critical step in preparing to inform your clients of the impending change. Clients need to be protected from your distress or adversity and focused instead on reviewing their options and resolving their relationship with you. Providers want to avoid drawing upon clients' sympathy or trying to align them on your side in opposition to your employer. It is more important to prepare to answer questions about the reason for the separation, and to explain things with an appropriate degree of professional perspective. It may be helpful to practice what you plan to say to clients with a trusted colleague to evaluate the impact of your delivery. Making recommendations that will help clients choose what to do about therapy pending your departure is a priority. As you help each one size up their personal situation, you can list the options and thus assist in the orderly transfer or resolution of care.

If the relationship between you and the employer is highly contentious, it is important not to retaliate in any way that involves or could harm the clients. For example, it would not be prudent to dramatically quit on the spot, walk out, and never return, thus abandoning your clinical responsibilities. Restrain any impulses to destroy records, slander the other staff or administration to the clients, or take any other action that might express your anger but damage your professional integrity. If your employer wants an immediate separation and insists that you leave promptly, make it clear that you are ethically obligated to assist in the orderly transfer of care. If the organization plans to have another staff member handle the transfers, you should know which person is designated for the task, and provide your follow-up contact information to that person so that clients can reach you if they wish to do so.

It may be pertinent to remind your employer that it is unethical to deny employment solely on the basis of being the subject of an ethics complaint (APA, 2002, 1.08). Even if a clinician must cease practice as determined by a formal disciplinary order issued by a state licensing board, clients should be allowed the opportunity to handle termination issues. For example, in an Agreed Order that suspended a psychologist's license for unprofessional conduct and other charges, the state of Tennessee (6/11/2004) stipulated a 30-day period before the suspension took effect "to allow for the orderly transfer of clients."

Sometimes the provider is unsure of their obligations to provide client care when their employment by an agency or third party is discontinued. Beyond fulfilling the ethical obligation of a clinically appropriate termination with transfer or referral as needed (APA, 2002, 3.12; 10.10), the provider has no direct obligation to provide further services. Depending on the provider's subsequent practice arrangements, it may be possible for clients to follow the provider to a new location if they wish to do so. This is a discretionary matter and may depend largely on financial options and the structure of the provider's new practice (see Chapter Five, therapist needs and limits). Clients are not commodities that can be owned by a practice or agency, so they are free to discontinue and transfer at will.

At the same time, the professional relationship is a contract, not a liability that must be carried forward until it is retired. Changes in the provider's ability to provide services under the original contract nullify that contract. If the employer or agency wants to continue serving those clients, it is their responsibility to arrange for adequate staffing by qualified providers to fulfill any obligation they hold or to entice the clients to remain. The departing clinician is not obligated to find his or her own replacement or to continue to provide care without pay until the employer decides to hire new providers. However, in the event that the employer fails to prepare for the clinician's departure and in the provider's opinion there will not be adequate staff for continuity of care, the provider is obligated to refer the client to other resources for care.

So you've tended your wounds yet retained your professional composure and not drawn your clients into the fray, organized the care of your clients, and resolved your obligations. Now it is time to move on. Maybe you didn't like what happened and your clients didn't either, but this is not a good reason to become stuck in regret over a lost opportunity (see section on forced terminations below). Learn from it what you can, by all means. But don't neglect your own closure with this experience. Let yourself terminate and move fully into your present opportunities.

Fired by the Client   There are many possible explanations why a client might boldly utter the words "You're fired" or their equivalent (e.g., "We're through; I'm done!"). This could be the culmination of your attempts to satisfy the unsatisfiable client, it could be the client's way of handling stress, it could be part of the client's illness, or it could be a clear statement that you or your therapy are not the right match for this client. For example, a substance-abusing client with Bipolar Disorder would regularly fire various providers (psychologist, psychiatrist, general physician) whenever she was entering a manic phase and increasing her substance abuse. Or the client could be angry with you for something that you did or did not do as per their expectations. Maybe you were late, you were early, you failed to attend to something, you were too intense, you weren't intense enough, somehow you failed to save them from themselves, or you did what they asked you to do but you should have known better.

The tasks for dealing with this type of termination are essentially the same as in employment termination. In addition to following the six essential steps of termination, you will want to (a) deal with your own crisis, (b) protect the client from negative impact as feasible, (c) clarify your obligations, and (d) move on. There are a few concerns that are particular to this uniquely stressful occurrence.

One element of this crisis is the elevated potential for adverse action by the client. This is especially true if the client makes a verbal statement to that effect, as in "You're fired, and I'm going to report you." This statement is a vague but definite threat, and if possible you want to clarify what the client means by reporting you. To whom and for what do they plan to report you? It could be just a way of saying "I'm really mad at you," but it implies some intent to complain through formal channels.

Regardless of your guilt or innocence of any wrongdoing, which is another aspect of the crisis to sort out, there is an elevated risk of some adverse action when the client is both angry and willing to take aggressive action. Your central task is to determine how to contain your panic and marshal an effective defense. Consultation is invaluable in determining whether it is wise to have further contact with the angry client, and if so, how to structure that contact. As a general rule, all contact with the client should immediately cease once the client has threatened any adverse action, directly or indirectly (e.g., "I'm going to report you;" "I'm calling my lawyer;" "I'll see you in court;" "You will be sorry;" "You will pay for this."), and it is clear this is not said in jest or as a symptom of decompensation. Also as a general rule, your crisis mobilization should also include seeking legal consultation. It is important to avoid taking any impulsive or retaliatory actions that further inflame the situation. Calling the client to talk things over, writing defensive letters, apologizing or counter-attacking are rarely if ever productive efforts. As far as obligations are concerned, if the client has fired you, that releases any obligation to offer termination notice and counseling. It is over, and you now realize that providers do not have the same protections as clients when it comes to notice and opportunity for resolution. For your own sake in moving on, review the case with a consultant, note this in the client's record, and address the task of resolving your emotional closure. One final question might be whether or not it is advisable to accept this client's return once you've been fired. In most cases it is *not* wise to do so (Younggren & Gottlieb, in press). You may have a strong clinical rationale for resuming therapy, but remember that it is best to review such judgments with a consultant whenever there are elevated risks of harm to you or to the client by inadequate therapy. If the client has made direct threats to harm you, do not accept their effort to return to therapy.

My Client Has Suddenly Died

Professional therapists have an elevated risk of grief and loss that extends beyond their personal social network. Current or former clients form a special network of those with whom the provider holds a meaningful relationship. Clients might die at any age from a range of causes, including illness, accident, or traumatic event, and when they do, we mourn their loss. Some of the very problems that precipitated the client's therapy may play a role in his or her death. Therapists who work with terminally or chronically ill patients may have the greatest exposure to client loss through death. Suicide of course has the greatest impact on the provider, particularly if there is any direct cause or negligence in the provider's actions.

With termination due to client death, the therapist should address two primary concerns: maintaining confidentiality and dealing with personal grief and emotional response. These two concerns are intertwined and need to be simultaneously considered. First, the death of a client is an emotional event for the therapist, perhaps intensely so. Yet any actions to express or acknowledge these feelings are attenuated by the demands of the professional role and the need to continue to protect confidential information. Second, the context of the patient's death and how it is disclosed to the therapist will have an impact on therapist distress level and options for support. For example, a terminally ill patient who gradually fades away as the disease progresses may leave the therapist with a wistful longing for the continuation of life, but able to accept this anticipated end. There may even be other treatment team members with whom the provider can share the grief. But a situation of abrupt or precipitous death by a medical complication in a client who was not terminally ill could precipitate the therapist's feeling shocked, angry, and upset by the lost opportunity to help the client. Here the provider will most likely have a need for support in processing the emotional impact of this termination experience.

One particular challenge is that there are no systematic means by which providers can expect to be informed of a client's death unless prior arrangements have been established. Only with terminally ill clients are we apt to have any prearranged plans for notification. Otherwise, the provider may only learn of the event through public announcement (e.g., newspaper obituary), unless a family member happens to think of calling. The impact of a client's death by accident or trauma may be magnified by the way the news is delivered. It is entirely possible that the therapist might open the morning newspaper and find that her client was murdered the night before, encountering this traumatic loss via an impersonal media report. There may be no way to share the shock and grief without potentially compromising confidentiality. Yet the need to comprehend and process this bombshell may compel the therapist to talk with *someone*. Thus, it is crucial to recognize our own emotional needs, and in this case to seek support within the bonds of professional confidence, either via consultation with a qualified colleague or through personal therapy.

If you are fortunate enough to learn of the client's death prior to the funeral, it can be extremely helpful to attend this event or some portion of the publicly offered opportunity of acknowledgment such as a wake or visitation. This is apt to be difficult but helpful in accepting and experiencing the loss of this person. However, this is not just anyone's funeral, so one must remain vigilant not to inadvertently disclose information about the client or the therapy. Condolences can be offered to the family, and even a card or flowers might be appropriate as a matter of provider discretion. Extended discussions, on the other hand, need to be avoided. It may be possible to attend the funeral by anonymously blending into the crowd and thus sidestepping any challenging conversations while benefiting from the shared public experience.

On the other hand, if the therapy relationship was well known among the patient's significant others, an intuitive friend or relative may be able to spot the therapist in the crowd, even if no one has ever directly met you. You could find yourself plucked from your discrete distance and handed around among the various attendees like an honorary member of the family. This is a rare opportunity to connect all the names with faces, as you may be meeting people with whom you already feel a great familiarity and who may feel a great familiarity with you due to the client's therapy. Nevertheless, you control the social response of blurting out personal condolences, keeping your tongue mostly in a locked position, and murmuring something about sharing their sense of loss. Depending on your personal comfort with open expression of emotion, tears might be perfectly acceptable in this context of shared grief.

If the family reaches out to you to help them understand their loss, it can be reasonable to respond in a designated professional context. Set up a specific meeting with them that is confidential and directed toward this explicit purpose. A family member is the legal representative or has personal authority to waive confidentiality in most states, but be certain that this applies before proceeding. With this waiver, you can discuss issues with the family and try to help them achieve a sense of closure. If you are highly distraught, you may want to postpone any meetings with the family until you can achieve a reasonable level of composure. Usually the family will appreciate an open, humane, and caring response. Taking this stance can reduce your risk of legal action in the event of death by suicide (Bennett et al., 2006).

Perhaps the most traumatic termination of all is a client's suicide. In the event of suicide as a possible cause of death, it is especially important to seek support, but to do so only in the context of a legally protected discussion with an attorney or personal therapist. Suicide is an occupational hazard of being a provider. If a colleague has this unfortunate experience, it is helpful to offer your support, even if only in a brief call or sympathetic note (Bennett et al., 2006). If you are the provider with the loss, however, be careful to avoid verbalizing statements of self-blame concerning the event. Confine your explorations of these issues to the context of personal therapy. If you are offering support to a colleague, avoid probing the question of "what do you think happened" and stop the colleague if they begin to make disclosures that could be self-incriminating if the case should ever result in legal action. Presume the absence of any professional error and as an observer do not attempt to verify this presumption. Leave that analysis to the provider and to any formal review processes that may occur.

Suicide risk is a red flag for taking extra care in constructing clinical progress notes. Of course, all of your records are carefully created, but this is a circumstance where extra caution is worth the energy it takes. If the client commits suicide, the record is all that you have left. For both clinical and risk-management reasons, it is especially important that your record provides a general understanding of what you did, why you did it, what you chose not to do, and why not. Imagine this record from the perspective of a review team or jury and their need to understand that your actions fulfilled a reasonable standard of care. Imagine trying to satisfy the inquiry of the jury of you. In the unfortunate event of the client's actual suicide, this record will be invaluable not only to your own personal review but as a means of protection should your actions be called into question by others. Now here's the rub: This record can not be created after the client has completed the act. It has to already be in place. Otherwise it becomes a post-hoc attempt to cover up your potential wrongdoing.

A parsimonious note in the patient's chart that specifies termination of treatment and the relevant known parameters of death, if there are any, without any further speculation or embellishment is appropriate documentation of the death. For example, the record might simply state, "Treatment is terminated due to the patient's death in an automobile accident." The therapist may find it helpful to review the patient's record as part of the process of grieving and gaining some closure. However, one should resist temptation to alter any part of the existing record or to add speculative comments, because as already noted, this could suggest an attempt to conceal negligence or other error should the record ever come under review.

SELF-MANAGEMENT CHALLENGES

Emotionally provocative terminations call upon the provider to have adequate knowledge and clinical acumen as well as sufficient skills of self-management and self-care. Self-care skills refer to what you do with and for yourself to effectively deal with your emotional reactions to termination and to work in general. The primary objective in considering these self-management challenges is not just to deal with a single situation, although that may be the immediate focus of your attention. The primary objective is to add to your tool kit of best practices for protecting your overall well-being and professional longevity.

I Can Not Seem to Let Go

Providers are not immune to the error of holding on when it is time to let go. As we have discussed, over-attentiveness and worry are a powerful dynamic that can become a barrier to termination. Feelings of over-attachment, over-responsibility, and over-reliance on clients as a source of social contact and reinforcement are all potential contributors to the dilemma of not letting go psychologically, not taking suitable action to terminate, or not regarding therapy relationships with a sufficient degree of emotional objectivity. Trouble letting go when it is appropriate and necessary to do so can happen for a variety of reasons. Some of these are:

- The provider is focused on what might have been, or the lost opportunity to help this client (psychological over-attachment).
- The provider thinks reasonable efforts and reasonable results are inadequate (unrelenting standards).
- The provider does not know where to stop (compulsive effort).
- The provider is over-reliant on clients for social and emotional gratification (self-neglect and boundary problems).

Let's consider each of these possible reasons in greater detail.

Letting Go of a Lost Opportunity. Suppose that as the provider, you have done everything possible to reduce the risk of early termination. You've created a practice profile and screened clients so the chances of an appropriate client-provider match are increased. You've discussed therapy length and termination policies and you've talked with the client about setting a treatment plan with specific goals. You've specifically identified the early sessions as a time for orientation and the client's socialization to therapy seems promising. You've put together some great ideas on how to help, and it looks as though things are on track. Then the client terminates or fails to return. You are confronted with the discouraging reality that, despite your best efforts, some clients are still going to check out early or quit.

When a client terminates prematurely, the therapist might wonder, "Why are they doing this to me?" Well, it is probably not really about you. The therapist might also wonder, "How can I stop them from doing this?" They have their reasons, and it may be better to try to understand them than to believe you can completely control them.

Perhaps providers are prone to the retrospective "woulda, coulda, shoulda" thinking described by Freeman and DeWolf (1989). In this mode of thought, we become preoccupied with regrets, mistakes, and missed opportunities with the clients who slipped away or who were afforded only a brief settlement in our care. We can't stop thinking of what we might have been able to accomplish, if only given enough time or control. But if we had more time, how do we know it would have been productive? Could we be absolutely sure that the client would have been benefited from the work? Sometimes we ruminate over the small mistakes or errors that, if done differently, could have kept the client in therapy long enough to appreciate its workings. Well, perhaps those small errors were indeed trivial and had no real bearing on the client's disposition. We could have done everything perfectly and still obtained the same outcome. Or it may have become painfully evident that trying to keep an uncommitted client in therapy is an even bigger mistake than some minor error that dislodged them.

Maybe we regret having lost an opportunity to help someone in obvious need. It is surprising that this feeling can persist, despite the obvious conclusion that the client's departure signals a *lack* of opportunity. Just because we thought it might have been an opportunity to help does not mean there actually *was* an opportunity. The opportunity was decided by the client, and their behavior has communicated that decision.

Letting Go of Unrelenting Standards. Perhaps you hold yourself to an extremely high performance standard and believe that you must do *everything* possible to help your clients. Limited efforts are not "enough." Modest goals are not "enough." Providers as a group tend to believe that, where therapy is concerned, more is more. And in their self-expectations, they tend to hold a superlative, labor-intensive level of performance as their benchmark for "acceptable." The provider with unrelenting standards continually thinks that they should be doing more in therapy—more exercises, giving more information, assigning more homework, providing more information, etc. The client may feel overwhelmed and so does the provider. But therapy can not stop because there is always something more to do.

Scientific focus can serve as a "self-righting" skill for gaining some alternative perspective on the problem of striving to do everything and do it all to the highest level. The scientific perspective reminds us to think carefully about our presumptions, remain cognizant of the limits of our beliefs about people and change, and make it a practice to challenge our judgments. Clinical standards of care do not stipulate extreme effort or perfect results. The standard of care requires a reasonable effort to provide due care. Instead of trying to do everything possible at the most intensive or thorough level, perhaps we can think about making each session a valuable contribution to the client's overall skills of self-management. It may be helpful to consider the possibility that less is more. In the end, the decision of how much therapy is "enough" is a task of the individual therapeutic alliance.

Letting Go of Compulsive Effort. This termination difficulty is closely related to unrelenting standards. Sometimes providers get caught in the loop of continuing to try to make something work when it is not producing the expected results, or continuing to do more when the maximum benefits have probably been reached. The provider might believe that more effort is needed or that stopping the effort is not a permissible option. Even though the treatment is not effective or is no longer beneficial, the provider feels compelled to persist. Immediate reasons might focus on not letting the client down, not wanting to give up too soon (when plenty of time has been invested), not wanting to discourage the client or fearing (erroneously) accusations of abandonment. If we explore the schema behind these persistent strivings, we may discover how much of this is really about ourselves. We want to be powerful enough to make things better, to be affirmed by the achievement of optimal results, to feel secure in our competence, to avoid disappointing others, to be above reproach, to control what happens, to fulfill our own ambitions, and to confirm our own beliefs about people and change.

There really is nothing wrong in wanting these feelings. In fact it makes sense because these are gratifying experiences and sometimes we get them. But we don't always get them and should not impose a need for them on clients. There are risks associated with not stopping when it is appropriate to do so. It is demoralizing to the client to continue an effort that is not working. It can contribute to the provider feeling ineffective and burned out. In addition, it is unethical to keep a client in therapy when it is not in their best interest. If we make it a point to focus on serving the client's best interests and accepting the inevitable limits of our methods, it becomes possible to let go of compulsive efforts to make treatment work.

Letting Go of Emotional Over-Reliance on Clients. Providers, by vast majority, are caring, self-sacrificing individuals who tend to work hard and defer gratification. Unfortunately, self-neglect can increase one's vulnerability to burnout (see below), and increase the risks of over-reliance on work for emotional gratification. Too little self-care and attention to a personal life can precipitate a blurring of adequate emotional boundaries within therapeutic relationships, where one is over-attached to clients, either certain ones or all of them. Although the presence of a so-called "slippery slope" is a topic of some debate (see Barnett, 2007; Zur, 2007), a slide down this slope is not a "fait accompli." There are warning signs of emotional over-involvement that can be spotted and corrected, if the provider is alert and willing to self-correct.

Several warning signs of emotional over-involvement have been identified by Koocher and Keith-Spiegel (1998). These include:

- Believing that you are the only one who can help this client
- Wishing the client could be your friend
- Thinking of your clients as the central people in your life
- Relying on clients for your self-esteem
- Resisting termination even when the indications are clear

If specific operative beliefs can be identified, the provider has an immediate mechanism for beginning to restore adequate emotional boundaries. Direct disputation may help with each distorted belief. For example, there are many providers who could potentially help a given client. Friend and therapist are incompatible as simultaneous roles, and it is best to keep this clear. Clients are significant in your life, but they are not "significant others." Our circle of friendships and significant close relationships should not overlap with our circle of clients. Reliable self-esteem depends more on effective self-regulation than external praise.

Letting go when appropriate is an important professional responsibility. Challenging the beliefs behind the emotional over-involvement with clients is only the beginning of restoring necessary boundaries. The matter of the provider's internal vulnerability still needs to be addressed. The best practice strategy for the long run is to develop self-care practices that balance work and personal living in a way that supports your overall well-being.

I Am Worried That I Mishandled Termination

Feeling uncomfortable with your professional actions is an important signal to take time for self-supervision and consultation. Perhaps you can start by recognizing the positive data. You are aware of feeling uncomfortable and attempting to understand what, if anything, might have gone wrong. This is evidence of a self-righting capability in action. You are evaluating the possibility of error, presumably so that you can take corrective action if needed now and learn how to avoid such errors in the future.

Several questions are pertinent to this particular task of self-evaluation. First, what is the evidence of mismanagement? In other words, what is triggering this worry? Is it the client's emotional reactions to the termination? Are you measuring this termination against some standard ideal of how termination "should" be conducted? Are you particularly vulnerable to thinking that you must be doing something wrong in general (see unrelenting standards)?

Some objective reference points might help with self-evaluation. Recall the six essential steps for establishing that you've done "enough" and assess your actions. This can be done as a self-review, but it may be very useful to include a reliability check with a consulting colleague. If the termination was initiated by you, did you first do a progress review and discuss it with the client? Did you pinpoint a reason for the termination and consider how the client would react to that reason? Did you review ethical and legal obligations? Did you consider the level of risk exposure, risk management, and need for consultation? If you had concerns with risk exposure and management, did you seek consultation to review your plan? Did you provide enough notice to the client so that there was time to discuss options and assist the client in processing thoughts, feelings, and plans? Was there a disposition or decision established and noted in the client's record? In the course of asking these questions, have you been able to identify any place where things got off track or mismanagement occurred?

If the termination was initiated by the client, the same steps can still be reviewed, but they take on a slightly different cast. First, did you review the client's progress and communicate an opinion to the client as to how you thought he or she was doing? Did you ask the client for his or her perspective on progress? Did you consider any clinical or ethical reasons to advise the client against termination (e.g., imminent risk of harm)? Did you evaluate the clinical, emotional, and professional risks that might be associated with terminating versus not terminating? Did you offer the client the option to return for a termination process session if so desired? Did you clarify the expected plan with the client and make a note in the clinical record (e.g., "client will call if needed upon returning to school in the fall")?

If the client terminated obliquely without notice, there are still a few steps that can be completed. Did you make a reasonable attempt to contact the client to discuss their plan to continue or withdraw? Did you assess the client's progress as of the last point of contact, perhaps noting a GAF score? Do you think there is any reason to believe the client is an imminent danger to self or others? Did you note the above in the client's clinical record?

Once you have identified any specific problems in the steps of professional management, your sense of mismanagement should be more behaviorally anchored. Perhaps any remaining worry stems from thinking that you must do things that you really do not have to do or that are a matter of discretion. This is a time to review your overall termination policy and check with others on relative standards. How do you usually handle situations like this one? What do others do? Does this particular situation suggest a revision to your policy?

Now it may be time to activate the emotional self-management skills involved in letting go. Consider some of the ideas offered in our discussion of getting fired, dealing with early terminations, and overcoming burnout (below). Is there some other reason why letting go is difficult with this client? Are you having trouble with professional perfectionism and applying extreme and exacting standards to your work? Everyone is going to have situations they wished they handled better. That is why it is called clinical "practice." Ask yourself what sense it makes to hold on to this experience by worrying over it. Consider the alternative of letting it become a memory of a learning episode and fade into the context of the past.

I Have Lost Control of the Therapy Relationship and Don't Know How to Terminate

Every provider will encounter risky times in their career and risky situations with certain clients and certain procedures (Bennett et al., 2006; Koocher & Keith-Spiegel, 1998). Everyone is going to make mistakes, not just the mythical subclass of dummies that skipped too many classes and does not care anyway. Staying competent and in control as a professional is a high-level skill that is acquired over many years and that requires ongoing maintenance. Even a seasoned provider can get blindsided by a situation they didn't predict or expect or by failing to appreciate their own vulnerabilities. Prevention is the key, of course. Here we will consider what to do if prevention was lacking or failed. The provider and client have veered off track and crossed significant boundaries to the point where their relationship has become personal and perhaps romantic or sexual.

Generally, therapy has to stop if it is unethical to continue. By far, the most frequent occurrences of sanctionable misconduct are those involving sexual relations with adults and, to a much lesser extent, other forms of nonsexual dual relationships (Bennett et al., 2006). Sexual intimacy in the context of psychotherapy always creates a conflict of interest and a loss of objectivity and thus is uniformly considered unethical. The first challenge the provider needs to address is any inner resistance to seeing the necessity of termination and obtaining personal help in self-correcting and redirection. Locating the right persons to help is important and should be carefully considered. The provider does not want to be treated like a dummy or a pariah, but does need someone to help them become more accountable to themselves and their professional identity. If there is a colleague assistance program within the profession, perhaps within the state, this is a good time to contact them and determine the availability of confidential service and support. An alternative is to independently seek a qualified therapist.

It is reasonable that a professional would be reluctant to solicit professional help under these circumstances out of fear of triggering a collateral disciplinary report and investigation. If there is any doubt, be sure to clarify the relationship between a colleague assistance program and any disciplinary bodies in the event of a voluntary enrollment in the program. Keep in mind that many providers are unclear or have vastly differing opinions about their responsibility to report ethical violations of this sort, even if they are affiliated with a colleague assistance program. It is wise to determine any legal requirement for reporting misconduct in your state before seeking services to know these parameters in advance of discussing them with a prospective therapist. A provider in this difficult situation needs assistance, but also needs certain protections from undue stress, judgment, and perhaps vigilante justice.

The next issue is how to actually terminate contact with the client. Confidential consultation on client management is a very important part of resolving a situation of professional misconduct. The place to turn for this is your professional malpractice insurance carrier, who will likely offer specific, expert consultation. This consultation will help you contain the risks to the client and manage your exposure to disciplinary and malpractice sanctions. Providers in such a difficult situation may be prone to myopic judgment that can lead to more severely negligent actions and other self-defeating maneuvers if they muddle through on their own. The lack of objectivity that goes along with sexual and personal involvement produces a desire to keep the relationship and prioritize its purpose, romantic or otherwise, over one's other personal and professional commitments. If you are trying to cope with this on your own, be advised that you are most likely caught up in a series of distortions, rationalizations, and bizarre arrangements that paste up the illusion of being able to make both relationships work. If you want to figure out how to conclude this destructive situation, you will need to be willing to examine the possibility of self-perpetuating misjudgments.

An obvious but difficult choice is to cease and desist from all contact with this client with no specific plans for reuniting. The provider must tell the client that therapy actually terminated at whatever point the original focus was lost, and now all contact must end. No cash settlements or bribes to induce the client away from filing a disciplinary complaint should be offered. Nor should any promises of being together in two years or whenever offered. The client should be given two or three names of alternative providers whom you believe are appropriate for the client's original problems and could offer tactful, sensible assistance in processing the client's feelings and reactions without overstepping the boundaries of confidentiality or respect for the client's autonomy. Also bear in mind that the recommendations of a malpractice consultant or defense attorney regarding a particular situation should trump any of the general suggestions offered here.

There are emotional sequelae to this transgression and potential legal and professional consequences as well. Every situation is different, but in general a sincere and conscientious effort to contain one's mistakes, to regroup and address one's vulnerabilities, and to cooperate with those who must protect the public and who are trying to maintain the integrity of the profession can help determine whether this will be a personal watershed or a personal undoing.

Other sorts of situations where the provider has lost control and does not know how to terminate likely pertain to clients with personality problems or disorders. These create a complex termination that requires more time and a more deliberate, systematic approach that addresses the client's primary beliefs about the provider, therapy, and the meaning of termination. Refer to chapters five and six for more extensive discussion.

I Am Feeling Burned Out—How Can I Get My Enthusiasm Back?

Burnout is an increasingly recognizable problem that refers to a syndrome of distress stemming from work demands. It is defined by Maslach, Schaufeli, and Leiter (2001) as a "psychological syndrome in response to chronic interpersonal stressors on the job" (p. 399). Burnout has three interacting components: emotional exhaustion, depersonalization of clients, and low sense of personal work accomplishment. Exhaustion has both mental and physical components, and it can occur when one is taxed beyond real or perceived physical limits. Depersonalization of clients occurs with the development of a cynical, detached, or uncaring attitude. Low accomplishment reflects feelings of uselessness, poor self-efficacy, and ultimately a deteriorated performance. Burnout is a state of diminished functioning where the provider feels little energy or enthusiasm for work and probably wants to quit, ruminates about escape, is cranky, sarcastic, and contemptuous of both clients and the system, prone to being scattered and lax about details and paperwork, and may be increasingly embittered about their personal career achievement. Good terminations are less likely to happen under these conditions.

The relative balance between work demands and viable resources for stress reduction and avoidance are thought to be critical ingredients in predicting burnout (Rupert, 2007). Work-related conditions such as autonomy and support as well as the clinician's personal coping strategies and life conditions are the major ingredients in one's risk for burnout. The association between a neglect of self-care and poorer functioning in the clinical setting is well known. Failure to develop the habits and techniques that foster a coping resilience increases the chances that you might disrespect clients, demean the importance of your work, feel distressed or make clinical mistakes (Pope & Vasquez, 2005), or become defensive, destructive, and demoralized in your approach to practice (Ronnestad & Orlinsky, 2005).

Greater control over work conditions and activities and more available support helps to mediate the risk of burnout. In a comparison between independent practitioners (solo or group) and agency providers, Rupert (2007) found that those in independent settings had an advantage because their control over work activities allowed for lower exhaustion, less difficult clients, and higher sense of personal accomplishment. Those in solo settings also had less support, greater over-involvement with clients, and higher risk for isolation or exhaustion. However, being in solo practice versus agency practice provided a greater advantage to women on the exhaustion dimension of burnout. The possible link may be that solo practice affords the option of more autonomy in balancing work and family responsibilities, a variable that may have greater impact on women's risk of burnout.

Internal resources are perhaps even more significant than specific conditions in preventing and mediating burnout. Internal resources are the characteristics and coping strategies that foster resilience and decrease levels of burnout in the face of work demands (Rupert, 2007). These coping strategies are variously described as self-care (Freeman, Felgoise & Davis, 2008; Mahoney, 1997; Norcross, 2000) or career-sustaining behaviors (Kramen-Kahn & Hansen, 1998; Stevanovic & Rupert, 2004). In a summary of the tactics preferred by clinicians and consistently cited across different studies, Rupert (2007) offers the following three general strategies for self-care or well functioning at work.

Key Strategies for Self-Care at Work

1. Use cognitive techniques to keep an objective perspective on psychological work. Specific tactics include maintaining a sense of humor and staying connected to one's professional identity and values.
2. Apply skills of awareness, observation, and reflection to yourself. Self-monitoring is a highly rated strategy and a fundamental step in organizing the constructive actions needed for self-regulation.
3. Keep a healthy balance between work and personal life. Spending time with significant others is important and should be a regular occurrence. Balance is also achieved by investing time in hobbies, vacations, and physical activities.

Thus, the path for recovering one's enthusiasm lies in adjusting work conditions to increase control and support and in attending to the care of you. Failure to do so risks one's present and future career. We might imagine that providers who commit egregious professional errors such as abruptly abandoning their practice are suffering some form of burnout to be so callous about their clients and detached from their professional identity.

If you are able to view termination as a professional task and know how and when to accomplish it, your sense of professional control and efficacy are likely to increase. Likewise, if you are attuned to your emotions and able to use them as a guide for constructive actions that include seeking support and consultation, your vulnerability will decrease. Being well grounded in the practical aspects of termination is likely to have a direct impact on your ability to keep a balance between working and other personal living. When you are able to end therapy appropriately and effectively, without undue vacillations, conflicts, or protraction, you will have more positive feelings about work and more time to go about doing the other things that generate positive affect in your day-to-day life. Ask yourself, "What have I done this week that has allowed me to relax, laugh, have fun, stimulate my senses, be creative, follow my spiritual practices, connect with others, or experience a state of flow?" If the answer is "Not enough," then consider if there might be some places to reduce your work demands by applying more effective termination skills.

SUMMARY POINTS FOR APPLIED PRACTICE

1. Termination is an emotionally provocative experience for the provider, yet it is a task to be accomplished with every client. Pay attention to your emotional reactions and use them as a source of information for guiding professional decisions and monitoring your emotional and behavioral competence.

2. Termination should be discussed with every client. The amount of discussion needed is highly variable and depends on the complexity of the issues, the client's level of functional organization, and the context in which termination occurs.

3. Interminable therapy needs a purpose check. Shared positive beliefs about worry can create a perpetual contract for meeting regularly but going around in circles. Productive therapy has a constructive view of the future and is actively pursuing it. Wishing that therapy would hasten to an end because of a difficulty in connecting with the client may be a skill issue, a personal sensitivity to something about the client, or an indication of burnout.

4. Persistence and adaptability as a provider can be liabilities with a chronically dissatisfied client. Check your limits on trying to gain the client's approval. Sometimes termination is the best option.

5. Oblique terminations can leave a provider dangling with uncertainty about how to proceed. The need for follow-up efforts can be determined on a case-by-case basis. An open invitation for the client to return with a low demand stance is a viable response for many situations. If there is no response from the client, providers must draw their own closure.

6. If you are fired by your client or your employer, deal with your own crisis first. Address the six essential steps for termination as appropriate to the context. Protect your client as a much as possible from the fallout, clarify your obligations, and don't forget to let yourself move on.

7. If an angry client fires you, it is probably in your best interest and theirs to accept the termination and not reverse it, even if the client wants to recant and resume therapy. If a client threatens you, therapy is definitely over and all further contact should stop.

8. Current and former clients form a special network of those with whom we hold a meaningful relationship. If termination is caused by the client's death, there will be grief to process. Death by suicide, an unfortunate occupational risk, requires grief processing and particular cautions in terms of managing professional liability issues.

9. Trouble with termination is a solvable problem. Review your work and tap your colleagues as a resource for checking your judgment. Even if you have lost control and don't know how to end an unethical or unworkable relationship, and don't want to do so, reasonable solutions are possible. You can make it better or make it worse, no matter where you are, depending on what you do next.

10. Self-care at work is a best practice strategy for career longevity. Effective termination skills can contribute to a provider's self-care tool kit by increasing one's sense of competence and efficacy, streamlining work demands, and managing time.

8

Termination with Couples, Families, and Groups

Key Questions Addressed in This Chapter

- How does termination differ when therapy involves more than one person?
- When should I recommend termination with couples?
- If one member of a couple or family terminates therapy, does that mean the other participants must terminate as well?
- Are there extra risks of abandonment in couples or family therapy?
- What should I do if I think couples' therapy should be terminated in favor pursuing individual therapy?
- How can I respond when a parent abruptly terminates the therapy of a child or teen?
- What about handling the opposite situation, when a parent essentially remands the child or teen to treatment?
- How can I minimize the disruption of early termination from a group?
- Is there a best way to end a group?

ATTENDING TO MULTIPLE INTERESTS

Termination takes on a different cast when there are multiple parties involved in therapy. The essential steps for termination remain the same, but variations in the mode of delivery create some differences. First, it is important that all participants understand the nature of the agreement to work together (informed consent), including how termination can be expected to occur and what typical reasons might trigger termination. This will help to reduce the risks of misunderstandings, although these issues still have to be reviewed from time to time to ensure current understanding and agreement among all clients. Second, it is important to establish that each participant has a shared responsibility for therapy progress and an individual right to terminate their participation. In other words, therapy proceeds most productively when everyone shares responsibility for its success, but each person has the right to stop his or her direct involvement.

Providers will generally set these notions out as part of the therapy "ground rules" so as to allay fears that someone could get capriciously voted out by the other participants. Ground rules will generally include requirements for effective participation that need to be met for therapy to proceed. The provider will explain in advance how non-compliance or disruptive behavior by a single participant will be handled. Just as no one will be forced out without a pre-established reason, no one should be forced into the process either. Providers are ethically obligated to clarify roles, responsibilities, and limits of confidentiality when providing services to several persons in a group setting or several persons who have a relationship with one another (e.g., spouses, parents and children) (APA, 2002, 10.02; 10.03).

How Does Termination Differ When Therapy Involves More Than One Person?

Termination should follow the original contract for therapy. If the contract was to provide couples therapy and one member of the couple drops out, the original contract is terminated by client default. If a new contract for continuing therapy with the remaining member of the couple is considered, the provider will want to carefully weigh the implications for any further marital therapy and clarify the new therapeutic relationship. Each time therapy changes format, the job changes and there is a new contract to establish.

If therapy starts out as family work and evolves into individual therapy, the original contract should be terminated and a new agreement that includes the informed consent of all parties set forth. The reasons for termination will follow along the same lines as those for individual therapy – the goals have been reached, the focus of therapy has shifted or is not working, financial limits have been reached, the provider is not the right person for the job, the circumstances have changed, or the conditions are untenable for safe or effective therapy. Each person who participated in the original contract should be given notice of the termination and provided with an opportunity to discuss it and come to an understanding of the resolution.

The provider might try to convene the original group for a termination session, but practical and clinical considerations can necessitate having separate meetings with participants. It is important that each person be given the opportunity to process the termination, even if he or she is unwilling to participate in a collective meeting or is ultimately uninterested in having the termination meeting. Offering an opportunity for a closing discussion demonstrates respect for each member of the original agreement. On the other hand, spouses or family members do not have to be involved in termination if their attendance occurred only in the context of providing collateral support to a client's individual therapy. These individuals were never enrolled as clients so they do not carry rights or responsibilities as clients. The exception to this is therapy with children, where the parent is included as a primary contributor to the intervention.

When Should I Recommend Termination with Couples?

Initiating termination of couples' therapy is a clinical judgment that should be based on the provider's assessment of the progress, potential for further improvement on their own, and the presence of any factors that would interfere with their ability to benefit from treatment. Termination because it is not safe or effective to continue is indicated if there is ongoing physical abuse or an ongoing extramarital affair (secret or revealed) (Gottman, 1999). Attempting marital interventions with a couple where physical abuse is ongoing can increase the physical risks to one or both partners. It also risks a misdirected conceptualization of the clinical problems as existing within the partner or marriage rather than being the responsibility of the person who engages in physically aggressive behavior. Conjoint therapy for couples with a pattern of ongoing physical abuse is generally thought to be contraindicated unless it is specifically designed as an abuse-reduction intervention. Couples who present with or eventually reveal a pattern of ongoing physical abuse should be referred to programs or providers who offer specialized services for problems of aggression, violence, and anger management (e.g., Geffner & Mantooth, 2000; Wexler, 2000).

Emotional abuse in the form of contempt is not automatically a reason for termination, unless the couple is unable to respond to confrontation of this corrosive process and has lost their positive affiliation toward one another. The tendency to argue should be clearly distinguished from psychological abuse, which is more contemptuous and degrading, with a corresponding low rate of positive affective exchange. Positive affiliation includes at least some elements of respect, affection, warmth, caring, interest, or attraction. Other problems may be corrected, but if the couple's shared system of fondness and admiration is dead, treatment of the marriage is unlikely to do much good, and the possibility of divorce should be considered (Gottman, 1999). If one partner remains in love but the other is not, there really is no shared system of positive affiliation remaining. Continuing the marriage, and continuing to attempt to treat the marriage, may be doing more harm than good to the spouses and any children who are trying to grow up in this context. The partners are apt to be emotionally disengaged, lonely, conflicted, and living parallel lives, emotionally connected by a thread of cold, contemptuous, or abusive exchange that is unlikely to change.

The absence of fondness and admiration is the key factor in triggering termination, regardless of the manifestation of abusive processes.

When emotional abuse occurs, it should be quickly and directly confronted as damaging and unacceptable, with a redirection toward more effective communication of feelings. Offering only support and empathy for the impact of such messages is not sufficient (Gottman, 1999). But when there is no positive affect to work with, the provider can initiate termination of the marital therapy and, if appropriate, offer to assist the couple in moving toward an amicable divorce and establishing cooperative and non-hostile parenting arrangements. Presumably this strategy would apply if either partner is lacking in positive affect toward the partner and the cause is not clinical depression, which could be treated. Otherwise, specific treatment of the depression would be an appropriate alternative.

In cases where the couple has a more constructive response to intervention, the options for a prospective or flexible termination are increased. The provider might recommend termination when the positive trajectory of the marriage has improved and the spouses have the tools to make their last conversation better on their own (Gottman, 1999). As with individual therapy, a fading component is very helpful in increasing the couple's autonomy and confidence in maintaining changes, while providing support and structure for those efforts. Follow-up is highly recommended, perhaps for as long as two years although meetings can be spaced at intervals up to six months apart (Gottman, 1999).

If One Member of a Couple or Family Terminates Therapy, Does That Mean the Other Participants Must Terminate as Well?

When one participant leaves a conjoint or family effort, termination decisions can be guided by the original contract for therapy. If therapy was established solely as couples' therapy, then this therapy would end if both members are no longer participating. When one member of a couple stops participating and the other continues, that couple's therapy has shifted to individual therapy, and the original purpose of treating the relationship has changed. This ends the original contract and precipitates the need to establish a new contract. If a participant just stops coming to sessions without making clear his or her intentions, the provider will probably want to determine if this was an oblique termination. If the remaining partner or family member wants to continue in individual therapy, the provider may want to send a letter to the absent participant to clarify termination prior to entering into any new contracts.

Any change of the regular participants is a point of re-evaluation and possible redirection of the therapy. A decision will need to be made regarding the disposition of the original plan for therapy and whether more couples work will be needed. When individual therapy proceeds subsequent to couples or family therapy, it is very difficult to shift back into the original modality. A new alliance is formed between the therapist and the continuing participant, one that excludes the absent others. If an attempt is made to resume couples' therapy, the objectivity of the provider may be affected because of the shift in the alliance. The sense of safety and fairness felt by the returning participants may be compromised, despite whatever confidence the provider may hold about keeping an even hand. On the other hand, the returning participant may have no problem with the new alliance and view the attempt to limit couples' therapy as a punishment for his or her ambivalence.

There are several possible resolutions to this dilemma that careful clinical judgment can help to resolve. In general, the provider needs to help each person determine their current needs and preferences and the options for best serving them. It is very difficult for the provider to shift between modalities such as couples to individual and back to couples because of the potential conflict between the duties owed to each client.

Family therapy is somewhat different in that there are often multiple participants who will be intermittently involved as collateral participants in the care of one or more identified client. The provider's duty will follow each identified client. Termination also follows the care of each identified client. When treating couples, families, significant others, or several persons who have a relationship with one another, it is always best to make it clear from the beginning which of the participants are identified clients, which ones are there as collateral participants, and what sort of relationship the provider expects to have with each person (APA, 2002, 10.02). If a conflict between roles develops, the provider must take reasonable steps to make the roles clear, modify their participation, or withdraw from incompatible roles (APA, 2002, 10.02 (b)).

In all instances, the provider needs to discern the wisdom and feasibility of serving as individual therapist to multiple persons with significant relationships to one another, whether that is two spouses, parent and child, chunks of siblings, multiple generations, or some other combination of a bonded cohort. Some clinical situations may be adaptable to this sort of intervention, whereas others are not, depending on the problems, the people involved, and the provider's skill set. This is a dynamic process and needs to be assessed on a case-by-case basis as the therapy progresses over time. The type of intervention and its goals play a part in these decisions as well. Intensive individual therapy with more than one member of a family is most complicated and least advisable. Switching of formats, for example from couples' to individual therapy with the same provider, is also ripe for confusion and may be best to avoid. In some family clinics where brief, solution-focused therapy is the model, intervention might take various forms including couples counseling, individual therapy for child or parent, parent counseling, family group therapy, group therapy for the child or teen, skills classes or multifamily group therapy. Contact with a family might continue with different family members as identified clients. For example, a family might come into therapy because of issues pertaining to the management of a child's chronic illness, and the child is the designated client. Parental emotional distress might precipitate additional designation of mom or dad as a client, with individual therapy included in the treatment plan. Then grandmother's deteriorating health becomes a family issue, and she is brought into the family consultation to determine if she needs individual psychological assistance, or if the family needs assistance in managing their reactions and worries about her, or both.

By this time, the child is happily moving forward so the child's therapy is terminated and placed in a follow-up mode. The focus of therapy now shifts to the older generation and mom's worried preoccupation with losing her mother, provided that these problems fall within the scope of the provider's competence. Perhaps mother is now the designated client, and grandmother attends some collateral therapy sessions with her to explore the family pattern of health-related anxiety, and husband attends some collateral sessions with her to discuss how this anxiety affects marital communication and satisfaction. At each decision point, the provider must determine the appropriateness of serving another family member as a client versus referring out to another provider or service setting.

There may be numerous contacts with various family members as follow-up when one issue overlaps with more intensive work on another. Because of the intermittent and accruing contact, the traditional sort of termination phase and a final good-bye does not really occur (Kreilkamp, 1989). There is less need to extensively process relationship loss at termination if the open option of a return as needed is offered. Because of the interconnected relationships, family members are also more likely to help one another retain a sense of connection to the provider and to the skills, beliefs, and practices that the provider encouraged among the members of the family. However, attention to the clinically and ethically appropriate termination process is still warranted. Usually the reason for termination is that an immediate goal has been met, the limits of the provider's competence have been reached, or the limits of reimbursement necessitate a flexible termination where therapy might be resumed at a future point.

Are There Extra Risks of Abandonment in Couples' or Family Therapy?

The risk of abandonment or perceived abandonment is elevated in couples' or family therapy. This is particularly true when there is a shift in the focus of the work and multiple members of the same family are clients. The provider will want to remain alert to the risk of inadvertently abandoning care of the originally designated client if therapy with various family members proceeds. Understanding the overall pattern of family roles and dynamics is important, so as not to play directly into any tendency to substitute one problem as a means of avoiding another. Sometimes family members will obliquely terminate as a means of relieving the stress of therapy and then ascribe this to abandonment by the provider. The client chooses to stop participating, but bases this decision on the belief that the therapist does not want them there, their presence is not needed, or the family has pushed them out and the provider has allowed this to happen. Because of this, it is incumbent upon the provider to ensure that he or she makes reasonable efforts to communicate about termination and to establish a shared disposition with each designated client. Clients need to be clearly informed on the matter of whether they are, in fact, a designated client.

In treating multiple members of a family, there is a risk that the original client might actually be abandoned as the focus shifts to another family member or family unit. In addition, one or more participants may be prone to perceive themselves as abandoned in this interpersonal context. To manage these risks, the provider has to keep track of the original goals as well as the participants and their perceptions of therapy progress. Recall that the definition of abandonment is the absence of a clinically and ethically appropriate termination process. If the focus of therapy is shifting, there should direct discussion of closure, concurrent management, or referral to another provider for treatment of the original problem.

In the previous example of a family originally referred for management of a child's chronic illness, there was a designated termination of the focused work on this problem, where family visits that included the child were faded out. This process was explicitly discussed with all participating members, and both parents and child understood what was happening with the child's therapy. The provider obtained follow-up reports on the child's development and functioning from the parents, and kept open the option for the child to return as needed. Providers want to avoid simply losing track of the original purpose of therapy and neglecting any termination discussion associated with that initial contract. As noted in chapters five and seven, the amount of termination discussion may be brief, depending on the overall context of therapy and the client's progress and functional status. The disposition may be quite flexible as to plans for further intervention or follow-up. The essential element is adequate communication or attempt at communication concerning treatment status, and notation in the record that this communication occurred.

Maladaptive personality styles and coping tactics often flourish in the family context, and family therapy is not an oasis away from these problems. Clients with paranoid, histrionic, borderline, or passive-aggressive tendencies may be particularly prone to misperceiving and distorting the provider's actions in a manner that confirms their beliefs about being mistreated in a family context. The provider will want to balance reaching out to correct misperceptions about rejection or slights with an expectation that the client should make reasonable efforts to collaborate in therapy. It is essential that the provider clarify his or her role with this client and provide sufficient structure to facilitate the experience for all participants.

Difficulties in personality functioning that are persistent and pervasive enough to indicate a personality disorder strongly suggest a need for more focused individual therapy in conjunction with or as an alternative to family therapy. Given the potential for risk and confusion of roles, it is advisable to involve a different provider for this individual work. A separate provider allows a dilution of intensity in the provider-client relationship and offers the client additional support, continuity over time, and reinforcement of basic ideas. However, the providers will likely find that both modes of therapy proceed more smoothly if they are able to share communications about the client on a regular basis. The individual client's ability to participate in a family therapy may be limited to a collateral role that varies with the level of the disturbance, the client's developmental concerns, and his or her ability to communicate with other family members. As noted with couple's therapy, any psychological abuse is a corrosive experience, and it should be confronted and redirected as a requirement for participation. The client may ultimately reject the recommendation for individual therapy with a different provider. However, the family therapist has established a clinically and ethically appropriate process was followed.

What Should I Do if I Think Couples' Therapy Should Be Terminated in Favor of Pursuing Individual Therapy?

Collaboration with the clients is a key element of successfully navigating any transition in the focus or modality of therapy. If provider and clients are not together on the direction of therapy, it is quite possible that the clients will strengthen their alliance with one another but turn against the provider and terminate therapy because of an incompatible agenda. Terminating one type of therapy for another is an appropriate choice only if it is clinically indicated and consistent with the wishes and expectations of the participating clients.

Shifting from a conjoint focus to an individual focus is a delicate maneuver and generally would not involve the original provider offering both services. This proposal can be easily misunderstood unless the clients readily grasp and agree with the clinical rationale. Without a clear, understandable, and acceptable rationale, the provider's motives become suspect and cause for distortion. Does the provider dislike one member of the couple? Does the provider favor a member of the couple or family? Or worse, does the provider think the problem really is all his (her) fault? Perhaps one partner or family member shows significantly greater individual difficulty, but is unwilling to enter individual therapy even though he or she may be the designated client. This client will react poorly to any suggestion of termination or transfer. Participating in therapy as a member of a couple is a safer and less stigmatizing way to be in therapy. For this client, the rationale of individual therapy is just not acceptable and to insist upon it is counterproductive. The most obvious exception to this would be the physically abusive client who can not continue in treatment that is contraindicated and potentially harmful.

If the rationale is not understandable, the clients may misconstrue the provider's actions as an effort to manipulate them. Even if the provider has no ulterior motives, the couple may think that the recommendation is insensitive to their stated preference for a relationship mode of intervention. They may see the provider's recommendation as an unprofessional distortion of their clinical needs to suit the provider's practice rather than offering the service that is in their best interests or referring them elsewhere. At worst, the couple may think that the provider is trying to split them up in order to pursue a personal relationship with the preferred partner. If any of these client perceptions is remotely true, the provider's standard of care is slipping below acceptable levels due to poor judgment and possible boundary violations (see Koocher & Keith-Spiegel (1998) for discussion of boundary violation warning signs).

Clinical Example: Isaac and Cleo were two highly accomplished professionals in a long-term marriage characterized by their similarly passionate and emotionally expressive personalities. They sought assistance for regulating the intensity of their interactions in the context of managing some new family stresses. The therapist, Dr. Blue, kept focusing attention on Isaac, to the point that Cleo felt excluded. In sessions, they never seemed to get around to the actual family stresses that brought the couple to therapy. Instead, Dr. Blue was interested in Isaac's work, Isaac's level of stress, Isaac's childhood, and Isaac's self-image. Overall, the interaction reflected Dr. Blue's interest in Isaac, but not the couple's relationship. After persisting with this line of inquiry for several sessions, Dr. Blue recommended that the couple's therapy be terminated in favor of continuing individual therapy with Isaac. Both Cleo and Isaac thought that Dr. Blue had been mildly flirtatious with Isaac, and they wondered if the agenda might be to isolate him in order to pursue an inappropriate relationship. They were puzzled as to why their initial goals for working on managing stress in their relationship were ignored in favor of identifying Isaac as a candidate for individual therapy. It is no surprise that they did not continue in either individual or couples' therapy, and they left with a distasteful feeling about therapy in general.

How Can I Respond When a Parent Abruptly Terminates the Therapy of a Child or Teen?

This is an awkward situation that deprives the youngster of a clinically appropriate process and instead creates an oblique termination. Ethically and legally, the provider can not go beyond the parent's authority to continue communications with the youngster, regardless of how clinically important they think a final contact is to the youth. Mature youth who have reached an age of consent for their own care, which in some states is younger than the standard age of majority at 18 (Sales, Miller & Hall, 2005), may be able to contact the provider on their own for a termination session. Otherwise, the provider's only recourse is to appeal to the parent for cooperation in completing at least a single termination visit. Providers may also want to offer an opinion on the advisability of continued treatment as clinically indicated. Depending on the parent's perspective, this could be a contentious situation, so it is important to handle any appeal wisely and simply request this as an important step in therapy completion. Warning the parent of potential damage to the child is not particularly helpful and may inflame the situation. Perhaps the parent has simply chosen to work with another provider and is not abandoning therapy altogether. Repeated attempts to get the parent to follow up can be inflammatory and not ultimately effective, as it could precipitate a formal complaint of harassment.

Although it may not always be possible to keep such an unfortunate turn of events from happening, preventive efforts are well worth the energy if they help to avoid this conundrum. Communication with parents as collateral participants in therapy from the very beginning is the primary step in such prevention. Continued contact with the parent, parents, or guardian also helps to ensure that everyone understands what is happening in therapy and agrees to its continuation. Touching base with those who are ultimately responsible for the child's welfare is vital to assessing the youngster's progress. The intensity or frequency of this contact may be considerably less as the teen's age moves toward the age of majority, depending on the client's maturity, type of problem, and family functioning.

Working effectively with family members as collateral participants can go a long way in managing the controllable reasons for this precipitous termination. The reality is that there can be other reasons for the occurrence of such actions that have nothing to do with the provider or the quality of care, but instead reflect central problems and conflicts within the family. At the outset of therapy, the provider may want to apprise the child of the parental authority to discontinue treatment at will without using a judgmental or negative tone. This creates a prearranged concept of this termination in the event that it should come to pass. The youngster then has an understanding of how parental controls might affect the course of therapy.

It may not be possible to predict this outcome, but the provider might be particularly alert in situations where there is one or more mistrusting, skeptical, or overly controlling parent. Sometimes this behavior is a functional stance that has evolved from dealing with a teen's problems and the parent has become increasingly stressed and impatient. Or perhaps a characteristically domineering parent abruptly ends therapy to restore an immediate sense of control over the child's problems or the family as a whole.

It may be that the parents are in deep conflict between themselves, if not outright war, and the youth's therapy becomes one more decision where one usurps the authority of the other. High-conflict families present special risks and call for specific risk-management strategies including caution in proceeding with therapy. It is always best to obtain consent from both parents and to abort the therapy if either parent objects. Consent of both parents should be considered mandatory when they are divorced but share joint custody (Bennett et al., 2006).

What about Handling the Opposite Situation, When a Parent Essentially Remands the Child or Teen to Treatment?

This is a clinical matter that concerns the interplay between the child's adjustment and the parent's struggle to fulfill their own self-expectations as parents. A parent who remands a child or teen to therapy may do so as a form of punishment, as a desperate effort to save the youth, as a personal cry for help, or as a way of rejecting their own sense of disappointment and loss in relationship to raising the child. The message to the provider, either implicit or explicit, is "Fix this kid so we can all feel better."

The child's resistance to the initial encounter is not unusual. Someone else is pushing for therapy as a solution, and the child may not exactly embrace the idea with enthusiasm. Perhaps the parent seeks treatment because of pressure from the school, repeated recommendation from the pediatrician, or prompting from the extended family. Anxious parents may overreact to normal developmental vicissitudes, have perfectionist standards, or be funneling their own concerns from other areas of their life into a preoccupation with the child. For whatever reason, they are feeling fragile as the caretaker who is responsible for preparing and ensuring the youth's success in a demanding world. Thus the youth lands in the provider's office, somewhere between bewildered about the point of being there, angry about being pushed around, or relieved to have access to some outside support. Maybe there is relatively little to actually "fix" in the child, and from this comes a potential termination dilemma of when it is appropriate to continue or end therapy due to the relative need or potential benefit.

All of these are matters for the skilled clinician to explore as much as the family will allow before coming to any conclusions on terminating therapy. Metaphorically, the provider does not want to miss the issues in the forest because the trees up front look fine. Quite often, the youth is less troubled than parents perceive, and it is the parent's concepts of the child's problems that need to be modified, yet the parent does not accept this perspective. The parent wants the therapist to find out what is troubling or "wrong" with the youth and repair it so that life will proceed as the parent expects.

An important tactic for such situations offered by Kreilkamp (1989) is to keep track of what has already been tried and to keep trying new things that may help to draw the issues out and provide support as the family development process moves forward. This can include various strategies such as psychological testing, group therapy, individual meetings alternating with family meetings, seeing different subgroups of the family together, and so on as a means of continuously gathering data and re-evaluating the problems in light of this new data. Throughout this process, however, the primary contract with the identified client is kept clear and if the focus of treatment shifts, the initial contract is terminated and a new one established.

On the other hand, it is entirely possible that the youth has serious, potentially life-altering problems that he or she avoids, minimizes, or blames on external sources. The parents may be deeply worried and struggling to help, or they may be embroiled in their own morass of concerns and unable to provide sufficient support. The likelihood of the client's benefit from therapy is questionable if there is a high degree of resistance and disengagement. However, the strategy of trying new things that haven't been tried may be quite applicable here as well. There are more options for trying different things with youth who have family members willing to be involved and lobbying for the therapeutic involvement than there may be with an adult client who denies the seriousness of their difficulties. So for the unconcerned or hostile youth who is at much greater risk than he or she perceives, one can potentially delay termination by trying different modes of engagement.

As always, the possibility of a clinically and ethically appropriate termination with the reluctant youth will be based on reasoned professional judgments taken in specific context. Rules about termination should not be oversimplified to the point that context of clinical judgment is lost. In this case, it may not be accurate to assume that an uncooperative youth has no likelihood of benefiting from therapy. Forcing the youth to come for intensive individual therapy may provide little benefit, but perhaps a useful alternative can be found amongst the array of possible interventions before reaching the termination conclusion.

TERMINATION AND GROUP THERAPY

How Can I Minimize the Disruption of Early Termination from a Group?

Group therapy is a modality that frequently includes exemplary efforts at informed consent and preparation for a prospectively determined termination. Membership composition and time boundaries are two dimension that determine the most important termination parameters in the group mode.

On the membership dimension, some groups operate with an open or rotating membership while other groups are established at the beginning and then closed to new members. On the dimension of time boundaries, some groups are open-ended with a broadly construed interpersonal or exploratory focus while other groups are specifically time-limited, often with a particular theme or skills-training focus. All types of groups (rotating vs. closed membership; open-ended vs. time-limited) have a stance toward termination that is apt to be spelled out in the informed consent process, but there are differences in that stance that parallel the structure of the group.

Groups with open membership acknowledge and plan for the transition of members in and out of the group. The boundary of being in or out is quite flexible, usually of some necessity, for example to accommodate patients as they are admitted or discharged from the hospital. In shorter-term groups with open membership, termination might be part of the group agenda at most if not every session as someone is always leaving or getting ready to leave. The group process predicts and contains this action, and it is not usually a disruption as much as it is part of the expected progress of the participants. In longer term, open-ended groups, termination will have more of a significant impact on the group because of the emotional investment and involvement among the members. An oblique or unexplained termination by one of the members is apt to have a more unsettling impact in this context.

Time-limited groups have a prospective termination point established from the beginning of the work. Members are prepared in advance and know when therapy will begin and end. Instead of members terminating one by one as suits their needs, the expectation is for all members to terminate at once when the group disbands. Oblique termination can have a distracting impact on short-term closed groups, particularly those with an interpersonal focus. In a skills-oriented group, the members might easily accept the absent member's termination as an impersonal event, attributable to such things as not benefiting from the material or needing a different approach.

An unplanned departure of a group participant prior to an expected point of ending causes some disruption for any group. Participants may be vulnerable to feeling personally rejected or perhaps personally responsible for the abrupt departure of a fellow participant. They may feel relieved if the departing member had strained the productive group process. Or they might feel angry at the person for not cooperating or participating effectively. Perhaps they feel guilty for wishing to hasten the troublesome participant's departure. Depending on how well the member was known by the others and how much members had emotionally bonded, a premature departure can trigger feelings of loss, disappointment, and perhaps devaluing of the group endeavor.

Because of these real and potentially upsetting effects, most providers of group therapy will undertake extensive efforts to select, screen, and prepare members for a group-therapy experience (Brabender, Fallon & Smolar, 2004). Clients who are unmotivated to participate in a group, who have extremely high levels of distress, who might have trouble adhering to the rules, and who have little capacity for empathy or connection with others should probably be excluded from the beginning. To qualify for selection, clients need to have goals that are compatible with the group purpose, and should have characteristics that will foster identification with at least one other participant. It is risky to include someone who represents a unique category that will be salient in the group, as this may isolate the individual and diminish his or her comfort, commitment, and benefit from the group (Brabender et al., 2004). Further efforts to prevent a distracting early departure include preparing the prospective members on what to expect from the group, how to participate effectively in the group, and how to address their realistic concerns or misconceptions.

What Is the Best Way to End a Group?

As is so often the case, there is no single answer to the question of how to best end a group. It depends on the group and its purpose. For a variety of compelling reasons, short-term groups are the increasingly favored and most practical applications of group therapy (Brabender, et al., 2004). One significant advantage of a short-term group is the inclusion of a prospectively established point of termination. This more closely parallels actual behavior, as clients tend to participate on a short-term basis even when the group is intended as a long-term intervention (e.g., Klein & Carroll, 1986). Because as many as 50 to 60 percent of clients return for additional therapy after termination (Budman & Gurman, 1988), many providers offer an option for renewed participation in subsequent time-limited groups. Each group then has a defined beginning and ending, and there is a termination process that marks the end of a specific group's tenure, regardless of whether the participant will end or continue with a new group. This helps individual clients to take stock of their progress, re-evaluate the effectiveness of the means they are using to achieve change (e.g., the group), and sharpen their immediate and longer-term objectives. Ideally, the planned termination helps members increase their motivation to take responsibility for changing, making specific efforts, and coming to terms with the realities of losses and limits.

Open-ended groups must deal with termination on a case-by-case basis. They do not, by definition, have any of the advantages that time-limited groups have with termination woven into the group structure. One trade-off may be that group continuity offers a source of stability for participants, and an opportunity to exercise more autonomy in determining their departure from the group. However, if the group norms establish continuous participation, members may experience considerable emotional stress in relationship to their personal decision about termination. There may be less encouragement of group members to get well and move on and more emphasis on staying involved and supportive of others in their ongoing struggles.

In some ways, we might see open-ended groups as actually biased against termination, as we know that group process is a powerful force that can alter individual judgment. This places more responsibility on the provider to ensure that there is a clear rationale for group continuation, that no one is being harmed, coerced, or simply pulled along by group force to continue in unnecessary therapy, and that the activities of the group continue to have a productive clinical focus. To be responsible to these issues, providers of open-ended group interventions should periodically review the potential termination needs within the group, following the same recommendations offered for evaluating extended individual therapy. Periodically reviewing termination issues with an outside consultant would be well advised.

In time-limited groups, the basic components of a clinically and ethically appropriate termination process are fairly well established in the process of setting up the group. The screening, selection, and preparation process ensures that all clients are notified of when and why termination will occur, and they presumably have access to the provider to assist in determining any needs and options for additional care. The provider makes note of the number of sessions remaining as the group progresses and thus alerts participants to impending termination. Prior to the final session, the provider might offer a plan for the designated termination meeting and enlist the participants in deciding how they would like to acknowledge the group ending (Shapiro & Ginzberg, 2002).

The actual techniques used to mark the final session as a termination meeting can vary considerably, depending on the theme or focus of the group, the proclivities of the provider, and the choices of participants. Some providers emphasize the importance of processing the emotional experience of loss in relationship to the support of the group and as a life theme (Brabender et al., 2004), while others emphasize awareness of new growth within oneself and generalization of that awareness to future intentions (Santorelli, 1999). The provider's leadership in turn guides the clients' choice of activities that reflect these different emphases. So some groups might end with a common ritual of members joining hands and having a go-round of statements about what they will remember about each group member and critical experiences within the group, thus highlighting the transition from togetherness to departure (MacKenzie, 1990). Other variations on these rituals include sharing written compliments that have been collected during the course of the group, or writing down the strengths-based comments that are shared during the last meeting and encouraging clients to post these ideas at home (Walsh, 2007). Other groups might end with a celebration of the experience by bringing food, stories or songs, and perhaps doing a group exercise of everyone writing a personal letter to themselves of what they have touched within themselves during the course of the group, to be mailed to them by the provider at some point in the next 6 to 12 months (Santorelli, 1999). Regardless of the chosen theme or activity, termination is clearly marked with a clinically and ethically appropriate process.

SUMMARY POINTS FOR APPLIED PRACTICE

1. The essential steps of completing a clinically and ethically appropriate termination process remain the same even when therapy involves multiple parties.

2. Termination should follow the original contract for therapy. In couples, family, or group therapy, each designated client should have a recognizable termination.

3. Collateral participants do not have to be involved in termination unless they are the parents of a child client.

4. Couples' therapy should be terminated if it is not safe or likely to be effective. Three fairly well established conditions for this are the presence of an ongoing extramarital affair, ongoing physical abuse, or the absence of any shared system of positive affiliation.

5. Termination of couples' therapy under conditions of positive improvement can be flexibly determined on the basis of the couple's preferences and their ability to improve their conversations on their own.

6. Termination in family therapy follows the care of each designated client. A single family might have multiple points of termination if the focus of therapeutic work shifts from one problem or set of issues to another.

7. The risk of abandonment is elevated in couples or family therapy when the focus shifts. The original intent of therapy and the matter of termination should not be lost or neglected as new problems emerge.

8. Some individuals are prone to a misperception of rejection or abandonment in the family context. This risk needs to be managed with a specific clinical plan that clarifies the participant's role as an identified client or as a collateral participant in the family therapy.

9. Clients who seek couples' or family therapy should not be pressured or pushed to switch to individual therapy. Efforts to persuade the client increase the risk that the provider's intentions will be misunderstood and the potential benefit lost. Referral to a different provider may be an acceptable alternative.

10. Precipitous and unilateral termination of a youth's therapy by a parent is a very awkward and unfortunate situation. It is probably best handled by preventive efforts such as preparing the youth to expect termination and engaging the parent as a collateral participant early in therapy.

11. Clinical skill is crucial in managing the situation where an unwilling or confused youth is delivered to therapy for repairs on the orders of exasperated parents.

The provider can attempt various means of engaging the family before determining termination is in order.

12. Time-limited group therapy usually has an appropriate termination process built into its structure. Specific methods of creating psychological closure in groups vary from acknowledging and mourning losses to celebrating and remembering growth. Open-ended groups need to be monitored for termination concerns to ensure a clinical focus and purpose is protected and participants are actively choosing to continue rather than being pulled along by the force of group consensus.

9

Supervisory Termination

Key Questions Addressed in This Chapter

- Should termination be included in the supervisory contract?
- Is there a clinically and ethically appropriate process of supervisory termination?
- When is supervisory termination complete?
- Should required ongoing supervision ever be formally concluded?
- When should multiple roles precipitate supervisory termination?
- What circumstances should precipitate a *supervisee's* termination?
- Are there situations that should prompt a *supervisor's* termination?
- Are there any particular challenges to expect in terminating supervision?

THE SUPERVISORY RELATIONSHIP

The supervisory relationship has many parallels to the therapeutic relationship, but also some crucial differences with implications for termination. The supervisory relationship has different priorities and responsibilities as compared to a therapeutic relationship. Depending on the level of training, a supervisee has relatively few degrees of freedom and limited autonomy in setting the parameters of the supervisory relationship. Supervision is a requirement, not a choice for those who are not (yet) licensed to practice independently *or* are licensed at a level of practice that requires qualified supervision. Supervision is a fiduciary relationship in which the supervisor holds greater power, responsibility, and trust that he or she will act in good faith, provide an appropriate role model, and act in the best interest of the supervisee (Gottlieb, Robinson & Younggren, 2007).

Supervision as it is described here follows the definition cited by Thomas (2007). Supervision refers to "an intervention provided by a senior member of the profession to a more junior member as part of the latter's training or rehabilitation. The supervision is required by some outside entity, and the supervisor assumes legal responsibility and ultimate authority for all or a designated portion of the supervisee's work. The external body determines the supervision's nature and duration. Conversely, consultation is not generally required by an outside entity and may be provided by a member of the same or an allied profession who possesses the desired expertise. An individual may seek consultation to develop expertise in some new area of practice or as a strategy to enhance his or her professional development. The duration is determined by the needs of the consultee, and the ultimate responsibility for clinical decisions rests with the consultee," (p. 221; cf. Bernard & Goodyear, 2004, p.8).

Clinical supervision is the primary means of acquiring the entry skills for work in any area of applied mental health practice (Campbell, 2006; Getz, 1999). To become qualified for independent practice, a clinician must obtain years of supervised experience. Thus, every clinician has the experience of beginning and ending multiple supervisory relationships over the course of their professional development. Although these relationships are designed to foster skill acquisition and acculturation into the profession (Handlesman, Gottlieb & Knapp, 2005), the primary aim of supervision must still be the assurance of quality of care and protection of the client's best interests (Falender & Shafranske, 2004). Despite the importance and the universality of the supervisory relationship, systematically describing its competencies and conditions is a fairly recent initiative. Recent efforts to spell out the models, methods, and current state of the art in supervision are a welcome advancement (e.g., Barnett, Cornish, Goodyear & Lichtenberg, 2007; Campbell, 2006; Falender & Shafranske, 2004; 2007).

The current standard of practice for clinical supervision now includes a supervisory contract that is executed either before supervision begins or within the first two weeks as part of an initial informed consent dialogue. This is similar to the process of informed consent in psychotherapy, although the specific details of the agreement and the contract are apt to be quite different. The established purpose of this consent process and its contract is to orient the supervisee to supervision, to explain roles, tasks, and requirements, and to create a shared understanding of the ethical standards of practice. The implied purpose is to help maintain boundaries, prevent exploitation, promote a sense of openness and safety, and provide a shared understanding of how learning will take place, how client care will be protected, and how any problems will be solved.

Should Termination Be Included in the Supervisory Contract?

Some orientation toward matters of termination should be considered an element of informed consent in supervision, just as it is in therapy (see Chapter Three). For decades, many training models followed a tradition of minimal informed consent or formal contracting for supervision. Supervisees were assigned to their rotations by a training director, and their task was to form some sort of cooperative and productive relationship with the designated supervisor. The supervisor's task was to take the trainee under his or her wing and provide whatever mentoring seemed appropriate. There was no formal contract between the trainee and supervisor. The only formal documentation occurred at the end of the placement when the trainee was evaluated. There was little systematic attention given to an informed consent process, perhaps because supervisees have such limited power to make choices that the need to provide information and obtain consent was simply not perceived.

Now, a written supervisory contract is required by most graduate training programs and some states before supervision can begin (Campbell, 2006). From practicum to internship to post-graduate supervision, a written document that spells out the terms of agreement is becoming more widely adopted as a useful tool and an explicit responsibility. The process of executing this agreement helps to structure the dialogue of informed consent as it applies to the supervisory relationship. Informed consent in supervision is critical to minimizing risk and maximizing benefit. Emphasis on this process is, however, a fairly recent development. It will likely be some time before informed consent and a formal contract becomes routine for all supervisory arrangements, but the standard of practice is evolving rapidly (Thomas, 2007).

The content of specific written documents will vary with the provider and the nature of the practice and training experience. As Campbell notes (2006, p.126), "The informed consent agreement and supervision contract may be separate documents or a combination of the two, depending on the supervisory situation. Each has a different aim and purpose." Although the supervisory contract is not a legally binding agreement like an office lease, it is useful for spelling out the implied legal aspects of the supervisory relationship (Campbell, 2006; Sutter, McPherson, & Geeseman, 2002). It specifies details of the agreement and establishes written verification that the information has been discussed. Informed consent, on the other hand, is an ongoing interactive process of exchanging information and making decisions about how to proceed (Bennett et al., 2006), thus fulfilling an ethical responsibility to respect the supervisee's autonomy and right to self-determination. A separate informed consent document might provide basic information that supports this purpose.

When combined as one contractual document, the informed consent portion of a supervisory contract is that which provides basic information about the provider, the nature of the practice experience, the process of supervision, any required administrative tasks, pertinent ethical or legal issues, evaluation procedures, and the means that will be used to resolve any difficulties (see Campbell, 2006, for excellent examples of informed consent agreement and supervision contracts; Falender & Shafranske, 2004, for a thorough outline of items to potentially include in a supervision contract). The informed consent documentation is, in brief, a summary of what the supervisee can expect from the experience and the supervisor.

Some training programs use a standard supervisory contract that articulates the important details pertinent to a variety of settings, supervisors, and clinical training experiences. This might be a highly detailed contract, or it can be relatively brief and supplemented with a more detailed document that outlines program policies and procedures (see Exhibit 9.1 and 9.2 for samples). Prospective termination is established in the contract by stating an anticipated date of completion. Any variations on this plan are then subsumed under the agreement to abide by all policies or procedures

Exhibit 9.1   Sample Policy On Graduate Supervision*

Guidelines For Students And Supervisors

Supervision should focus on specific case monitoring and skill training, and be fully consistent with the Rules Governing Psychologists as promulgated by the State Board of Examiners in Psychology. Students and supervisors are encouraged to review these rules, especially under the scope of practice stipulations in chapters 2–4, for further information concerning respective supervisory responsibilities under the law. To ensure that students receive supervision that conforms to these rules of practice and the APA ethics code (esp. Standards 3.05, 3.08, 7.04, 7.06, and 7.07), we require that a practicum contract be completed at the start of the placement, that 25 percent of the time at practicum be spent in individual and group supervision with never less than one hour per week of individual supervision, that communication occur regularly with the program faculty, that evaluations are completed in a timely manner, that any changes to the practicum contract be approved by the program faculty, and that appropriate boundaries be maintained with regard to potential multiple relationships or student disclosure of personal information. Students are not to engage in non-professional social, sexual, or any other potentially harmful multiple relationships with supervisors. Issues of personal reactions may be appropriate for discussion in supervision if pertinent to the monitoring of a specific clinical case. However, students should not be encouraged to extensively disclose private information in supervision, as the process of supervision should be clearly distinguished from individual personal therapy. If a student has personal problems that are interfering with competent performance of practicum duties, the Assistant Directors of Clinical Training should be notified.

In the spirit of collaboration and contribution to the students' overall professional development, we hope that most challenges encountered in meeting these requirements can be dealt with through discussion and informal adjustment. Raising sensitive issues should not be avoided, but rather viewed as part of our commitment to excellence in training. Please use the following protocol as a reference for communication between trainees, supervisors, and the training program faculty.

Protocol for Monitoring Professional Conduct

Students will regularly discuss their supervisory experiences with our designated academic program faculty. For sites where a training director oversees multiple supervisors, we also recommend that the trainee meet at least once per term with that training director to review his or her overall experience. This will enhance the learning process and allow discussion of concerns without having to reach a "problematic" threshold.

Trainees understand that supervisors must be kept fully informed about any consultations the trainee plans to seek concerning any case over which the supervisor holds direct responsibility. The trainee is responsible for fully informing the supervisor about any actions or consultations related to such cases.

If there is an impasse in communication with a supervisor, an ethical violation has occurred, or an ethical violation appears imminent, the training program practicum faculty should be contacted by the student, the supervisor, or site director (or all three). The program faculty will meet with the student, with the supervisor or training director, and possibly as a group to attempt to reach one of the following possible resolutions:

  a. A plan for guiding the student toward a more productive involvement at the current practicum placement may be outlined.
  b. The program faculty may encourage the supervisor to seek consultation or supervision.
  c. The student's practicum contract or relative duties may be modified.
  d. The supervisory assignment may be changed or modified.
  e. The student's term at the specific placement may be terminated, with appropriate provisions for transfer or termination of clients.
  f. Depending on the situation, the student may be subject to further review within the clinical training program if there appears to be any issue of willful unprofessional conduct. An ad hoc review committee consisting of representatives from the clinical area group and the DGS (Director of Graduate Studies) will review the facts and determine if further University review should be pursued. If so, the departmental ad hoc committee will refer the case to the Dean of the Graduate School, who will determine the appropriateness of review by either of two University committees, the Honor Council, or the Legal Council. Any student who is determined to have willfully committed an ethical or legal violation may be subject to dismissal from the clinical graduate training program.

(Continued)

g. The student may discuss any grievance issues with the DCT (Director of Clinical Training) or the DGS, and refer to the Department of Psychology Manual of Standard Operating Procedures.

h. If a personal issue relevant to the student's ability to continue or complete a practicum becomes known to the program DCT or practicum faculty, the program will contact the practicum site for further discussion and decision pending details specific to the situation. The program will attempt to assist any student who is experiencing physical or mental impairments that interfere with competent performance of training-related duties. Efforts to assist the student may include referral for evaluation and treatment as appropriate.

If an ethical violation involving a supervisor can not be resolved sufficiently through informal means, a report to the State Board of Examiners in Psychology will be made, provided that doing so does not violate client confidentiality.

*From the *Practicum Handbook of Requirements and Procedures for Clinical Psychology,* Doctoral Program in Clinical Science, Departments of Psychology and Psychology & Human Development at Vanderbilt University.

Exhibit 9.2   Sample Practicum Contract*

Name of Student

Student's Current Level of Training:

Name of Agency_____

Name of Primary Supervisor_____

Dates of Placement: Begin: ___/ ___/ ___   Intended Completion: ___/ ___/ ___

Credit hours to be earned for   Assessment_____   Therapy_____

Number of hours per week expected to be spent in practicum activity:

(Circle one)   4   8   12   16   20   other

Hours are to be apportioned as follows:

	Summer	Fall	Spring
Inpatient therapy	_____	_____	_____
Inpatient assessment	_____	_____	_____
Outpatient therapy	_____	_____	_____
Outpatient assessment	_____	_____	_____
Total	_____	_____	_____

In a typical week, the above number of hours will be spent:

____ hours of psychological evaluation (actual test administration)

____ hours of writing psychological assessments (report writing only)

____ hours of direct client contact in therapy

____ hours of intake interviewing

____ hours of clinical meetings (e.g., staffing, case conferences)

____ hours of individual supervision for therapy (see Guidelines)

____ hours of individual supervision for assessment

____ hours of group supervision

____ hours of didactic seminars

____ hours of documentation (e.g., maintaining charts, writing letters)

____ hours of case preparation (e.g., preparing for therapy sessions, formulating treatment plans)

____ hours of (specify)_____

____ Approximate number of therapy clients to be seen during placement

____ Approximate number of test batteries to be administered

(Continued)

Indicate which methods of supervision will be used:

____ Audio/video tape of sessions

____ Live observation

____ Case report

____ Co-therapy

____ Modeling and Demonstration

____ Team Feedback

____ Review of written reports/notes

List specific goals for overall training experience (e.g., able to select test battery, or learn to write a treatment plan).

1.

2.

3.

4.

Note: Clinical case materials may be used by the student to fulfill the requirement of a case presentation to practicum class. Relevant identifying information will be omitted.

My signature below indicates that I agree to abide by this contract and by the Practicum Requirements and Procedures as outlined in Handbook B. I agree to adhere to an ethical model of clinical practice and supervision. I understand that the clinical program faculty must be kept informed of all aspects of the training experience, including any changes to this contract. Program faculty is available for consultation at any time and should be contacted if there are any conflicts or concerns regarding either party in the supervisory relationship.

_____/_____   _____/_____
Student Signature   Date   Supervisor Signature   Date

*From the *Practicum Handbook of Requirements and Procedures for Clinical Psychology*, Doctoral Program in Clinical Science, Departments of Psychology and Psychology & Human Development at Vanderbilt University.

specified in other documents, such as a procedural handbook. The procedural protocol then identifies termination as a possible means of resolving difficulties in the supervisory relationship.

The supervision contract and its associated documents create a basic structure for clarifying respective expectations and commitments and establishing mutual consent. Executing the contract is a means by which supervisee and supervisor articulate what they want to accomplish and how they will work together to do so. This template hopefully is a springboard for further discussion about the setting, the supervisor's and trainee's respective background, their model or approach to supervision, what is expected for the supervisee to attain success in the placement, and how problems will be addressed. The contract is an indispensable tool for the apprenticing clinician to use in taking a more active rather than passive role in supervision right from the start. As Campbell (2006) notes, beginnings are important in successful supervision. Having a clear working arrangement from the outset builds the trainee's confidence and provides both participants with a good sense of direction. Under the auspices of graduate training, the contract also provides a means for the program faculty to document a basic level of quality control in the agreements being enacted between two clinicians with vastly different levels of experience and power.

When clinicians must obtain supervision at the post-graduate level to fulfill any requirements for professional licensure, a designated state regulatory board becomes the third-party monitor of the supervisory arrangement. The licensure applicant may be required by the state to obtain a temporary or provisional license that establishes the applicant's authority to engage in supervised practice. To obtain this license, the state might require the applicant to provide a signed and notarized contract for supervision. This supervisory contract simply attests to the existence of an agreement with a specifically named and qualified supervisor. Any requirements of the supervisory arrangement are spelled out in the state's rules and regulations of practice. Holding a license at any level means that both supervisor and supervisee have agreed to abide by those standards. Responsibility for informed consent and articulating the working details of the agreement now falls to the two clinicians who have forged the relationship, with no direct monitoring unless a disciplinary issue comes to the attention of the regulatory board. For their own protection, post-graduate supervisees are well advised to seek supervision from someone who provides a clear written agreement, engages in informed consent dialogue, and who is receptive to the supervisee's inquiries regarding these matters.

Personal contracts for providing supervision are likely to be brief and direct on the matter of termination. The contract may simply note that either party can terminate the agreement with designated notice (e.g., 30 days). The contract should also note a procedure for attempting to resolve disagreements, the most common being the use of an outside consultant or specified third party. Academic programs will typically follow a similar protocol, with the consultation provided by the faculty member responsible for monitoring trainee progress and quality of the supervisory relationship.

It is important to note either in the contract or in supporting documents that termination is a potential outcome of any problem-solving effort, as this is an element of informed consent. Although termination of a supervisory contract for some cause other than completion of the planned rotation is an unlikely event, it is well worth the supervisor's time to think through the operational terms of a threshold for precipitated termination in advance of any action being needed. This will help to reduce the supervisor's angst and struggle and ensure timely action on containing unproductive or potentially harmful situations. Likewise, post-graduate clinicians and program faculty need to have a sense of their limits regarding circumstances that will trigger termination of a supervisor.

Is There a Clinically and Ethically Appropriate Process of Supervisory Termination?

Appropriate supervisory termination can be managed by using the same parameters as therapy termination. Recall that this begins by formulating a termination strategy from the beginning of the relationship. Two primary objectives of the termination strategy are to talk about termination issues (collaboration) and to develop, update, and follow a reasoned plan for appropriate dissolution of the contract. The supervisor's collaborative efforts have a significant influence on the positive quality of the termination. This collaborative stance can be defined in terms of three basic elements: (a) the supervisor takes responsibility for initiating dialogue about the plan for termination, and he or she makes sure this plan is sufficiently addressed at strategic points and revised as needed; (b) the supervisor offers and asks for feedback concerning the supervisee's progress and discusses any reasons or circumstances affecting the existing termination plan; (c) the supervisor establishes a final disposition for the supervisory relationship.

The types of termination may be more limited in supervision as compared to therapy. Recall that therapy terminations can be described as prospectively planned, flexibly implemented in response to the client's immediate needs and circumstances, complex in the nature and extent of communication needed, oblique and unilaterally enacted by the client or unprofessional when the provider fails to uphold basic standards of conduct. Most supervisory termination is prospective in that it is planned for a specific point in time (e.g., end of an academic term) or a specific clinical juncture, such as when the clients have all completed their work or when a certain number of supervisory hours have accrued. The supervisory relationship can be flexibly terminated or temporarily discontinued, but this would most often involve some sort of emergency situation. An example of this might occur when the supervisor is taken ill or has to have surgery or finds that responsibilities must be adjusted because of changed circumstances. In this case the supervisee(s) should be notified and alternative supervisory arrangements established.

A complex termination is any termination that is not readily anticipated, easily managed or imminently reasonable, and acceptable to both parties. Termination of supervision is apt to become more complex and involved when problems escalate and the supervisor either does not have a plan for attempting resolution, or more likely when the supervisee does not respond to efforts offered. Not all conflicts can be anticipated in advance, and perhaps the challenges we end up dealing with are not the ones we anticipated. However, an overall protocol for resolving difficulties can guide the supervisor through managing these various challenges. Complex supervisory termination is a situation where an ounce of prevention and planning is worth a pound of cure.

Supervisors might expect oblique, unilateral termination by the supervisee to be a rare event because the apprentice clinician can not advance to the next level without successful completion of the supervised work. However there are times that supervisees avoid supervision and do not do what is expected in terms of appropriate professional communications. Having a supervisee disappear, fail to show for appointments, or repeatedly cancel meetings without adequate explanation is an urgent situation in need of prompt attention. The supervisor's primary duty is to protect the clients' welfare and because of this, he or she must be continuously apprised of the clients' clinical status. The supervisor can not risk letting the supervisee slide out of contact so far that the supervisor loses track of what is going on with the supervisee's clinical work. This circumstance should activate a pre-established protocol for investigating, confronting, warning, or otherwise containing this questionable, risky, and unprofessional conduct.

In consideration of unprofessional termination, we can return to the concept of abandonment. As you may recall, abandonment in therapy is defined as the absence of a clinically and ethically appropriate process of dissolving the professional relationship (Younggren & Gottlieb, in press). Termination of supervision that occurs prior to prospectively established points without adequate provisions for transfer of responsibility would appear to fall under the definition of abandonment. An example of this would be the supervisor who stops meeting with the supervisee at appointed times and does not make arrangements for other supervisory coverage. Another example is the previously mentioned situation of a disappearing trainee who doesn't show or makes repeated excuses to cancel. Either party could be the initially negligent clinician, but both are liable for abandonment of the supervisory relationship if they fail to address this important situation in a timely manner. Abandoning a supervisory relationship is also abandoning the duty to the client to provide service that meets an appropriate professional standard of care.

There are other examples of unprofessional conduct on the part of either supervisor or trainee that may be cause for termination, but we are concerned at this point with handling of the termination per se in a professional manner. Aside from abandoning the relationship, an unprofessional termination might occur if there is a failure to follow a reasoned course of action. The termination action must include resolution of the contract with the trainee as well as disposition on all of the clients under the trainee's care. Here again, the six essential steps for ensuring an appropriate termination process in therapy can be used as a guideline. These steps are (a) review progress and discuss with supervisor/supervisee; (b) assess the reasons for termination and the supervisor/supervisee's potential concerns; (c) identify any compelling legal or ethical obligations to the supervisee or to the clients; (d) evaluate the level of risk exposure, risk management, and need for consultation; (e) notify and discuss termination with the supervisor/supervisee, and participate in pre-termination counseling; and (f) establish a final disposition with the supervisee and for each client and complete relevant documentation. The use of consultation is extremely important in resolving any complex termination in therapy and the same is true in supervision.

The best assurance of a clinically and ethically appropriate termination of supervision appears to be a well-specified plan that is spelled out in a supervisory contract and in any supplemental informed consent documents and presented at the outset of the endeavor. One caveat to keep in mind, however, is that the best laid plans are only useful to the extent that they are remembered and followed.

What Needs to Happen for Supervisory Termination to Be Complete?

Good endings are as important as good beginnings in therapy and in supervision. Supervisory termination follows a similar process, but the tasks and meaning associated with its completion are quite different from therapy. Supervisory termination often marks a shift in the supervisee's professional identity and in the relationship with the supervisor. Because supervision provides an evaluative, gate-keeping function for the profession and for the protection of the public, there are significant judgments and endorsements involved in completing supervision. The supervisee must have achieved the designated competencies at a satisfactory level to receive a favorable endorsement upon completion. In this way, the closing evaluation helps determine the supervisee's fitness for more advanced duties, highlights areas for further growth or even remediation, and flags problematic areas that signal caution in allowing the supervisee's advancement. Ending a supervisory relationship typically means that the supervisee has progressed in his or her professional developmental milestones, perhaps even crossing a major threshold. This turning point also signals the opening of a window of opportunity for developing a different, more collegial relationship with the now former supervisor.

Hopefully any problems in the supervisee's performance have already been recognized and addressed as an issue of developing competence. Termination evaluation is not the time for surprises, as *initial* negative feedback given at the end is both disturbing and less helpful than it could be with better timing. However, it is possible that certain problems crystallize only at the end and must be addressed for the first time as termination approaches. For this reason, supervisory termination should be a time of heightened awareness of important tasks, risks, and opportunity for learning. The supervisor does not want to allow time pressure or trainee expectations to distort their professional judgment and cause them to minimize or overlook something new in this final evaluation process.

Supervisory termination must subsume the priority task of attending to the termination process of the supervisee's clientele in order to ensure that each client receives proper care and appropriate disposition. Assuming that pro-active strategies, such as those outlined in this volume, have been in place throughout the duration of the training period, the primary closing tasks are to make certain that the supervisee has given each client notice, discussed a clinically appropriate disposition, provided pre-termination counseling and referral as needed, and completed all final documentation. This final step, the completion of all final documentation, can become a stumbling block for some supervisees as the demands of transition causes some tasks to "fall through the cracks." Experienced supervisors are often alert to this risk and routinely plan to withhold necessary evaluation of the trainee until after all required administrative work is completed.

Discussion of the supervisee's evaluation usually takes place at or just before a final supervisory meeting. This is the time to wrap-up any final details, to share feedback with the supervisee, and to ask for closing feedback on the supervisory experience. The supervisee might be asked to complete a formal rating form, either by the supervisor or by the external monitor of the experience such as their graduate program. The supervisor might also take this opportunity to solicit the supervisee's suggestions for ways to improve the experience for future supervisees.

The relationship changes that might occur with supervisory termination are unique. Supervisory termination entails shifts in the power structure that do not occur in psychotherapy, although it is not possible to know how long the supervisory power differential continues or how it will change over time (Gottlieb et al., 2007). Clinicians are aware that therapy entails a certain power structure that does not dissolve at termination and because of this they are alert to possible fiduciary duty in any future dealings with their clients. It is not quite the same with supervisees. The supervisor will always have more years of experience and perhaps perceived power in the eyes of the supervisee. However, the supervisee is accruing power, responsibility, and independent standing as a colleague within the mental health profession. Continuing a collegial working relationship with the former supervisor is not only permitted, it can be encouraged as a vehicle for positive professional development, as long as prudent ethical regard still prevails.

Many supervisors like to mark the completion of supervision with an activity that signifies change, such as going out for a meal or a drink together. An activity like this is a common strategy for denoting the opportunity to develop a more mutual and friendly relationship. Timing is important, however, as is advance discussion on ways to mark the end of supervision and change in the relationship. Any special activities should take place after evaluations are completed so there is no implied message that the supervisee must be friendly and go out socially with the supervisor or give the supervisor gifts in order to receive a favorable evaluation (or that doing so will produce a favorable evaluation). The supervisee's level of accomplishment often determines his or her readiness to accept a shift in the supervisory power structure. Those who are young in their career (but not necessarily young in their chronological years) may feel most reluctant and awkward about collegial-type activities, while those who are more advanced and closer to independence have an easier time enjoying such gestures and benefiting from this mentoring effort.

Should Required Ongoing Supervision Ever Be Formally Concluded?

When supervision is a job requirement or a standard for practice rather than a focused training experience that will lead to eventual independent practice, its continuation might be assumed in perpetuity. In agencies or groups, it might be assumed that the contract is open-ended and will continue until someone is fired or takes another job. Should such arrangements ever be formally concluded? Good reasons to say yes are offered by Campbell (2006). Conclusion in this context follows the idea of termination as a point of re-evaluation, and possible renewal of a contract. It does not necessarily mean stopping or dissolving the relationship but it might be a point of discontinuation or redirection. Routinely planning an ending, such as on a yearly basis, creates structure, ensures evaluation of the experience, fosters growth over stagnation and allows people an opportunity to make changes without having to develop problems or personal reasons to change. It also promotes goal setting, positive motivation, and greater agency among the participants. Supervisory groups, even open-ended ones, can benefit from setting such time limits as well. A new beginning for individual or group supervision may pick up right where the ending left off, but participants have had some breathing space and opportunity to evaluate the productivity and direction of their efforts.

PROBLEMS IN SUPERVISORY TERMINATION

Assuming that supervision will always terminate without incident is a risky position to take, even if the supervisor has decades of experience to support this assumption. The risks of adverse events do not diminish over time and may, in fact, increase. Part of the reason for increased risks is that rules and regulations of practice and the standards to which supervisors are held are, like the tax code or the Medicare manual, expanding and becoming more complex. One of the most significant risks in being unprepared for problems in supervisory termination is the emotional distress and turmoil that can result from having to grope your way through an unpleasant and professionally threatening situation. Supervisors need to be well versed in risk management strategies and actively engaged in preventive efforts.

Any lack of supervisory preparation for termination is more apt to be the result of few resources and little attention to the topic rather than outright disinterest or willful neglect. Although supervision is the means by which all practical mental health skills are taught, few supervisors have formal training or supervision in the development and use of this particular skill set (Campbell, 2006). Instead, most supervisors rely on the skills drawn from their own experiences as a supervisee. Not only does this present the real possibility that supervisors will perpetuate any mistakes of their mentors, it suggests that those trainees who matriculated practica without incident will have an experiential deficit in knowing how to spot problems and deal with them. The fortunate few are those who either have had or observed problems that were dealt with effectively, thus forming experiential reference points, or those who have had some guidance in developing these important supervisory skills. In the sections to follow, some of the possible reasons why supervision might need to be terminated for cause are explored.

When Should Multiple Roles Precipitate Supervisory Termination?

Conflict of interest in supervision is difficult to crisply discern. To answer this question about when multiple roles cause a conflict of interest, we need to consider issues pertaining to sexual and romantic relationships, professional development and maturation, mentorship, and role boundaries, crossings, violations, and overlap.

Sexual and Romantic Relationships.   Some role boundaries are clearly marked and firm while many others are discretionary and determined by contextual factors. Current professional standards require that explicit boundaries be maintained for sexual or close personal relationships that obviously present a conflict of interest with the supervision. Sexual relationships with supervisees are expressly prohibited as a matter of professional ethics (e.g., APA, 2002, 7.07; ACA, 2005, F.3.b) while other non-professional relationships with supervisees are discouraged (ACA, 2005, F.3.a). Although some ethical guidelines only discourage supervision of a close relative, romantic partner, or friend (ACA, 2005, F.3.d), institutional policy or state law may specifically forbid direct supervision between persons with such relationships. For example, Tennessee rules of practice for psychologists prohibit a supervisor from holding a dual role such as close relative, spouse, or therapist of the supervisee (Rule 1180-2-.01 (7) (d) 2.).

Keeping a clear boundary with sexual and romantic interaction is the responsibility of the supervisor (Herlihy, 2006). If this line is crossed, it is up to the supervisor to take appropriate and decisive action toward promptly ending the supervision. Depending on the level of repercussions expected for this termination, it is not too surprising when both parties want to avoid ending either relationship. However, the further this goes, the deeper the trouble in terms of unprofessional conduct. From a disciplinary standpoint, making a mistake is one thing but failing or resisting corrective action suggests a more serious pattern of willful disregard of professional standards.

Professional Development and Maturation.   There are other interactions that fall under the notion of multiple relationships between supervisor and supervisee which can not be avoided and instead must be appropriately managed (Herlihy, 2006). It is inevitable that there will be some contact outside of clinical supervision during the course of attending meetings, conferences, workshops, classes, and collegial social events. Multiple relationships occur frequently, are not unethical per se, and are a realistic part of professional life (Gottlieb et al., 2007). They are part of the desired course of professional acculturation and maturation. Some distinctions are necessary, however, to see the differences between positive, risky, and harmful relationships in the professional context.

Often the same person provides multiple levels of supervision as professor, researcher, employer, and clinical supervisor. An academic clinical supervisor might employ the trainee in a research capacity, provide training and feedback for assessment and intervention skills, supervise the trainee's own research, collaborate on publications, and contribute to the programmatic evaluation of the student. In an agency setting, the clinical supervisor might also be an administrative supervisor. All of these roles still fall within the scope of a professional relationship that is intended to accomplish professional objectives and contribute to the supervisee's professional development. Supervisor and supervisee might work together in the research lab, attend the same workshop, or go out to dinner together with a group at a conference without losing their professional focus. This is because these interactions are all consistent with an established hierarchy of fiduciary supervisor and apprentice supervisee and none of the various activities alters the basic professional contract.

Mentorship.   *Mentorship* can be confusing because on the surface it might resemble an inappropriate relationship. Mentorship is an emotionally connected, dynamic, and enduring personal relationship that unfolds and develops intensity over time. A clinical supervisor may become a mentor but this is not defined at the beginning because the mentoring relationship must develop over time through mutual participation. However, the process of mentoring incorporates a deliberate and active concern for the trainee's professional development that goes beyond simple acquisition of clinical skills (Johnson, 2007). Mentors are defined by their support, encouragement, affirmation, personal interest, and frequent interaction with the supervisee across multiple contexts. This requires considerable competence and maturity in the supervisor and careful attention to protecting the supervisee from any harm or exploitation as well as willingness and effective collaboration of the supervisee. When the supervisor possesses the necessary internal restraints and wisdom, and there is a synergistic reaction with the supervisee, mentorship is a very positive and desirable relationship (Johnson, 2007). There is no need to discourage this relationship or terminate it as long as proper caution is observed by both participants.

Role Boundaries, Crossings, Violations, and Overlap.   Termination of supervision might be warranted if the multiple relationships between supervisee and supervisor cause harmful or inappropriate deviations from their respective professional roles. The rules that define expected behavior when interacting in one's professional capacity are considered *role boundaries*. Whether interacting with clients or in supervision, there are general boundaries for the permissible amount and timing of contact (both face-to-face, telephone, and e-mail), range of topics to be discussed, physical closeness allowed and non-verbal behavior that is appropriate, territory or range of physical spaces shared, and extent and type of emotional disclosure considered acceptable (Walsh, 2007).

Departing from the normal expectations for role behavior is considered a *boundary crossing*. This is common and probably part of an ordinary learning process. Boundary crossings help identify limits or prompt adaptive role adjustments. However, boundary crossings should not be too large, careless, or ignored. Such actions can quickly develop into *boundary violations*, depending in part on the perceptions and reactions of the supervisee. For example, a supervisor might ask the supervisee for a lift to the car repair shop at the end of their meeting, provided the supervisee is willing and not inconvenienced by this unplanned task. This is a boundary crossing that should have no ill effects and may even contribute to a sense of collegiality. If the task causes the supervisee to miss class, however, it causes some harm. If the supervisor insists on taking the supervisee out for drinks at happy hour as thanks, the boundary crossing is large and risky. Some potentially risky boundary crossings include excessive touching, needless self-disclosure, inappropriate attire, inappropriate jokes, or special treatment, gifts, or friendship (Gottlieb et al., 2007). *Boundary violations* occur when role variations (boundary crossings) cause impaired judgment or loss of objectivity, exploitation of the supervisee, disruption of clinical supervision, or other foreseeable harm (For more in-depth examination of boundaries, see Zur, 2007).

It is easy to see the potential confusion between mentoring, boundary crossing, and boundary violations. A distinction can be made by the level of coercion perceived by the recipient, the relative contribution that the role variation makes to the supervisee's overall professional needs and interests, and finally in the accumulating impact of the interactions between supervisor and supervisee on both parties as well as their larger professional community. For example, a supervisor who offers a talented student a special opportunity to do fee-for-service evaluations to earn extra money and gain additional hours of supervision without any coercion to do so is offering a mentoring experience. Compare this with a supervisor who adamantly insists that the student accompany him to a weekend workshop that will include considerable personal self-disclosure. When the student tries to refuse, citing cost as a factor, he offers to pay for everything and makes teasing jokes about the student's (non-existent) "compulsive fears of being real with emotions."

It is difficult to create a firewall between working with a supervisee in one area and judging his or her efforts in another without any cross-influence or intrusion of one's self-interest. *Overlap* between the roles can increase the risk of misjudgment and diminished objectivity. For example, when a supervisee does a superlative job in the research lab and produces multiple publications, he or she might acquire a certain "halo effect" that causes the supervisor to overlook the supervisee's naiveté and overconfidence in clinical matters. Perhaps the supervisor, motivated by his or her own desire to achieve tenure, is tempted to use the supervisory contact to exploit the clinical supervisee's skill with statistics and data analysis. In the professional hierarchy, trainees do not typically feel empowered to say no to such requests, particularly when accompanied by flattery and approbation.

On the other hand, supervisees also have blinds spots, and they might fail to see the harm in accommodating the supervisor's vulnerabilities or demands. Perhaps the supervisee offers to "help" an overworked clinical and administrative supervisor ease his or her time burdens by canceling supervisory meetings, telling the supervisor that all is well and no consultation is needed. Perhaps the supervisee offers to "fill in" the supervisor's signature on records so that documentation can be kept up to date while saving the supervisor the inconvenience of actually reviewing it. Overly submissive, attentive care-taking behavior is not unusual when one is in a subordinate position and dependent upon the favor of the superior for advancement.

Or it may be that there is no grossly impaired judgment, loss of objectivity, or exploitation, but the supervisory pair neglects the primary focus of supervision by allowing their other shared interests to predominate their interactions. Supervision time is spent happily chatting about research ideas, projects, conferences, or personal interests while matters of client welfare are overlooked. The problem is not necessarily the expanded range of their discussion, but rather that it has supplanted the cardinal focus on client care and development of clinical skills. Problems with such blurring of multiple professional roles are often solvable and do not necessarily indicate termination of one role or another unless corrective efforts are denied, refused, or not effective.

Can We Be Friends? Things get more complicated when the boundaries of professional roles begin to overlap with non-professional roles, yet there is still a legal responsibility for actions that involve third parties. The stakes become greater as the number of roles increases. The risk of harm or exploitation is increased when multiple roles are more incompatible or conflicting (e.g., personal and evaluative roles) (Gottlieb et al., 2007; Kitchener, 1988). Although some social contact is inevitable and important to a maturing collegial relationship, it is risky to cross the barrier between business and friendship when one party continues to hold significant evaluative authority and legal responsibility for the actions of the other in clinical matters.

The expected behaviors that build a friendship—being available, uncritically supportive, generous, and tolerant of shortcomings—often conflict with an evaluative stance where one must ensure that certain standards are met. Confrontation has a different tone and meaning in a personal context, and problem resolution generally involves more negotiation and accommodation between friends. Clinical supervisors, on the other hand, must ensure that standards are met, be ready to enforce limits, and deliver sanctions if necessary. The role conflict between being supervisor and friend presents significant potential for risky boundary crossings, boundary violations, and harm to the third party (clients).

Age proximity can make a friendly relationship seem like a natural extension of the supervision, but the risks are even greater when both clinicians have relatively little experience in maintaining their professional roles. Young supervisors (interns, post-docs, post-graduates within the first five years of independent practice) often still identify more with the supervisee role, feel uncomfortable with being a member of the "establishment," and have an underdeveloped grasp of their role of authority. The finer, more subtle differences between mentoring and potentially harmful multiple relationships may be difficult for younger supervisors to distinguish in their actions. For the sake of their own development and to appropriately fulfill their ethical and legal responsibilities, young supervisors are well advised to avoid role overlap in relationships where they must perform an evaluative function. Clear boundary maintenance is most salient when the supervisor is experiencing any difficulty that requires monitoring (Gottlieb et al., 2007). This point can be logically extended to younger supervisors who may not be having particular problems but are still learning how to carry the evaluative role. Supervisees are safer when the supervisor keeps the evaluative capacity clearly in mind.

When a supervisee rises through the ranks and becomes a supervisor for a former peer and friend, there is a very conspicuous issue of potential role conflict that should not be dismissed as trivial. The supervisor may feel capable of being objective and fair, but feeling capable does not necessarily establish *being* capable. Whether this role conflict can be managed will depend on the relative maturity and autonomy of both people and the degree of authority and legal responsibility involved in the supervision. For example, a clinician who has just obtained her license for independent practice, now working in the clinic where she trained, would be a poor supervisory match for her friend who is just a year her junior and needing post-doctoral supervision. As a supervisor, she has little distance from this subordinate role, yet would be assuming responsibility for evaluating her friend's fitness to enter independent practice and sharing legal responsibility for her friend's actions. The stakes are high and the relative autonomy and career maturity of both participants is moderately low.

Compare this with a situation where two clinicians have worked together in an agency for five years. They are friends at work and away from work, and both have the capacity to practice independently. Dr. A proposes a contract to receive supervision from Dr. B for a period of six months to expand her clinical skills in a specific area. Dr. B assumes legal responsibility and ultimate authority only for the four clients that he will supervise and only for the agreed period of time. His evaluation of Dr. A, while it could strain their friendship, will have no direct impact on her employment or her general career status unless she engages in some sort of unprofessional or negligent conduct. This is no different from the collegial relationship that already exists. There is little reason to believe that the pre-existing friendship would necessarily conflict with this defined and limited role of supervisor.

In the end, it seems reasonable to assume that supervision should be terminated if clear boundary violations have occurred or are an ongoing problem that can not be adequately resolved. Supervisor and supervisee do not have to repel like the North and South poles outside of the consulting room, but they do need to respect the professional hierarchy within their relationship. Slight boundary crossings can provide opportunities to learn how to manage the professional role without slipping into non-professional or incompatible roles, as long as the crossing is noted with self-reflection and redirection if needed.

What Circumstances Should Precipitate a *Supervisee's* Termination?

A precipitated supervisee termination will depend on how any problems with the supervisee's performance are defined (Campbell, 2006) and what happens in the course of a due process attempt to rectify those problems. Poor performance that can be remedied with supervisory intervention can be distinguished from character issues or clinical impairment that requires something beyond the scope of supervision. Ethical or legal mistakes or clinical blunders can result from inadequate preparation, obstinacy, deviance or resistance to professional acculturation, or stress-related conditions and clinical decompensation. By definition, supervision is expected to be an experience of learning as the trainee acquires new skills and improves performance. Thus it should be expected for the supervisee to make some mistakes and need corrective feedback. However, supervisee incompetence is not expected or tolerated. Supervisee impairment calls for collegial assistance and referral.

Some mistakes are more alarming than others, though, and should trigger elevated supervisory vigilance and intervention. Such actions could indicate a *possible* dismissal from supervision or even a training program. Behaviors that create harmful, unethical, or unproductive conditions include the following actions summarized by Campbell (2006) and Thomas (2007):

Potential Cause for Supervisory Dismissal

- Noncompliance with supervisory directions
- Refusing to help and withholding service or support from clients
- Belittling, harassing, attacking, or manipulating clients for one's own benefit
- Abandoning clients
- Breaking confidentiality
- Engaging in fraud
- Promoting boundary violations (sexual relationships, going into business, etc.)
- Using inappropriate diagnosis or intervention strategy
- Failing to recognize a need for referral
- Withholding or misrepresenting information about self or client to the supervisor, particularly in crisis situations
- Frequent tardiness or absence
- Inability to practice with reasonable safety or skill

Efforts to deal with problems should be guided by the dual priority of ensuring that client welfare is protected and that the supervisee is afforded an understanding of the problem, reasonable time to change, and assistance or guidance in making needed changes. There is no standard time frame for trying to sort out and remediate supervisee problems before enacting termination. Instead, this can be based on implementing an established remediation protocol that includes the following steps (Herlihy, 2006):

Steps for Supervisee Remediation

- Specific feedback is offered to the supervisee that outlines problem behaviors or deficits
- An opportunity for and assistance in improving are offered
- A remediation plan with specific objectives and a timeline is agreed upon
- Evaluative feedback regarding the efforts to improve is offered both orally and in writing
- Supervisory consultation is obtained
- An appeal process is made known to the supervisee

Sometimes there is confusion about what constitutes an adequate effort to help the supervisee make remedial changes. Common tactics might include assigning additional readings, videotapes, training sessions, adding group supervision, requiring self-study courses or modules, helping the supervisee work through ambivalence about changing and moving forward and encouraging the supervisee to problem solve and find ways to manage stress and reduce situational burnout. Having an outside consultant review the situation to suggest other ideas for resolving relationship impasses and to provide a reliability check for the supervisor's judgment is extremely useful.

If the supervisee does not follow through on such remedial efforts, nothing changes, or the changes are unsatisfactory in terms of the agreed objectives and timeline (too little, too late), the gate-keeping function of supervision should be triggered, even if the supervisee wails and gnashes and threatens to sue. The supervisor has offered a reasonable learning experience but in the end must protect the public from the risk of an inadequate, incompetent, or dangerous provider (Campbell, 2006). By now, this turn of events should be no surprise to the supervisee. The possibility of termination was addressed in the supervisory contract and the supervisee has been notified, warned, and given an opportunity to regain control of the situation.

When it appears that the supervisee's problems are placing clients at risk and the resolution is beyond the scope of supervision (e.g., character problems, clinical impairment), the supervisor may have to choose between recommending an immediate leave of absence to resolve the problems with a possible return pending sufficient remediation *or* a closed termination without the option of returning. If a distraught supervisee takes any of these outcomes poorly and appears to present an imminent danger to self or others, appropriate protective actions should be set in motion.

Are There Situations That Should Prompt a *Supervisor's* Termination?

Supervisors often begin with a certain handicap because until recently there has been little structured training and few resources to support the acquisition of this specific competency. Often problems in supervision are not the result of a bad supervisor so much as inadequate supervisory development. Many problems in supervision can be remedied with better support for the supervisor in the form of information, structure, consultation, and strategic feedback. Termination does not need to be a first resort when difficulties are encountered, but it may be a reasonable and viable alternative. Termination is necessary if it becomes apparent that the supervisor is incompetent, persistently unethical, or impaired.

Incompetence is a lack of requisite skills and should be distinguished from unethical judgment or impairment related to substance abuse, psychopathology, or burnout (Falender & Shafranske, 2007). Competence, on the other hand, is a continuously developed, dynamic, and situation-specific phenomenon. Boundaries of competence are broadly defined by having "education, training, supervised experience, consultation, study or professional experience" (APA, 2002, 2.01 (a)). Clinical competence is a matter of degree that is greatly affected by the supervisor's degree of professional involvement, ongoing practice, and participation in continuing education.

Inadequate supervisory performance is a paramount concern, but one that is somewhat difficult to detect and evaluate. Supervisee's assessments provide some information, but in most instances a single supervisee's comments should be taken in a context of other data when evaluating the performance and competence of a supervisor. Supervisees typically have idiosyncratic responses that are colored by their own needs, traits, and coping style, and they are not fully qualified to provide an objective evaluation of supervisory functioning. Performance evaluation is one of the skills that they are beginning to acquire but this competence is in its nascent stages. Their feedback is relevant, but it becomes more compelling in cumulative form, when a pattern of supervisor behavior becomes evident. Depending on the supervisee's level of maturity and experience, they also tend to be somewhat naïve in judging the nuances of professional standards. They are still forming their understanding of what is and is not ethical judgment or adequate performance. One supervisee might raise vaguely grounded concerns about a supervisor's competence while another bonds with the same clinician as their favorite role model. Their concepts of professional standards are not fully formed, and they need further opportunities to test their perceptions, usually with someone other than the supervisor (Gottlieb et al., 2007). One study of supervisee perceptions of supervisor's ethical behavior found that over half reported at least one perceived ethical violation by their supervisor

(Ladany, Lehrman-Waterman, Molinaro, & Wolgast, 1999). However, it comes as no surprise that many supervisees turned to other resources to discuss the matter, with 54 percent discussing it with someone other than the supervisor and only 35 percent talking with the supervisor.

It is important to evaluate supervisory competence on a prospective basis to judge whether the supervisor's self-assessment of competence (Falender, Cornish, et al., 2004) adequately matches the needs of the supervisee. For trainees at more subordinate levels, this evaluation needs to be done by someone qualified to make the judgment. Supervisees at a post-graduate level must take more personal responsibility for using the process of informed consent to screen the supervisor's competence for the task. Difficulties with competence that arise during a supervisory relationship may be a function of a mismatch of skills and needs, poor management skills, or escalating supervisor impairment. Irritable or erratic behavior, cynicism, significant distraction, and loss of interest are but a few of the potential signs of supervisor impairment, along with more serious ethical slippage. If competency issues arise during the course of a supervisory relationship, it might be reasonable to involve a consultant and develop a plan for remediation. Otherwise, a switch to a different supervisor might the wisest course of action.

Supervisees may be the first to spot blatant problems of harmful and unethical behavior that should precipitate termination of the supervisor, even though their subtle judgment is still unrefined. Examples of such behavior (in addition to sexual intimacies) include misusing power to meet their own personal and professional needs, being vindictive, treating the supervisee with derision or malice, demeaning them publicly or privately, or showing blatant prejudice or favoritism based on race, gender, sexual orientation, age, education, or discipline (Ellis, 2001). Such harmful behavior can cause emotional trauma of a short- or long-term nature, and can significantly impact a supervisee's career and personal development. The worst outcome would be if the behavior caused the supervisee to drop out or leave the field entirely. However, their relatively low position of power makes it difficult for supervisees to speak up and blow the whistle on supervisors. Supervisors in this situation are often highly resistant to any feedback and if confronted by their supervisee will retaliate and escalate their behavior (Campbell, 2006).

Thus it is crucial that all supervisees have some safe means to speak up and test their perceptions concerning the supervisor's potentially incompetent or unethical actions, misuse of power, or erratic behavior. This safety net can be established by identifying a third-party monitor or consultant at the outset of supervision when the contract is established so that the supervisee knows what direction to turn when questions arise. It is also imminently helpful for the consultant to have an additional line of consultation ready to provide a second opinion, particularly in highly charged situations where jobs, careers, and reputations hang in the balance.

Other formal advisory resources, such as the ethics committee of a professional association or a malpractice insurance consultant, can help the third-party monitors evaluate their decisions and actions. State licensing boards are generally not equipped to handle advisory matters and members serving on such boards must be careful not to render casual advisement on cases that could possibly rise to a formal disciplinary level. However, it may be appropriate to file a complaint with relevant disciplinary board if the supervisor's peers have cause to believe the clinician presents a risk to the public and the issue has not been resolved through less formal collegial intervention. This will trigger a formal disciplinary investigation that will be evaluated by the designated regulatory board.

Are There Any Particular Challenges to Expect in Terminating Supervision?

The reasons for ending supervision are roughly similar to the reasons for ending therapy, and they follow a similar challenge profile. Ending because the work is complete is a positive if somewhat poignant conclusion. No real problems are likely to occur, and it may even be that a mentoring relationship continues. Ending supervision for other understandable reasons is apt to be unremarkable in terms of any particular challenges. If schedules just aren't working out or the supervisor has to take a medical leave or the supervisee wants to take advantage of a different opportunity that has opened up, no one is particularly perturbed as long as there is an orderly termination process. Determining that the supervisor is not the right person for the job does not have to be particularly traumatic if the situation is handled with tact, diplomacy, and maturity by all involved.

The primary challenges are apt to be in situations with highly charged emotions, when the supervision or the supervisory relationship is inappropriate, harmful, and inadequate or below minimal standards. Both supervisee and supervisor are apt to experience some distress, regardless of the source of error. Few situations are more wrenching than having one's competence or ethical behavior called into question by fellow professionals, no matter whether they are subordinates, peers, or superiors. And although it may be hard to believe it, anyone who has ever had to fire, dismiss, or discipline a fellow professional understands the angst of rendering such negative consequences. Administering sanctions is antithetical to our usual helping role. When this occurs in a supervisory context, the emotional intensity is magnified by the significance associated with this particular professional relationship. We know that getting fired or dismissed by a client is an occupational hazard that happens sometimes despite our preventive efforts. We come to accept, eventually, that some therapy efforts are just not going to work. But with supervision, we tend to have much higher expectations for success along with greater vulnerability to distress at failure. Allegations of wrongdoing, incompetence, impairment, or other unethical conduct in the process of teaching or acquiring professional skills cuts right to the core of the clinician's professional identity, source of livelihood, and personal future. It is no wonder that such situations arouse defensive anger and possible retaliation.

Emotional turmoil is apt to be a bigger challenge than any threatened lawsuit, ethics complaint, or other forms of external reprisal. If the termination action has included a due process and conformed to expectations for a clinically and ethically appropriate process, formal actions are unlikely to proceed beyond the investigation stage. Gossip and other peripheral interest that reverberates from the termination are usually evident for what they are and at most have minimal and fading impact. The power of an influential person to discredit a supervisee or a consultant is often greatly feared, and although retaliation is possible it is often less probable than fear makes it seem. Internal emotional processing may continue for some time though, with varying degrees of turbulence, self-doubt, or recrimination of self or others. The impact of harmful behavior on supervisees can be profound, as can the consequences for engaging in such behavior or poorly handling the supervisory termination.

The best defense against emotional disruption and turmoil is a series of pro-active efforts to reduce the risk of misunderstandings and have contingencies plans ready for action. Key pro-active efforts include using informed consent and a supervisory contract, outlining a protocol for spotting and managing potentially problematic behaviors as soon as possible, and keeping professional roles separate from incompatible nonprofessional roles.

SUMMARY POINTS FOR APPLIED PRACTICE

1. Supervisors have a fiduciary role that holds the greater power, trust, and responsibility for defining the beginning and ending of the professional relationship and the supervisee's learner role.

2. A written supervisory contract that spells out terms of agreement, including termination contingencies, is an emerging standard of practice.

3. The clinically and ethically appropriate process of supervisory termination follows a close parallel to the process of therapy termination. Supervisory termination is more extensive in that it includes reaching a disposition with each of the supervisee's clinical cases and endorsing the supervisee's competence.

4. Most supervisory termination is prospective, but it can be flexible as well. It can become complex, especially when problems have escalated without effective intervention. Oblique termination of supervision is unprofessional and should not happen.

5. If either or both parties stop meeting without an appropriate termination or transfer, supervisory abandonment has occurred. The supervisor has, in effect, abandoned all of the supervisee's clients as well.

6. Supervisory termination is uniquely defined by a professional re-evaluation and redefinition of the relationship. When supervision ends, the supervisee's professional status and identity change. This may or may not change the power and evaluative hierarchy within the relationship.

7. Boundary violations cause termination of the supervisory relationship. Boundary crossings are common and offer opportunities for learning how to stay in a professional role across different contexts.

8. Trying to avoid any multiple relationships or multiple roles with a supervisee is unrealistic and probably not desirable. Multiple contacts are part of professional acculturation and development and do not cause problems for stable supervisory pairs. Problems emerge when either party is unstable, unethical, or unclear about the professional hierarchy or when roles multiply and overlap in incompatible ways. The most significant risks occur when there is an attempt to combine professional and non-professional roles.

9. Poor performance can be remedied but negative behaviors that cause supervision or therapy to be unsafe, unethical, or unproductive are cause for dismissal. Remember to follow due process in working through any problem to determine if remediation is possible prior to dismissal.

10. Supervisees need a safe third-party consultant with whom they can test their perceptions of supervisor behavior and learn to distinguish the boundaries of acceptable and unacceptable professional actions.

10

A Consumer's Guide to Ending Psychotherapy[1]

Beginnings and endings are important. As a consumer of professional psychotherapy, you want to make the most of your experience. The more informed you are about how psychotherapy works and how it ends, the better prepared you will be to work with your therapist toward a satisfying experience and a positive conclusion.

The following are frequently asked questions that can increase your understanding of how psychotherapy is structured. This will help you in making decisions about when and where your therapy should end. It can also help you to work effectively with your therapist and have the best possible experience from beginning to end.

1. What is psychotherapy termination, and when does it happen?
2. How do I know if I've had enough therapy?
3. Are there any other reasons to stop therapy?
4. What does it mean to "end on a positive note"?
5. Shouldn't I stay in therapy until I feel totally together?
6. I really depend on therapy. Do I have to let it go?
7. Should I quit therapy if I feel lost or stuck?
8. I can not seem to talk about ending therapy. What should I do?
9. Doesn't my therapist have to continue therapy until I feel ready to stop?
10. Will my therapist stop working with me if my problems are too difficult?
11. I am angry and disappointed in therapy. What are my options?
12. Will I be able to return to therapy if I feel the need?
13. What happens to my records after I stop therapy?
14. Can my therapist talk about me once therapy ends?
15. Can my therapist and I be friends after therapy?
16. I think my therapist and I have a mutual attraction. Can we get together after therapy?
17. Should I let my therapist know how I'm doing after we stop therapy?
18. Will we have some sort of graduation at my last session?

19. Should I bring a gift to mark the ending?
20. Can I refer my friends or other family members to my therapist?

Special Concerns for Kids and Teens

1. How long do I have to be in therapy?
2. Once I stop, can I ever go back to my therapist?
3. Will the therapist report my problems to my school or college?
4. Does ending therapy mean that I am normal?

UNDERSTANDING HOW TO END ON A POSITIVE NOTE

Frequently Asked Questions

1. What Is Psychotherapy Termination, and When Does It Happen?
Termination is a formal word for ending therapy. Usually this means that regular meetings with the therapist are no longer scheduled, although sometimes follow-up visits are made on an "as needed" basis. It used to be that most therapy lasted a long time and termination was a special phase that took several months. Now there is a greater range of time for therapy, from weeks to months to years in some cases. It is also common to have more than one episode of shorter-term therapy. For some people, contact with a therapist, either the same one or a new one, may continue over many years, with several endings and new beginnings. Most therapists think of termination as not just one big conclusion but rather a point of re-evaluation and redirection that may occur several times over. The discussion about how long therapy should take and when it should end actually begins in the first visit. This is when the purpose of the therapy is identified. Deciding when, how, and why to end this work is a task that you and your therapist will discuss together, bit by bit, until you reach a conclusion.

2. How Do I Know if I've Had Enough Therapy?   There is no single answer to this question. Everyone is different in how much therapy they might need or want at any given point in time. What constitutes "enough" therapy depends on the changes you hope to make, the extent of the problems you are trying to overcome, the energy you have available to put into those changes, your overall readiness to actively work on these issues, and your interest in the tools and support offered by psychotherapy.

The best way to determine a point of "enough" therapy is to be specific about what you want. If your main goal is something clear-cut and discrete, such as deciding whether to attend a family reunion, you will know that you have had enough therapy when your decision is settled. Therapy goals are usually broader than this, however. If your main goal is something more complex or extensive, such as understanding your family dynamics, it will be harder to draw a specific line on when "enough" therapy has occurred.

Your therapist can help you to set some more specific sub-goals for the broader ones that you want to undertake. Many complex problems are dealt with in segments or "chunks" of therapy over time, so the issue of "enough" becomes one of "enough for now." Signs that you may have had enough therapy for now include:

- Feeling ready to move on from a particular issue after resolving some important feelings or thoughts
- Having a sense of relief or accomplishment about what you have discussed so far in therapy
- Thinking that something important has been reworked in a new way
- Feeling better overall
- Doing better in your life activities and roles (family, work, school, personal)
- Feeling like you don't really have anything to work on
- Getting a little bored and restless with therapy
- Thinking that you might be ready to stop

Some of these can also be signs that you are avoiding bigger or more difficult issues. It is helpful to ask yourself about this possibility, discuss it with your therapist, and then decide whether to stop therapy. You may not be ready to work on that bigger issue. Even though it is there, it could be that you have had enough therapy for now. This is not meant to imply that you will inevitably need more therapy. Many if not *most* problems are resolved without the formal support of psychotherapy. Change is a self-directed process, and formal therapy is only one option to assist you on this path.

3. Are There Any Other Reasons to Stop Therapy? Sessions can be stopped for many reasons. The most common is that certain goals have been reached or you both decide that the work has served its original purpose. Other potential reasons for terminating therapy are:

- Financial limits have been reached
- Scheduling does not work out
- Too many other demands on your energy
- Job or life changes make it impractical or impossible to continue
- This provider is not the right person for the job
- The therapy does not seem to be helping
- Some other kind of service or solution is needed
- A conflict of interest has developed
- Maximum benefit from this particular therapy has been reached

Your therapist is alert to these possibilities and will initiate a discussion of your progress every so often to help you evaluate possible reasons for ending. This is not meant to push you out of therapy. It is intended to help you make the best and most efficient use of your time and money.

Most therapists are fairly careful *not* to bring up termination *too* often out of concern for giving you the opportunity to raise the issue when you are ready. If your therapist has not raised the issue in a while, you should feel free to bring it up. It is especially important to talk about termination if you have any questions, you wonder if therapy is worth it, you are thinking about wrapping things up, or you do not want to return. If your insurance benefits specify a particular number of covered visits, you should work with your therapist to keep track of these limits so you will know if you have to stop for financial reasons.

4. What Does It Mean to "End on a Positive Note"?   Ending on a positive note means that you and the therapist have talked about the decision to stop meeting and the reasons why, even if only briefly. Discussing your thoughts and feelings about ending therapy and what you have gotten out of it is part of the conclusion. Taking time to do this can help you recognize what was most and least helpful and what you still want to address, either now or at some future point. This conversation contributes to a sense of psychological order and control that is called "closure." Psychological closure occurs when thoughts and feelings are organized and expressed in a way that draws out the benefits of the experience, identifies reasons for the decision, settles conflicts, and encourages moving on in a positive, peaceful way.

As a consumer, you always have the right to end sessions at any time, no matter what the reason. You do not owe the provider an explanation, nor do you need their approval. At the same time, psychological closure is usually easier when you discuss ending with the therapist. It is helpful if the decision is agreeable to both of you, but not absolutely necessary. Just talking about it can increase your closure, even if some disagreement remains.

5. Shouldn't I Stay in Therapy Until I Feel Totally Together?   If feeling totally together was the main criteria for ending therapy, probably no one would ever stop. The notion of feeling totally together is a bit of a stereotype that arbitrarily separates the so-called weak from the strong or the confused from the confident. There are many times in life when it is normal to feel unsettled and not together, particularly when going through major changes or transitions. The length of time anyone needs to be in therapy is highly variable and depends on many things.

In general, therapy that lasts for several months or longer may provide more benefits than extremely brief therapy, although the benefits tend to accumulate more slowly as time goes on. Staying in therapy until you feel completely confident, however, may be a set-up for disappointment. First, there is no real definition of "totally together," so it will be hard to know when you have reached that goal. Second, if you decide you feel totally together and stop therapy, you may feel disappointed, demoralized, or scared by the normal ups and downs that are going to come up further down the road.

Today's approach to therapy emphasizes self-help more than ever, and there are many strategies that you can learn to use. Instead of staying in therapy until you feel totally together, consider the alternative goal of staying in therapy long enough to develop your resilience and your skills for dealing with emotional challenges in living. Letting go of therapy and learning to rely on you is part of any effective treatment. Having a strong relationship with a therapist who is empathic and reliable is very important, but hopefully the objective is to help you help yourself. Your therapist can assist you in recognizing progress and the changes you've made for the better. He or she can also support you in coming to terms with the uncertainty that is part of ending. To aid this process, many therapists recommend a time of "fading out" sessions so that you can develop confidence through practice at handling stresses on your own. Sessions are scheduled with longer and longer intervals in between to provide support while you are consolidating your skills.

6. I Really Depend on Therapy. Do I Have to Let It Go?   Therapy is a professional, contractual service that should serve a necessary purpose. It should continue only as long as it serves that specific purpose. It is not intended to be a continuous direct support throughout your life but rather a tool to increase your independent functioning in meaningful ways. There are a variety of reasons why therapy ends as already noted, the most common being that it has served its immediate purpose. There may be other reasons why it is no longer beneficial, safe, or feasible to continue. If you are benefiting from therapy and don't want to stop, that is a valid reason to continue. However, therapy might still have to end if you are unable to afford the cost, if the logistics just don't work, or if the provider is not going to be available. In addition, your therapist has to agree that therapy really is helping you to make progress in order to ethically continue the work.

Therapy is intended to build your strengths, confidence, and self-esteem. If you depend mainly on the provider's strength, wisdom, and perspective, you are short-changing yourself in the long run. You could be learning to use internal strengths that will always be with you. This will help your overall self-esteem and stability much more than reliance on the therapist. Hopefully your therapist will encourage you to develop the skills of independence and will keep nudging you in that direction. If therapy has become prolonged because you are reluctant to let go, it might be a good idea to consider taking a therapy "vacation" for a brief time to get some perspective on your reliance on the provider. A good step toward becoming more self-reliant is to discuss your feelings of dependence with the therapist and brainstorm some ideas about what you can do to develop balance.

Beyond the fading process already discussed, many clinicians offer an indefinite opportunity to return for booster visits or consultation as needed. In other words, the therapist is like many other professionals in your life on whom you might call for specific services—accountant, physician, lawyer, and so on. You don't need them all the time, but if and when you need them, you can call. Your contract or agreement for working on certain goals might end, but the option of returning for further work might remain if you need it. This is something that you should discuss with your provider to see if this is an option. It may help a great deal with the task of letting go.

7. Should I Quit Therapy if I Feel Lost or Stuck?   Feeling lost or stuck might mean that therapy should stop, but not always. If you wonder about what you are doing in the therapy and why you are there, bring this up with your therapist. Perhaps your objectives were not clear to begin with, or they have become fuzzy or lost along the way. Some frank discussion about what you want from therapy could refresh and redirect the effort.

This may also be a good time to think about your own treatment goals and termination plan. Therapy is most satisfying and productive when you identify something specific that you want to get out of it. In other words, what would you like to learn or accomplish—in concrete terms—before you stop therapy? Let's say you came to therapy because of mood problems—you were anxious or depressed or both. Now you are feeling better. What else might be important to address before you stop therapy? Some possible goals that you may want to consider are to:

- Improve your performance at work.
- Get along better with your family (or other specific people).
- Improve your parenting skills.
- Make a relationship lasting and fulfilling.
- Use your time more productively.
- Improve your ability to handle stress.
- Do a better job of managing your physical health.

The most common reason why people get less out of therapy than they could is that they do not understand the importance of actively setting goals and pursuing them. Your therapist may suggest goals, but ultimately you must decide what you want to get out of therapy. Your initial goals might be too global or unworkable, but your therapist can help you to whittle those ideas down into something that is possible. When this happens, the purpose of therapy is much clearer. From there, you can decide how long you will work on these issues and at what point you will stop. This is your termination plan. Termination plans can be tied to different anchors such as any of the following examples. You might plan to terminate when:

- You reach a certain point in time—maybe the end of the summer or school term
- You accomplish a particular task or milestone—perhaps a positive work evaluation
- You establish a new pattern of behavior—for instance arguments with family occur infrequently or less than once per week
- You experience a change in your inner or subjective feelings—such as feeling more satisfied with your marriage or friendships or happier about your future.

When you reach any of these possible termination points, you and your therapist can re-evaluate your concerns and decide if you want to stop there or set some new goals.

8. I Can Not Seem to Talk about Ending Therapy. What Should I Do? If you want to stop therapy but do not know how, it is important find a way to bring this subject up for discussion. It is not in your best interest to keep going to therapy when you want to stop, nor is it optimal to just disappear without saying anything. First, keep in mind that therapists are trained to help you express your feelings and thoughts about difficult subjects. All you need to do is say something that indicates an interest in talking about termination, although being direct is often easiest and most effective. Here are some ideas to get you started. For example, you might say,

- "I have something to bring up that is hard for me to discuss."
- "There is something I want to talk about, but I'm not sure what to say."
- "I think I am feeling anxious about stopping therapy."
- "I have been thinking about when to end therapy and want to talk this over."
- "I want to talk about stopping therapy."
- "I have mixed feelings about continuing our sessions."
- "Can we talk about when therapy should end?"

You may want to think about the reasons why you are considering termination so that you can discuss them with your therapist. If you are not really sure, you can just say so. If you think the work has run its course, or has gotten off track in some way and is not very useful to you lately, it is fine to say that as well. If you don't like something the therapist is doing or need something different, it is helpful to explain this. Hints, complaints, criticisms, or total avoidance are hard to interpret, yet these tactics sometimes pop up when one is worried about the possibility of hurting the other person's feelings. Try to avoid these less-effective communication strategies and use a more direct, assertive approach, as shown in the examples.

Therapists are human too, and their feelings can be hurt, but they are expected to take a professional perspective and learn from the feedback they receive. Usually, a therapist is a caring person who wants to know more about your reasons for stopping therapy. If you take a chance and speak up, you might be surprised to find out that your therapist understands your reasons and wants to help make the best decision for you.

If the problem is you really don't want to stop therapy and that is why you can not talk about it, you may be experiencing separation anxiety. Perhaps you feel emotionally overwhelmed at the thought and dread the therapist's efforts to bring it up. It may help to realize that the therapist is not trying to get rid of you or make you feel bad. The same advice offered earlier applies here. Remember that the therapist is trained to help you deal with difficult thoughts and feelings. The basic issues are a bit different, however. Instead of your desire to stop, the issues to discuss are your feelings of anxiety and dread and how hard it is to talk or maybe even think about ending. Getting this out in the open is the first step toward reducing your distress and working out the best plan for you.

9. Doesn't My Therapist Have to Continue Therapy Until I Feel Ready to Stop?   Both client and therapist have rights and responsibilities when it comes to continuing or ending therapy. You should understand that some circumstances require your therapist to initiate termination and perhaps even insist on it, even if you disagree with the idea. Providers must curtail any service that is not necessary or beneficial to you, in their professional judgment. Clients are expected to actively participate and comply with the terms and conditions of the professional relationship in order to benefit. Low participation or noncompliance on your part can create unsafe conditions or make it unlikely that you will benefit, so the responsible provider must consider termination. It is also possible that your problems are mild enough that treatment is no longer necessary. In addition, your therapist may have reached the limits of what benefits he or she can offer you and needs to conclude the relationship.

In any termination, you can expect your therapist to make a very thoughtful and deliberate decision, one that takes your wishes into account as much as possible. If the provider thinks it is necessary to end therapy, he or she should give you some notice (under most circumstances) and provide you with an opportunity to discuss the situation and decide if you need information on alternative resources or providers. It will be up to you to take advantage of the opportunity offered by your therapist to discuss termination and to choose among the available alternatives. Although it may be uncomfortable or disappointing to have to end therapy, there is some compelling reason that is ultimately meant to protect your best interests in the long run. If this comes up in your therapy, try to approach the situation with a cooperative attitude. It is fine to raise questions and discuss the matter, but it may be that further negotiation is not possible. Your wishes, although they are always a priority for the provider, can not dictate that the provider overrule his or her objective professional judgment.

10. Will My Therapist Stop Working with Me if My Problems Are Too Difficult?   Therapists are prepared to deal with difficult problems and help you find solutions to the things that are challenging or overwhelming you. They will work with you as long as it is safe, effective, and reasonable to do so. At the beginning, the therapist will evaluate the type of problems that you have and determine whether or not he or she has the appropriate skills and experience needed to effectively help you. If your problems do not seem to be improving as expected from therapy, the therapist must review this and may recommend termination or transfer. It may be that you could get more benefit from a different level of care, type of therapy, or different provider.

Effective participation is important in getting what you want and need out of therapy, no matter how tough your problems. To participate effectively you need to:

- Attend sessions as planned.
- Prepare for sessions as directed by your therapist.
- Be forthcoming with important information.
- Try to focus on important rather than tangential issues.
- Follow through on ideas discussed in session.
- Pay agreed fees in a timely manner.
- Treat the provider and any staff with respect.

If your participation or behavior is an issue, the provider should bring this up and give you an opportunity to make adjustments before terminating therapy. The exception to this is if you or someone with a relationship to you (e.g., spouse, parent) threatens the provider or does something that creates conditions that are unsafe for the clinician or others working in the same location. Behavior that threatens others will trigger a unilateral termination, usually without any additional warning or opportunity to make adjustments.

For example, if you make repeated phone calls to your therapist's house, he or she will advise you on whether or not this is acceptable and what you should do instead. If you don't follow that advisement, your therapist may insist on termination. On the other hand, if you stalk your therapist, steal from his or her office, threaten homicide or legal action, or take some form of threatening action, your therapist will stop contact with you. In the second situation, it is actually the client who ends therapy through actions that pose a threat to others. The provider has no option other than to end contact because the relationship of trust has been violated.

11. I Am Angry and Disappointed in Therapy. What Are My Options?   This is an unfortunate situation. Most therapists are highly committed to client satisfaction and will work with you to the best of their ability to provide a beneficial experience, if it is possible to do so. The best way to reduce the risks of anger and disappointment is to become informed at the beginning of therapy about what the therapist can offer, how therapy works, and what you can do to make it a successful experience. If you have expectations that are not being met, by all means bring this to the attention of your therapist as soon as possible.

If you are disappointed in therapy, getting angrier and angrier will probably not improve the situation. Coercion and emotional intensity can make it more difficult to think creatively or solve the problem. If you find your frustration escalating, it may be time to stop therapy or at least take a break and think it over. Sometimes anger and disappointment are signposts of the very issues that brought you to therapy in the first place. On the other hand, it could be that this particular therapist is not the right person for the job of working with you. Rather than struggling to get something that can not be gotten, it may be better to end this relationship and move on. There are many types of therapy and even more types of therapists.

If the source of your anger and disappointment is some potentially unprofessional conduct by your therapist, you may want to seek a second professional opinion to sort this out. This confidential consultation is probably the best way to get an objective, professional perspective on the things that have bothered you. Another provider can help you to see if the situation was clearly unprofessional, as in the provider tried to date you or get you to invest money in business schemes. It could also be that the provider's questionable actions really fall within the scope of a normal range of professional judgment, but did not fit well for you. Therapy is not a standard procedure, and there is significant variability among the judgments and strategies that you might encounter from different providers. You might not like or agree with the provider's opinions or tactics, but that does not necessarily mean that the provider acted in an unprofessional manner. It may simply mean that this provider is not a good match for you.

You have the option of filing a complaint with the state board that licenses the provider if you think that professional disciplinary action might be important to protect other members of the public. In this process, you give a detailed report of your complaint to the appropriate state board (for example, social work, psychology, medicine, nursing, counseling; often these are grouped into health-related boards), and they will conduct a formal investigation. This is a serious legal process that you can not stop or retract once it is set in motion. It will often take months to years to resolve and may lead to disciplinary action or not, depending on the facts of the case and what happens during the provider's due process.

Another legal option is a formal malpractice lawsuit. This might be appropriate if you have been directly harmed by the therapist's actions. Both of these formal legal actions are adversarial in nature, so you should realize that taking either action will sever your relationship with the provider. It will no longer be possible to talk with the provider directly to work things out, nor can you ever return to therapy with this person. However, if the circumstances warrant legal action, it may be helpful to you and to others to pursue this option.

12. Will I Be Able to Return to Therapy if I Feel the Need?   Yes, most of the time a return to therapy is relatively easy. However, there are some things that may affect your return. These include the practice policies of your therapist or the agency where he or she works, your financial or insurance arrangements, the availability of your provider, and your overall needs. You might be seen on a follow-up basis for intermittent visits as needed, or you might come back for a new segment of therapy with new goals. If the provider or agency has a waiting list, you might have to re-enter as a new applicant and wait for an opening. These are all practical matters that you might want to review towards the end of your current therapy. As just noted, any adversarial process means that you would not be able to return to that particular therapist or agency.

13. What Happens to My Records after I Stop Therapy?   Providers are bound by law to create and keep some sort of formal record of your therapy, and not to destroy it before a certain period of time has passed. The minimum length of time that records have to be kept varies state by state. Your record will be kept in a secure area for a designated length of time, usually about seven years after your last contact with the provider. Records for children and teens are usually kept at least that long, or until one year past their reaching the age of majority, whichever comes later. Either your provider will keep track of your record, or the agency where you received services will keep your record.

If you want to access your record, you have a fairly long window of time in which to make requests for information. After this time, your record may be destroyed in a confidential way—for example it is shredded or deleted. Your therapist or agency can not destroy a record at your request, or at the request of anyone else, before the minimum time has passed. However, it is assumed that after a long period of time it is safer to destroy the record than to try to keep it indefinitely protected. Keeping a record indefinitely is an option, and it could be advisable if there is a known reason that the information will be useful at a future point. For instance, if a client is convicted of a crime and receives capital punishment, therapy records might be relevant to his or her legal appeals. Providers must weigh the risks of attempting to keep and protect confidential information against the potential likelihood of it being relevant and useful beyond the basic window of a seven-year time lapse.

14. Can My Therapist Talk about Me Once Therapy Ends? Information that identifies you is confidential, even after you stop coming for sessions. There is no expiration date on this rule. Your therapist can not discuss you or details of your therapy with others in their social circle or yours, regardless of whether therapy is active or ended. Occasionally therapists discuss their work in a context of professional teaching or consultation. When they do this, they are careful to limit the amount of information revealed, and they do so only for a clear professional purpose, not to gossip or entertain others. Their consultants or students are other professionals or professionals-in-training who understand the rules of keeping information confidential and respecting your privacy. In all situations, your identity is protected unless you have given permission for the discussion to take place. When therapists give lectures or produce written works, such as professional articles or books that include case examples, they will usually create "hypothetical" clients that are made up from a blend of real people so the information rings true but no one person's identity is revealed. The purpose of these materials is to instruct and inform others, and not in any way intended to misuse your personal information.

15. Can My Therapist and I Be Friends after Therapy? Because the basis of therapy is a personal confiding relationship, ending it can seem like breaking ties with a dear friend or family member. Even when you feel ready to wrap-up, you might still feel uncomfortable or sad about losing contact with someone you value and like. So it is natural to want to continue this positive relationship in some form. Friendship can seem like a normal progression, especially if your therapist is similar to other people in your life who are your friends. Maybe you share a lot in common or have similar interests. There are some circumstances where friendly contacts and even closer friendships are possible after therapy ends. However, there are important reasons why you want to think carefully about crossing this boundary.

One reason to hesitate is that it is basically impossible to switch back and forth between being friends and being client-therapist. If you make the switch to friendship, this means that your therapy relationship is permanently closed. There are plenty of times that providers and clients might have incidental contact outside of the therapy situation—for example when they run into each other on the street or any other of the vast number of possible crossings in a shared community—and they might or might not greet one another as acquaintances. This does not change or interfere with their therapy relationship.

However, closer social or business relationships create a conflict with the therapy relationship that can affect the provider's objectivity, cause the purpose of therapy to become fuzzy or get lost, or cause some unforeseen harm. Therapists have to keep a separation between their personal and professional relationships because of this potential conflict of interest. So while you might think your therapist would make the perfect friend, acquiring this person as a friend essentially means that you are giving up access to this therapist.

Another reason to hesitate on the friendship idea is the awkwardness that might go along with trying to switch into a different sort of relationship. Acquiring your therapist as a friend might not actually be as perfect as you think. Maybe what you are imagining is really a continuation of therapy, but in a more casual setting. Shifting to a different relationship means that the expectations and assumptions about how to behave with each other have changed. How comfortable will you feel if your former therapist is now inattentive, moody, or opinionated? Disagreements might be especially distressing, given the emotional charge to the relationship. Either of you might be misjudging the viability of a friendship. Disappointments and conflicts with the former therapist could have a negative influence on the therapeutic work after the fact. Rifts in this relationship as a friendship might be more difficult and distressing than ending the therapy. Even though such complications are not especially likely or readily predictable, there is some risk.

Providers and clients who live and work in rural or suburban communities or even in smaller communities within urban areas often find they have incidental contacts or overlapping roles. These experiences are not a problem as long as they remain compatible or non-interfering with the therapy relationship, even if it is inactive. But the shift into incompatible simultaneous roles of therapist-friend is where things can get very complicated and unworkable. Although your social impulses are well intended, there is merit in hesitation and cordial limits.

16. I Think My Therapist and I Have a Mutual Attraction. Can We Get Together after Therapy? The idea of a romantic or sexual relationship has all of the risks of a potential friendship, but to a greatly magnified degree. The ethics and rules of professional practice explicitly prohibit this because of the potential exploitation of the client-therapist relationship. Therapy is not a dating service. There are a few limited circumstances where a relationship that is not exploitive or potentially harmful might develop long after brief and uncomplicated therapy has ended, but this is the rare exception. If you have expressed interest in your therapist, and he or she has declined this interest, you should understand that this is normal. For most therapists and under most circumstances, any romantic or sexual attraction is something that will not be pursued because it is just too risky to both of you. It's better to learn from that attraction and move on to more available partners.

It is unprofessional for your therapist to ask you to end therapy so that the two of you can enter a romantic, sexual, or business relationship, or to try to pursue any such contact with you after therapy is over. This is a situation you might consider reporting to the state licensure board. On the other hand, it is professionally appropriate for your therapist to end therapy if an unavoidable personal conflict develops without any action from either of you. For example, let's imagine your therapist's son starts dating your daughter, and they seem to be developing an involved relationship. If you have any questions about such a situation, it is best to get a second professional opinion.

17. Should I Let My Therapist Know How I'm Doing after We Stop Therapy?   Most providers appreciate hearing something of your progress as time goes on. It is fine to send a card or a note. Telephone calls may be appropriate as well, although many providers today have considerable time pressures at work and do not have much opportunity to catch up with you over the telephone. Expect a phone call to be kept brief. If you want to have some interaction with the therapist, it is best to see if you can schedule a follow-up visit. You don't have to formally re-enter therapy just to have a follow-up visit unless your provider's policy stipulates otherwise. Be prepared to schedule an office visit if you want to have time to talk and review your progress.

Understand that all follow-up contacts should occur in a professional context and be handled in a professional manner. Therapists are generally discouraged from accepting an informal request to meet over coffee or lunch to catch up with you because this tends to confuse the boundary between personal and professional contact. At the same time, if you happen to pass on the street, it is okay to stop him or her to say hello if you want to do so. It is fine to let your therapist know how you are doing, but realize that this is still part of the tail end of therapy where you are thinking about your issues from the therapist's perspective and your therapist is still in the provider role.

18. Will We Have Some Sort of Graduation at My Last Session?   Ending therapy is an important step, one that is good to acknowledge in some way. Usually this is done through an informal wrap-up session where you will review your experience with your therapist. Depending on how long your therapy has lasted, you may spend time reviewing and looking ahead over several sessions. The ending of therapy may feel like a graduation because it is a point of re-evaluation and redirection, but the ending is not something marked by any specific formality. Sometimes group therapy includes special activities to mark the end of the shared experience. In individual therapy, you and your therapist will focus on the feelings, issues, and meaning connected to ending your regular work together.

19. Should I Bring a Gift to Mark the Ending?   Gifts are certainly not expected. Large gifts can not be accepted. If you want to give the provider a small gift, that is entirely up to you. Providers will accept small gifts according to their personal discretion. Some providers will accept food items or something simple like a book or plant. Others make it a policy to discourage all gift-giving to avoid the potential complications associated with such material influences. The provider's intent in accepting any gift is primarily to acknowledge the graciousness of offering and the feelings of gratitude or attachment being expressed. Do not feel compelled to bring a gift, but if you want to do so be sure to keep it simple.

20. Can I Refer My Friends or Other Family Members to My Therapist?   Providers have different policies on this issue. Some welcome personal referrals while others want to keep firm boundaries where there might be possible conflicts of interest. If a provider has multiple clients with a known relationship to one another, he or she must still keep the boundaries of confidentiality for each one. This can be a complicated task, but it might be manageable, depending on the closeness and nature of the relationships. Your therapist and the potential clients will have to be the judge of that issue. Finding a compatible therapist is both important and challenging, so most providers understand the value of a personal recommendation and want to accommodate if they can. Usually there is no problem in your passing along the provider's name and number to other potential clients. The provider will typically ask new clients how they were referred and evaluate the situation from there. If the provider does not think he or she is the right person for the job, they can offer your friend or family member further assistance in finding someone who can meet their needs. If in doubt about your provider's policy, it is always best to ask.

Helping Kids and Teens End Therapy on a Positive Note

Kids and teens don't have the same level of independence or authority in making decisions about their care as adults do. Even though they may ask fewer questions about the process of therapy, they still need to be informed about how therapy works and how it ends. The following are some added concerns from kids and teens about termination issues.

1. How Long Do I Have to Be in Therapy?   Therapy is meant to help you figure out a problem. These are some of the problems or reasons why kids and teens go to therapy.

- Feeling sad or scared a lot
- Feeling sick and not able to do things
- Having a hard time in school
- Worrying too much about things
- Trouble with other kids
- Family problems
- Fighting with others
- Getting into big trouble
- Cutting or self-harm
- Using drugs or alcohol
- Problems with eating
- Not liking yourself or feeling excessively insecure
- Dealing with a bad or sad event or situation
- Feeling "stressed out"

Therapy is not meant to be punishment or time-out for bad behavior. Your therapist cares about you and wants to spend time talking or playing special therapy games to help you express your feelings and learn more about the things that bother you. Your therapist can also give you ideas about new choices that you can use to make your problems change. Lots of kids and teens like going to therapy. They enjoy telling their therapist things and talking about different ways to think and act.

Therapy usually ends when you are feeling better and doing better with your problems. You don't have to rush to finish therapy. But you probably want to feel better as soon as you can. You can talk to your therapist about why you are coming to therapy, what you can do to make progress, and when you might expect to stop coming for visits. You might feel better just knowing more about what to expect.

2. Once I Stop, Can I Ever Go Back to My Therapist?   This depends on the therapist and the type of therapy. Lots of kids and teens return to their therapist for check-up visits or for more therapy if it seems like that would be useful. You might stop therapy, but that does not mean that you can never go back. Talk to your parents and your therapist if you think you might want to continue or return to see the therapist sometime. Talk to them if you do not like going to therapy and want to stop as well. They can help you work out a plan.

3. Will the Therapist Report My Problems to My School or College?   Usually therapists explain how information might be shared as part of your introduction at the beginning of therapy. It is fine to ask questions about this at any time. The things you talk about with your therapist are kept private most of the time, but there are some things that might be shared. First, if school and learning problems are part of the reason you are working with the therapist, the therapist will probably get permission from you and your parents to talk with certain teachers or counselors at your school.

Second, if you are in any serious danger of physically hurting yourself or someone else, your therapist will take whatever steps are needed to protect people from physical injury. That might mean letting your school know of these serious risks so they can help protect you or whoever else could be hurt. If you are thinking about hurting yourself or someone else, be sure to tell your therapist so he or she can help you decide what to do next. Talking this over will allow the therapist to figure out the best way to protect your privacy and keep everyone safe from harm. This is important even if you are scared to admit these ideas.

If you leave home and go to see a therapist at college, the new therapist might ask your permission to get records of your last therapy. Your last therapist won't release any information without your permission. Therapists do not just send reports to schools or colleges without an OK from you. You have a right to refuse to give permission for information to be shared, so you can say no if you want to. The only time the therapist would overrule your refusal to share information would be in a situation where someone's life is threatened, for example, if you might kill yourself or someone else.

4. Does Ending Therapy Mean That I Am Normal? For many kids and teens, being normal means being like other people they know, or being like the popular kids. But you could be different from the popular kids or other people in some important ways and still be very normal. Another way to think about being normal is to think about what is normal for you. If you and your family eat tacos for breakfast every day, that is normal for you. It is normal for you even if your friends eat eggs and toast and would never have a taco before lunch. Eating different kinds of foods is normal, but having NO food in your house or never eating is abnormal or a problem.

Going to therapy is a normal thing to do, like going to the doctor if you break a bone or have strep throat. Lots of kids and teens go to therapy for help with problems or difficult situations. When your moods or behavior change in some important ways, we call that "abnormal" because you are not being your normal self. The reason you go to therapy is because there is something abnormal going on. Either you are not *feeling* like your usual self, or you may be *acting* in ways that are risky or dangerous to your healthy development or growth, or both.

When you end therapy, hopefully you feel more normal, able to be more like your usual self. The following are some of the things that you might get from participating in therapy.

- Feel happier and healthier
- Feel more sure of yourself
- Be less worried
- Improved habits and behavior
- Able to get along at home
- Able to do better with schoolwork
- Have more fun
- Fit in better with other kids or find the best group for you

All of these things can be worked on in therapy. You might want to quit going to therapy sometimes or forget the point, so it is important to remember the things you would like to accomplish. Stick with therapy long enough to figure out what to change and how to accomplish these things. You will be ready to stop therapy when you are feeling better and doing things that are healthy for you.

Note

1. Purchasers of this book have permission to use this chapter, whole or in part, in their own personal clinical practice provided that the original author's copyright is cited.

References

Abrams, M. (2001). Resilience in ambiguous loss. *American Journal of Psychotherapy, 55*(2), 283–291.

American Association for Marriage and Family Therapy (AAMFT). (2001). *AAMFT code of ethics.* www.aamft.org.

American Association of Pastoral Counselors (AAPC). (2005). *Code of ethics.* www.aapc.org.

American Counseling Association (ACA) (2005). *Code of ethics.* www.counseling.org.

American Heritage Dictionary, 4th Edition (2001). New York: Houghton Mifflin Company.

American Psychiatric Association (ApA) (2000). *Diagnostic and statistical manual of mental disorders: DSM-IV-TR* (4th ed., text revision). Washington, DC: Author.

American Psychiatric Association (ApA) (2006). *The principles of medical ethics with annotations especially applicable to psychiatry.* Arlington, VA: Author.

American Psychological Association (APA) (1993). Guidelines for providers of psychological services to ethnic, linguistic, and culturally diverse populations. *American Psychologist, 48*(1), 45–48.

American Psychological Association (APA) (2002). *Ethical principles of psychologists and code of conduct.* www.apa.org.

American Psychological Association (2003). Guidelines on multicultural education, training, research, practice, and organizational change for psychologists. *American Psychologist, 58,* 377–402.

Anthony, W. A. (1993). Recovery from mental illness: The guiding vision of the mental health service system in the 1990's. *Psychosocial Rehabilitation Journal, 16,* 12–23.

Barlow, D. H. (2001). *Clinical handbook of psychological disorders* (3rd ed.). New York: Guilford.

Barnett, J. E. (1998). Termination without trepidation. *Psychotherapy Bulletin, 33*(2), 20–22.

Barnett, J. E. (2007). Whose boundaries are they anyway? *Professional Psychology: Research and Practice, 38*(4), 401–405.

Barnett, J. E., Cornish, J. A. E., Goodyear, R. K., & Lichtenberg, J. W. (2007). Commentaries on the ethical and effective practice of clinical supervision. *Professional Psychology: Research and Practice, 38*(3), 268–275.

Barnett, J. E., MacGlashan, S. G., & Clarke, A. J. (2000). Risk management and ethical issues regarding termination and abandonment. In L. Vandecreek & T. Jackson (Eds.), *Innovations in clinical practice: A source book* (Vol. 18; pp. 231–245).

Baumeister, R. (2001, April). Violent pride. *Scientific American, 284*(4), 96–101.

Baumeister, R., Bushman, B., & Campbell, W. K (2000). Self-esteem, narcissism, and aggression: Does violence result from low self-esteem or from threatened egotism? *Current Directions in Psychological Science, 9,* 26–29.

Beauchamp, T., & Childress, J. (2001). *Principles of biomedical ethics* (5th ed.). New York: Oxford.

Beck, A., Rush, A., Shaw, B., & Emery, G. (1979). *Cognitive therapy of depression.* New York: Guilford.

Beck, A. T., & Beck, J. S. (1991). *The Personality Beliefs Questionnaire.* Bala Cynwyd, PA: Beck Institute for Cognitive Therapy and Research.

Beck, A.T., Butler, A. C., Brown, G. K., Dahlsgaard, K. K., Newman, C. F., & Beck, J. S. (2001). Dysfunctional beliefs discriminate personality disorders. *Behaviour Research and Therapy, 39*(10), 1213–1225.

Beck, A. T., Freeman, A., Davis, D., & Associates (2004). *Cognitive therapy of personality disorders* (2nd ed.). New York: Guilford.

Beck, A. T., & Weishaar, M. E. (2008). Cognitive therapy. In R. Corsini & D. Wedding (Eds.), *Current psychotherapies* (8th ed; pp. 263–294).

Beck, J. (1995). *Cognitive therapy: Basics and beyond.* New York: Guilford.

Bennett, B. E., Bricklin, P. M., Harris, E., Knapp, S., VandeCreek, L., & Younggren, J. N. (2006). *Assessing and managing risk in psychological practice: An individualized approach.* Rockville, MD: The Trust.

Bernard, J. M., & Goodyear, R. K. (2004). *Fundamentals of clinical supervision* (3rd ed.). Boston: Pearson Education.

Bernstein, B. E., & Hartsell, T. L. (2000). *The portable ethicist for mental health professionals: An A-Z guide to responsible practice.* Hoboken, NJ: Wiley.

Bordin, E. S. (1979). The generalizability of the psychoanalytic concept of the working alliance. *Psychotherapy: Theory, Research and Practice, 16,* 252–260.

Brabender, V. A., Fallon, A. E., & Smolar, A. I. (2004). *Essentials of group therapy.* Hoboken, NJ: Wiley.

Brogan, M. M., Prochaska, J. O., & Prochaska, J. M. (1999). Predicting termination and continuation status using the transtheoretical model. *Psychotherapy, 36,* 105–113.

Brown, G.K, Have, T. T., Henriques, G. R., Xie, S. X., Hollander, J.E., and Beck, A. T. (2005). Cognitive therapy for the prevention of suicide attempts: A randomized controlled trial. *Journal of the American Medical Association, 294*(5). 563–570.

Budman, S. H., & Gurman, A. S. (1988). *Theory and practice of brief therapy.* New York: Aronson.

Butler, A. C., Brown, G. K., Beck, A. T., & Grisham, J. R. (2002). Assessment of dysfunctional beliefs in borderline personality disorder. *Behaviour Research and Therapy, 40*(1), 1231–1240.

Campbell, J. (2006). *Essentials of clinical supervision.* Hoboken, NJ: Wiley.

Carpenter, J. (2002). Mental health recovery paradigm: Implications for social work. *Health and Social Work, 27*(2), 86–94.

Chambless, D., Baker, M., Baucom, D., Beutler, L., Calhoun, K., Crits-Christoph, P., Daiuto, A., DeRubeis, R., Detweiler, J., Haaga, D., Johnson, S., McCurry, S., Mueser, K., Pope, K., Sanderson, W., Shoham, V., Stickle, T., Williams, D., & Woody, S. (1998). Update on empirically validated therapies, II. *The Clinical Psychologist, 51*(1), 3–16.

Chambless, D. L., & Ollendick, T. H. (2001). Empirically supported psychological interventions: Controversies and evidence. *Annual Review of Psychology, 52,* 685–716.

Curtis, R. (2002). Termination from a psychoanalytic perspective. *Journal of Psychotherapy Integration, 12*(3), 350–357.

DiClemente, C. C. (2003). *Addictions and change: How addictions develop and addicted people recover.* New York: Guilford.

DiClemente, C. C. (2006). *Matching intervention strategies to the process of change.* Workshop presented at the 40th annual convention of ABCT, Chicago, IL. November 18, Chicago Hilton.

Drake, R. E., Merrens, M. R., & Lynde, D. (2005). *Evidence-based mental health practice: A textbook.* New York: Norton.

Dryden, W. (1986). Eclectic psychotherapies: A critique of leading approaches. In J. C. Norcross (Ed.), *Handbook of eclectic psychotherapy.* New York: Brunner/Mazel.

Duckworth, A. L., Steen, T. A., & Seligman, M. E. P. (2005). Positive psychology in clinical practice. *Annual Review of Clinical Psychology, 1,* 629–651.

Dutton, D. G., & Hart, S. D. (1992). Risk markers for family violence in a federally incarcerated population. *International Journal of Law and Psychiatry, 15,* 101–112.

Ebert, B. W. (2006). *Multiple relationships and conflict of interest for mental health professionals: A conservative psycholegal approach.* Sarasota, FL: Professional Resource Press.

Ellis, M. V. (2001). Harmful supervision, a cause for alarm. Comment on Gray et al. (2001) and Nelson and Friedlander (2001). *Journal of Counseling Psychology, 48*(4), 401–406.

Ensworth v. Mullvain, 224Cal.App.3d 1105, 274 Cal.Rptr. 447 (1990).

Erikson, E. H. (1963). *Childhood and society* (2nd ed). New York: Norton.

Erikson, E. H. (1968). *Identity: Youth and crisis.* New York: Norton.

Falender, C. A., Cornish, J. A., Goodyear, R., Hatcher, R., Kaslow, N. J., Leventhal, G., et al. (2004). Defining competencies in psychology supervision: A consensus statement. *Journal of Clinical Psychology, 60,* 771–787.

Falender, C. A., & Shafranske, E. P. (2004). *Clinical supervision: A competency based approach.* Washington, DC: American Psychological Association.

Falender, C. A. & Shafranske, E. P. (2007). Competence in competency-based supervision practice: Construct and application. *Professional Psychology: Research and Practice, 38*(3), 232–240.

Fisher, C. B. (2003). *Decoding the ethics code: A practical guide for psychologists.* Thousand Oaks, CA: Sage Publications.

Fiske, S. T. (1998). Stereotyping, prejudice, and discriminiation. In D. T. Gilbert & S. T. Fiske (Eds.), *The handbook of social psychology,* Vol. 1 (4th ed.; pp. 357–411). New York: McGraw-Hill.

Fossati, A., Maffei, C., Bagnato, M., Donati, D., Donini, M., Fiorelli, M., & Norella, L. (2000). A psychometric study of DSM-IV passive-aggressive (negativistic) personality disorder criteria. *Journal of Personality Disorders, 14*(1), 72–83.

Freeman, A., & DeWolf, R. (1989). *Woulda, coulda, shoulda: Overcoming regrets, mistakes and missed opportunities.* New York: Harper Collins.

Freeman, A., Felgoise, S., & Davis, D. (2008). *Clinical psychology: Integrating science and practice.* Hoboken, NJ: Wiley

Frisch, M. B. (2006). *Quality of life therapy: Applying a life satisfaction approach to positive psychology and cognitive therapy.* Hoboken, NJ: Wiley.

Fulero, S. M. (1988). Tarasoff: 10 years later. *Professional Psychology: Research and Practice, 19*(2), 184–190.

Garfield, S. L. (1994). Research on client variables in psychotherapy. In A. E. Bergin & S. L. Garfield (Eds.), *Handbook of psychotherapy and behavior change* (4th ed., pp. 190–228). Hoboken, NJ: Wiley.

Geffner, R. & Mantooth, C. (2000). *Ending spouse/partner abuse: A psychoeducational approach for individuals and couples.* New York: Springer.

Getz, H. G. (1999). *Assessment of clinical supervisor competencies. Journal of Counseling and Development, 77*(4), 491–497.

Glicken, M. D. (2006). *Learning from resilient people: Lessons we can apply to counseling and psychotherapy.* Thousand Oaks, CA: Sage.

Goldfried, M. R. (2002). A cognitive-behavioral perspective on termination. *Journal of Psychotherapy Integration, 12*(3), 364–372.

Goldfried, M. R. (2007). From ABCT to evidence-based therapies: What's in a name? Letter to the Editor: *The Behavior Therapist,* January, 3–5.

Goldfried, M. R., Davison, G. C. (1976). *Clinical behavior therapy.* New York: Holt, Rinehart & Winston.

Gordon, K. A. (1996, June 20–23). *Infant and toddler resilience: Knowledge, predictions, policy and practice.* Paper presented at the Head Start National Research Conference, Washington, DC.

Gottlieb, M., Robinson, K., & Younggren, J. (2007). Multiple relations in supervision: Guidance for administrators, supervisors and students. *Professional Psychology: Research and Practice, 38*(3), 241–247.

Gottman, J. M. (1999). *The marriage clinic: A scientifically based marital therapy.* New York: Norton.

Greenberg, L. S. (2002). Termination of experiential therapy. *Journal of Psychotherapy Integration 12*(3), 358–363.

Handelsman, M., Gottlieb, M., & Knapp, S (2005). Training ethical psychologists: An acculturation model. *Professional Psychology: Research and Practice, 36*(1), 59–65.

Hansen, N. D., Pepitone-Arreola-Rockwell, F., & Greene, A. (2000). Multicultural competence: Criteria and case examples. *Professional Psychology: Research and Practice, 31*(6), 652–660.

Helbok, C. M., Marinelli, R. P., & Walls, R. T. (2006). National survey of ethical practices across rural and urban communities. *Professional Psychology: Research and Practice, 37*(1), 36–44.

Henry, D. L. (1999). Resilience in maltreated children: Implications for special needs adoptions. *Child Welfare, 78*(5), 519–540.

Herlihy, B. (2006). Ethical and legal issues in supervision. In J. Campbell, *Essentials of clinical supervision* (pp.18–34). Hoboken, NJ: Wiley.

Hjelt, S. (2007, August). *Termination and abandonment: Civil and administrative law implications.* Paper presented at the annual convention of the American Psychological Association, San Francisco, CA.

Hollon, S. D., Stewart, M. O., & Strunk, D. (2006). Enduring effects for cognitive behavior therapy in the treatment of anxiety and depression. *Annual Review of Psychology, 57,* 285–315.

Huppert, J. D., Barlow, D. H., Gorman, J. M., Shear, M. K., & Woods, S. W. (2006). The interaction of motivation and therapist adherence predicts outcome in cognitive behavioral therapy for panic disorder: Preliminary findings. *Cognitive and Behavioral Practice, 13*, 198–204.

International Council of Nurses (ICN) (2005). The ICN code of ethics for nurses. www.icn.ch/.

Jakobsons, L. J., Brown, J. S., Gordon, K. H., & Joiner, T. E. (2007). When are clients ready to terminate? *Cognitive and Behavioral Practice, 14*, 218–230.

Johnson, W. B. (2007). Transformational supervision: When supervisors mentor. *Professional Psychology: Research and Practice, 38*(3), 259–267.

Joyce, A. S., Piper, W. E., Ogrodniczuk, J. S., & Klein, R. H. (2007). *Termination in psychotherapy: A psychodynamic model of processes and outcomes.* Washington, DC: American Psychological Association.

Kassinove, H., & Tafrate, R. C. (2002). *Anger management: The complete treatment guidebook for practitioners.* Atascadero, CA: Impact.

King, L. A., & Hicks, J. A. (2007). Whatever happened to "what might have been"? Regrets, happiness and maturity. *American Psychologist, 62*(7), 625–636.

Kitchener, K. S. (1988). Dual role relationships: What makes them so problematic? *Journal of Counseling and Development, 67*, 217–221.

Klein, R. H., & Carroll, R. A. (1986). Patient characteristics and attendance patterns in outpatient group psychotherapy. *International Journal of Group Psychotherapy, 36*, 115–132.

Kleinke, C. L. (1994). *Common principles of psychotherapy.* Pacific Grove, CA: Brooks/Cole.

Knapp, S. J., & VandeCreek, L. S. (2006). *Practical ethics for psychologists: A positive approach.* Washington, D.C.: American Psychological Association.

Koocher, G. P. & Keith-Spiegel, P. (1998). *Ethics in psychology: Professional standards and cases* (2nd ed.) Oxford: New York.

Kramen-Kahn, B., & Hansen, N. D. (1998). Rafting the rapids: Occupational hazards, rewards, and coping strategies of psychotherapists. *Professional Psychology: Research and Practice, 29*, 130–134.

Kramer, S. A. (1986). The termination process in open-ended psychotherapy: Guidelines for clinical practice. *Psychotherapy, 23*(4), 526–531.

Kreilkamp, T. (1989). *Time-limited intermittent therapy with children and families.* New York: Brunner/Mazel.

Kroger, J. (2007). *Identity development: Adolescence through adulthood.* Thousand Oaks, CA: Sage.

Kuyken, W., Kurzer, N., DeRubeis, R. J., Beck, A. T., & Brown, G. K. (2001). Response to cognitive therapy in depression: The role of maladaptive beliefs and personality disorders. *Journal of Consulting and Clinical Psychology, 69*(3), 560–566.

Ladany, N., Lehrman-Waterman, D., Molinaro, M., & Wolgast, B. (1999). Psychotherapy supervisor ethical practices: Adherence to guidelines, the supervisory working alliance, and supervisee satisfaction. *The Counseling Psychologist, 27*, 443–475.

Lambert, M. J. & Barley, D. E. (2002). Research summary on the therapeutic relationship and psychotherapy outcome. In J. C. Norcross (Ed.), *Psychotherapy relationships that work* (pp. 17–32). New York: Oxford University Press.

La Roche, M., & Maxie, A. (2003). Ten considerations in addressing cultural differences in psychotherapy. *Professional Psychology: Research and Practice, 34*(2), 180–186.

Leahy, R. L. (2003). *Roadblocks in cognitive-behavioral therapy: Transforming challenges into opportunities for change.* New York: Guilford.

Leahy, R., L. (2007a). *Using cognitive therapy on ourselves. Advances in Cognitive Therapy.* Bala Cynwyd, PA: Academy of Cognitive Therapy.

Leahy, R. L. (2007b). Schematic mismatch in the therapeutic relationship: A social-cognitive model. In P. Gilbert & R. Leahy (Eds.), *The therapeutic relationship in the cognitive behavioral psychotherapies* (pp. 229–254). London: Routledge.

Levinson, D. J. (1996). *The seasons of a woman's life.* New York: Knopf.

Linehan, M. (1993). *Cognitive behavioral therapy for borderline personality disorder.* New York: Guilford Press.

Linehan, M. M., Cochran, B. N., & Kehrer, C. A. (2001). Dialectical behavior therapy for borderline personality disorder. In D. Barlow (Ed.) *Clinical handbook of psychological disorder*s (3rd ed.; pp. 470–522). New York: Guilford.

MacKenzie, K. R. (1990). *Introduction to time-limited group psychotherapy.* Washington, DC: American Psychiatric Press.

Mahoney, M. J. (1997). Psychotherapists' personal problems and self-care patterns. *Professional Psychology: Research and Practice, 28,* 14–16.

Marchand, A., Goyer, L. R., Dupuis, G., & Mainguy, N. (1998). Personality disorders and outcome of cognitive behavioural treatment of panic disorder with agoraphobia. *Canadian Journal of Behavioural Science, 30,* 14–23.

Marlatt, G. A., & Gordon, J. R. (1985). *Relapse prevention: A self-control strategy for the maintenance of behavior change.* New York: Guilford.

Maslach, C., Schaufeli, W. B., & Leiter, M.P. (2001). Job burnout. *Annual Review of Psychology, 52,* 397–422.

McCullough, J. P. (2000). *Treatment for chronic depression: Cognitive behavioral analysis system of psychotherapy (CBASP).* New York: Guilford.

Merikangas, K. R., & Kalaydjian, A. (2007). Magnitude and impact of comorbidity of mental disorders from epidemiological surveys. *Current Opinion in Psychiatry, 20,* 353–358.

Merriam-Webster's Dictionary of Synonyms. (1984). Springfield, MA: Merriam-Webster, Inc.

Miller, W. R. (1995). Increasing motivation for change. In W. R. Miller and R. K. Hester (Eds.), *Handbook of alcoholism treatment approaches: Effective alternatives* (2nd ed.)(pp. 89–104). Needham Heights, MA: Allyn & Bacon.

Millon, T., & Davis, R., (1996). Negativistic personality disorders: The vacillating pattern. In T. Millon, *Disorders of personality: DSM-IV and beyond* (2nd ed.; pp. 541–574). New York: Wiley.

National Association of Social Workers (NASW) (1999*). Code of ethics.* www.social workers.org.

Nezu, C. M., & Nezu, A. M. (2003). *Awakening self-esteem.* Oakland, CA: New Harbinger.

Nickelson, D. W. (1998). Telehealth and the evolving health care system: Strategic opportunities for professional psychology. *Professional Psychology: Research and Practice, 29,* 527–535.

Norcross, J. C. (2000). Psychotherapist self-care: Practitioner-tested, research-informed strategies. *Professional Psychology: Research and Practice, 31,* 710–713.

Novick, J., & Novick, K. K. (2006). *Good goodbyes: Knowing how to end in psychotherapy and psychoanalysis.* Lanham, MD: Jason Aronson.

O'Connor, R. (2001). Active treatment of depression. *American Journal of Psychotherapy, 55*(4), 507–530.

Oordt, M., Jobes, D., Rudd, M. D., Fonseca, V., Runyan, C., Stea, J., Campise, R., & Talcott, G. W. (2005). Development of a clinical guide to enhance care for suicidal patients. *Professional Psychology, 36*(2), 208–218.

Orlinsky, D., Grawe, K., & Parks, B. (1994). Process and outcome in psychotherapy: Noch einmal. In A. Bergin & S. Garfield (Eds.), *Handbook of psychotherapy and behavior change* (4th ed.), (pp. 270–376). New York: Wiley.

Pekarik, G. (1992). Relationship of client's reasons for dropping out of treatment outcome and satisfaction. *Journal of Clinical Psychology, 48(1),* 91–98.

Persons, J. B., Burns, B. D., & Perloff, J. M. (1988). Predictors of drop-out and outcome in cognitive therapy for depression in a private practice setting. *Cognitive Therapy and Research, 12,* 557–575.

Pilkonis, P. A., & Frank, E. (1988). Personality pathology in recurrent depression: Nature, prevalence, and relationship to treatment response. *American Journal of Psychiatry, 145,* 435–441.

Pope, K., & Vasquez, M. (2005). *How to survive and thrive as a therapist: Information, ideas and resources for psychologists in practice.* Washington, DC: American Psychological Association.

Prochaska, J. O., & DiClemente, C. C. (1982). Transtheoretical therapy: Toward a more integrative model of change. *Psychotherapy: Theory, Research and Practice, 20,* 161–173.

Prochaska, J. O., & DiClemente, C. C. (1992a). Stages of change in the modification of problem behaviors. In M. Hersen, R. M. Eisler, & P. M. Miller (Eds.), *Progress in behavior modification* (pp. 184–214). Sycamore, IL: Sycamore Press.

Prochaska, J. O., DiClemente, C. C., & Norcross, J. C. (1992b). In search of how people change: Applications to addictive behaviors. *American Psychologist, 47,* 1102–1114.

Prochaska, J. O., DiClemente, C. C., & Norcross, J. C. (1994). *Changing for good: A revolutionary six-stage program for overcoming bad habits and moving your life positively forward.* New York: Avon Books.

Prochaska, J. O., & Norcross, J. C. (2003). *Systems of psychotherapy: A transtheoretical analysis* (5th ed.). Pacific Grove, CA: Brooks/Cole.

Reis, B. F., & Brown, L. G. (2006). Preventing therapy dropout in the real world: The clinical utility of videotape preparation and client estimate of treatment duration. *Professional Psychology: Research and Practice, 37* (3), 311–316.

Renk, K., & Dinger, T. M. (2002). Reasons for therapy termination in a university psychology clinic. *Journal of Clinical Psychology, 58,* 1173–1181.

Roberts, L. J., & Marlatt, G. A. (1998). Guidelines for relapse prevention. In G. P. Koocher, J. C. Norcross, & S. S. Hill (Eds.), *Psychologists' desk reference* (pp. 243–247). New York: Oxford University Press.

Rodgers, M. L., Norell, D. M., Roll, J. M., & Dyck, D. G. (2007). An overview of mental health recovery. *Primary Psychiatry, 14*(12), 76–85.

Ronnestad, M. H., & Orlinsky, D. (2005). Therapeutic work and professional development: Findings and practical implications of a long-term international study. *Psychotherapy Bulletin, 40*(2), 27–32.

Rupert, P. A., & Ken, J. S. (2007). Gender and work setting differences in career-sustaining behaviors and burnout among professional psychologists. *Professional Psychology: Research and Practice, 38,* 88–96.

Sales, B. D., Miller, M. O., & Hall, S. R. (2005). *Laws affecting clinical practice.* Washington, D.C.: American Psychological Association.

Sanderson, W. C., Beck, A. T., & McGinn, L. K. (1994). Cognitive therapy for generalized anxiety disorder: Significance of co-morbid personality disorders. *Journal of Cognitive Psychotherapy: An International Quarterly, 8,* 13–18.

Santorelli, S. (1999). *Heal thy self: Lessons on mindfulness in medicine.* New York: Bell Tower.

Sedaka, N., & Greenfield, H. (1962). *Breaking up is hard to do.* RCA. (2007, Razor & Tie).

Shapiro, E. W., & Ginzberg, R. (2002). Parting gifts: Termination rituals in group therapy. *International Journal of Group Psychotherapy, 52*(3), 319–336.

Singer, J. A. (2005). *Memories that matter: How to use self-defining memories to understand and change your life.* Oakland, CA: Hew Harbinger.

Small, I., Small, J., Alig, V., & Moore, D. (1970). Passive-aggressive personality disorder: A search for a syndrome. *American Journal of Psychiatry, 126*(7), 973–983.

Smith, M. K. (2000). Recovery from a severe psychiatric disability: Findings of a qualitative study. *Psychiatric Rehabilitation Journal, 24*(2), 149–158.

Sommers-Flanagan, R., & Sommers-Flanagan, J. (1999). Suicide Assessment. In R. Sommers-Flanagan & J Sommers Flanagan (Eds), *Clinical interviewing* (2nd ed.) (pp. 244–275).

Sperry, L. (2007). *Dictionary of ethical and legal terms and issues: The essential guide for mental health professionals.* New York: Routledge.

Stevanovic, P., & Rupert, P. A. (2004). Career-sustaining behaviors, satisfactions, and stresses of professional psychologists. *Professional Psychology: Research and Practice, 41,* 301–309.

Sutter, E., McPherson, R. H., & Geeseman, R. (2002). Contracting for supervision. *Professional Psychology: Research and Practice, 33*(5), 495–498.

Thomas, J. T. (2007). Informed consent through contracting for supervision: Minimizing risks, enhancing benefits. *Professional Psychology: Research and Practice, 38*(3), 221–231.

Tryon, G. S., & Kane, A. S. (1995). Client involvement, working alliance, and type of therapy termination. *Psychotherapy Research, 5,* 189–198.

VandeCreek, L., & Knapp, S. (2001). *Tarasoff and beyond: Legal and clinical considerations in the treatment of life-endangering patients* (3rd ed.). Sarasota, FL: Professional Resource Press.

van Velzen, C. J. M., & Emmelkamp, P. M. G. (1996). The assessment of personality disorders: Implications for cognitive and behavior therapy. *Behavior Research and Therapy, 34*(8), 655–668.

Watchtel, P. L. (2002). Termination of therapy: An effort at integration. *Journal of Psychotherapy Integration, 12*(3), 373–383.

Walsh, J. (2007). *Endings in clinical practice: Effective closure in diverse settings* (2nd Ed.). Chicago: Lyceum Books, Inc.

Weiner, I. B. (1998). *Principles of psychotherapy* (2nd ed). New York: Wiley.

Wexler, D. B. (2000). *Domestic Violence 2000: An integrated skills program for men*. New York: W. W. Norton.

Young, J. E., Weinberger, A. D., & Beck, A. T. (2001). Cognitive therapy for depression. In D. Barlow (Ed), *Clinical handbook of psychological disorders* (3rd ed.). New York: Guilford.

Younggren, J. (2007, August). *Termination and abandonment: A risk management approach*. Paper presented at the annual convention of the American Psychological Association, San Francisco, CA.

Younggren, J., & Gottlieb, M. (2004). Managing risk when contemplating multiple relationships. *Professional Psychology: Research and Practice, 35*(3), 255–260.

Younggren, J., & Gottlieb, M. (in press, 2008). Termination and abandonment: History, risk and risk management. *Professional Psychology: Research and Practice*.

Zinkin, L. (1994). All's well that ends well. Or is it? *Group Analysis, 27*, 15–24.

Zur, O. (2007). *Boundaries in psychotherapy: Ethical and clinical explorations*. Washington, DC: American Psychological Association.

Zwick, R., & Attkisson, C. C. (1985). Effectiveness of client pretherapy orientation videotape. *Journal of Counseling Psychology, 32*, 514–524.

Subject Index

Author Index

Lightning Source UK Ltd.
Milton Keynes UK
UKOW06f0817291015

261629UK00001B/35/P